You Should Have Seen the Caterpillar

'unease'
Gender dysphoria
Transexuality

You Should Have Seen the Caterpillar

Faye Helen Wardle

Copyright © 2013 by Faye Helen Wardle.

ISBN:	Softcover	978-1-4836-1795-4
	Ebook	978-1-4836-1796-1

All rights reserved. No part of this book may be reproduced or transmitted in any form or by any means, electronic or mechanical, including photocopying, recording, or by any information storage and retrieval system, without permission in writing from the copyright owner.

This book was printed in the United States of America.

Rev. date: 04/01/2013

To order additional copies of this book, contact:
Xlibris Corporation
0-800-644-6988
www.xlibrispublishing.co.uk
Orders@xlibrispublishing.co.uk
306208

CONTENTS

Acknowledgements..9
Prologue...11

Chapter One: A Time of Pain, Contemplation, Fulfilment,
      and Recollection...13
Chapter Two: Childhood Remembrances...................................16
Chapter Three: Puberty and Teenage Confusion 25
Chapter Four: Per Ardua Ad Astra..29
Chapter Five: This Sporting Life 41
Chapter Six: Discovering the Dales and a Little of Myself 47
Chapter Seven: The Dancing Years 54
Chapter Eight: Family Life and the Study Years.......................67
Chapter Nine: A Time of Change..79
Chapter Ten: Faye Emergent at Long Last 87
Chapter Eleven: The Problems at Home and at Work 95
Chapter Twelve: Faye's Early Days 113
Chapter Thirteen: The Press and Life on My Own 123
Chapter Fourteen: Love as a Female in a Strange, New,
      and Wonderful World 130
Chapter Fifteen: Early Retirement...138
Chapter Sixteen: Fulfilment 159
Chapter Seventeen: The Deep Pain of Lost Love 176
Chapter Eighteen: A Settled Life at Last?................................193
Chapter Nineteen: Whither Now the Butterfly? 215
Chapter Twenty: Epilogue 225

Dedications

To those I have loved and lost with my heartfelt sorrow and deepest regrets that my unavoidable change of circumstances caused any pain and suffering, especially to my former wife, my two lovely sons, and my beautiful daughter, all of whom I miss deeply. God bless them and keep them all safe and well.

And to all those dear friends and relatives who have stood by me through all the trials and tribulations that my journey occasioned. Your friendship, love, and understanding helped me beyond comprehensible measure to eventually find my way.

God grant me the serenity
to accept the things I cannot change,
the courage to change the things I can,
and the wisdom to know the difference
What we cannot change, we must accept
what we can change, we must

ACKNOWLEDGEMENTS

To my dear wife for the twenty-four years of our marriage and for three wonderful children, God bless you all.

To Dr Joe Borg-Costanza and Dr Russell Reid for their help and guidance.

To Mr Michael Royle and the wonderful caring staff of the Sussex Nuffield Hospital.

To my dear sister Barbara and dear late brother Bernard for being there when I needed you most.

To my dear friend Jackie, who has been a constant friend and guide.

To Terry, have a pint on me.

To all the girls at 'Fatclass', thanks for the acceptance and friendship.

To all at Yorkshire Housing, your friendly acceptance at work helped see me through.

To the people of wonderful St Neot, and especially dear Mandy, who became a good close friend before passing away recently Thank you all for the friendship and hospitality.

And finally to my very dear 'emmit' friend in the West Country. Keep the white rose and the palm trees flourishing.

PROLOGUE

Pain is varied and relative. There is a physical pain which can be endured and can be fleeting, reducing with the passage of time—the great healer. Then there is a mental pain, an anguish, which is more difficult to endure, which creates a lifetime's burden, gnawing at one's very soul until located, confronted, acknowledged, and appeased.

—Faye Helen Wardle

CHAPTER ONE

A Time of Pain, Contemplation, Fulfilment, and Recollection

To lay in Dreams, so safe, secure
In Morpheus's cloak of darkest night
To wake complete, to dream anew
In Springtime's brightest Shining Light

—Faye Helen Wardle

The date was 2 May 1996, and I was immersed in yet one more strange world. It was an unreal world of semi-consciousness, a world without care and problems, and a world apart where anything is possible. It was the day when I had finally parted company with my manhood, the day when medical science had made me as complete a female as I could ever be.

The place was the Sussex Nuffield Hospital, high on England's lovely South Downs at Woodingdean, just to the east of Brighton.

I was vaguely aware of change, of numb, aching sensations, and of immobility and an underlying feeling of relief and deep contentment.

I was also aware of reflected warm evening sunshine filtering through the partly drawn vertical slat blinds to the windows close to my bed as the outside world greeted the new spring, the season of promise and new birth. Even the time felt right and appropriate.

I could hear the rustle of a gentle breeze through the nearby flowering cherry trees, and I visualised the scattering of the blossom fall like an unseasonal snowfall. This was accompanied by an evening birdsong from a nearby lone songbird—a gentle trilling ballad to welcome me back to the conscious world.

Inside the room, I was aware of the concerned attentions of the nursing staff, then blissful oblivion as I sank once more into sleep . . .

This was it at last. I had finally undergone the major physical operation on my long journey from a biological male to a non-biological female, or to give it its erroneous, often-used misnomer—the sex change.

I had completed over two and a half years of living in the female role to fulfil the requirements of 'the real life' test, two and a half roller-coaster years of deep lows and exhilarating highs, of deep sorrows and frustrations, and of rich contentment and happiness.

Years of losses and gains, and of finding my way in a completely new, strange, and wonderful world.

Years of fading old loves and friendships and blossoming new ones.

Years of discovery and of regrets at the number of years it had taken to find my true self.

Years of battling against age-old misconceptions and prejudices.

Years of discovery and strange, new emerging emotions.

Years of vastly varying family attitudes.

Years of protracted legal mayhem and financial losses.

Years of much laughter and a lot of tears.

Years of Chanel and Roses.

And just where did it all start?

It is impossible to place any precise date on any beginnings of feelings of 'difference'. I can recall these feelings from a very early age, feelings which I learned to hide away and suppress, for this was an age of a total lack of understanding, when suggestions of a mistake of gender were seen as a mental disturbance and were treated accordingly. This treatment was usually a course of painful electric shock aversion therapy, followed by a spell in the local mental home. To admit to such feelings would mean social ridicule, condemnation, isolation, and chastisement. So you keep quiet and learn to cope, but it doesn't go away. It just hides, quietly nagging and waiting to claim acknowledgement and its rightful place in the world . . .

I was conscious again, aware of being surrounded by a room full of cards and beautiful flowers from friends and relatives. An ocean of fragrant floral profusion and good wishes from around the country, which conveyed loving wishes on me just when I needed such a boost.

Had I really finally got this far? Had the long-felt impossible dream finally come true? It seemed all so unreal and unbelievable, like a lovely dream from which I was shortly to awake to a world of harsh reality. But this was all real. I was here at last, and it was all happening to me.

The confirmation was only too painfully obvious, as my movements were restricted by dressings and various tubes that ran from different parts of my body to points both above and below my bed: two drainage tubes and a catheter tube from my dressings and a liquid drip into my hand. My dressings encased me like a giant nappy, and my throat felt as though I had swallowed a bus! I remember thinking that I must look a mess without the benefit of make-up that can normally hide a multitude of sins.

Something inside said I should return to sleep and drift back to a world of dreams, to a state of recollection and contemplation, and away back to the land of Morpheus, where society did not file people in neat little pigeon holes coloured strictly blue or pink only. Clear thought was difficult, but the message from my body was clear. I should sleep, rest, and emerge complete at last, at last . . .

CHAPTER TWO

Childhood Remembrances

Through mists of time and sirens wail
And innocence of youth
A search begins to find one's self
From doubts, to dawn, to truth

—Faye Helen Wardle

The date was 12 February 1937.

The time was evening, and the elements were welcoming the birth of one more infant to pre-war Britain by providing a fierce freezing blizzard across the north of England.

It's small wonder that on such a night, Mother Nature wasn't quite on top form, for as she delivered a healthy, bouncing baby of over nine pounds in weight, she hiccupped on one small point.

The birth certificate read as follows:

Name: Roy Harry Wardle

Sex: Male

Date of Birth 12 February 1937

At least the surname and date of birth were right. The Christian names were right for the perceived gender, and the purists may argue that the biological sex was also right. But what of the mind and soul, the vital, indefinable inner spark that drives us all through life? It was to be over fifty years before this particular aspect of my being was to find its way.

In the interim, gender is still laid down at birth by the 'Willy Test'. If the newborn infant has a 'Willy', it is designated male; if no 'Willy', then it is obviously female.

This test has been passed down since the time of the cavemen, and the science of gender identification has not changed, nor progressed since before the time that the wheel was invented! The infant is still held aloft by its ankles, and gender decreed according to appendage or no appendage.

Neither have many people's attitudes to the subject changed much in all this time. Some people's attitudes remain Neanderthal; the subject is seen as taboo and best not discussed. It was good enough for Neanderthal man in his cave, so why not for us?

Thank heavens that not all thought and concepts remain Stone Age! Just what is the main constituent of a human being? Is it the sentient mind or the frail shell of a body to which the mind is condemned for the duration of its time on this earth? The two are not always mutually compatible.

For what happens if the mind of a girl is born in a body equipped with a 'Willy' and a liberal dosage of testosterone? She is of course designated male by the infallible 'Willy' Test. Or what if an unfortunate male mind is condemned to a life in a body equipped with a vagina, enlarged mammary glands, and a liberal supply of oestrogen? He of course is designated female because of the absence of the ubiquitous 'Willy'.

Thus are imposed life sentences on confused and innocent infants. It can happen, but human society has decreed tough! Nature doesn't make mistakes of gender. If you have a 'Willy', you are male, no 'Willy', female. It has ever been thus from time immemorial. End of story . . . or is it . . . ?

My Christian names were derived from a reversal process to a well-known band leader of the 1930s—Harry Roy. My parents also wanted me to have names that could not be shortened, a principle that I was to employ in choosing my new names of Faye Helen (no, there wasn't to my knowledge a female band leader called Helen Faye!).

I was born at St Mary's Maternity Home in Leeds, Yorkshire, the sixth child of Kathleen and Arthur Wardle, preceded by two sisters and three brothers. It would be three years before my younger sister Wendy completed the seven children.

I remember my mother as tall, slim, dignified, prematurely grey, and with a waspish temper, which could cause her to mete out instant physical retribution on any of her offspring who caused offence. And yet there was an underlying maternal tenderness towards, and deep pride in, her children.

My father, an engineer born and bred in Leeds, was to die prematurely in late 1940 while still in his early forties, leaving my mother to struggle through life with seven children from twenty years down to three months old. I myself was three years old when my father died, and I have no memories of him. Neither have I any photograph of him as cameras were something of a luxury in those days.

With hindsight, the fact that my mother managed to cope and enable us to enjoy relatively privileged childhood, even through the austere years of the Second World War speaks volumes for her self-sacrifices, discipline, dedication to her family, and fortitude.

She had little or no social life, had few pleasures beyond her children, and dedicated her entire life to ensure that we lacked for very little. Small wonder that she was often given to tears and depression, which as young children we couldn't readily understand at the time.

At this point, I can hear all the sociologists amongst you declaring, 'Ah it was the absence of a father figure that brought about Faye's condition'.

Baloney! Social conditioning can cause a male to be effeminate or a female to be aggressive and butch. It cannot create the genetic condition of gender dysphoria or transsexuality. **This condition is a medical condition. It is an immovable part of our physical condition from birth. It cannot be generated nor changed by social conditioning.**

The condition is there lurking, nagging, and awaiting its opportunity from the word go. Apart from that, my three big brothers made sure I didn't lack male influence. As sportsmen, they all were to have a major influence on my formative years.

Just when did I sense any 'difference' in myself? (It is a favourite question of the psychiatrists.) The earliest recollections are from the infant school where I preferred playing hopscotch with the girls rather than climbing trees with the boys (a primeval exercise that I could never understand, more suited to monkeys than human beings).

I didn't like fighting, not because of cowardice or a fear of being hurt but because of an inbuilt resistance to inflicting pain on anyone else.

Physical conflict has always been something I have abhorred and seen as a pointless exercise. I nevertheless frequently got involved in scuffles more out of a desire to conform rather than out of choice and out of a growing need to prove that I could cope and exist with what nature had given me. I was committed to 'proving myself' from a very early age.

Someone once described the male need for physical conflict as latent homosexuality being rechannelled. Now there's an interesting thought that merits a separate study in itself!

I began to prefer my own company and was at my happiest with crayons and sketch pad or a jigsaw puzzle. To play with the girls got you a reputation as a sissy or a softie, and I had no particular desire to play with the boys, although I can recall making friends with one or two of the quieter boys.

My eldest sister, who was later to totally reject me, became my second mother, taking some of the burden from my overworked mum. I did not lack therefore for care and attention.

My infant and primary school was St Luke's, a Church of England school, in Beeston, South Leeds.

St Luke's comprised a series of red brick-built Victorian buildings, with concrete playgrounds, which housed the outbuilt exposed toilets. These antiquated school buildings have only in recent times been demolished, and the school moved to new purpose-built premises on the site of a nearby former workhouse.

Amongst my earliest recollections from the early 1940s were my 'coal' duties. One of my brothers worked at Middleton Broom Colliery in South Leeds, and a spin-off benefit from his duties was that from time to time, we had a ton of coal tipped outside our house from the colliery. This was a godsend to our household, which ensured that we always had roaring coal fires and a warm house.

An added benefit for mum was that she was never short of cooking fuel, as most of her cooking was carried out on the coal burning Yorkist kitchen range, which she kept immaculate by the application of copious amounts of black-lead polish. I also recall her regular efforts of washing down the outside steps and donkey stoning the edges. Such meticulous attention to the external appearance of premises was commonplace in those days. There were no televisions, washing machines, or microwave ovens. Nor were there many of the smaller kitchen gadgets that we now take for granted.

My duties when the coal arrived were twofold. Firstly, I had to shovel the coal, which was tipped in a heap outside the house, into our cellar. As the cellar was at ground level at the back of our through terrace house, it was quite a task as the coal had to be deposited through a small hole some five feet above ground level.

The major task for me at this time, however, was to deliver spare buckets of coal to our various neighbours for the princely sum of one shilling (5 p) per bucket. While this wasn't the done thing as far as the colliery was concerned, it was a small earner for my mum, helped the neighbours through cold austere times, and brought me odd treats of sweets and fruits (treats indeed in these times of strict rationing and food shortages).

In Leeds, the action of the Second World War by and large passed us by as a city. The air-raid sirens, however, frequently gave out their rising and falling succession of wails to warn of approaching enemy aircraft, and many a night's sleep was interrupted as we paraded down to the cellar to sit on a cold stone slab awaiting the monotone drone of the all-clear siren.

The air raids were usually not directed at Leeds, which made a difficult target to identify in its dark Pennine bowl. Generally, the enemy aircraft were passing over to the more lucrative targets of Merseyside and the industrial areas of western England.

This did not deter the nearby anti-aircraft ack-ack guns at Hunslet Parkside from opening up to intersperse the drone of the passing aircraft with the reverberating volley of heavy artillery which itself caused our house to shake and the sash windows to rattle in their frames.

On one particular night, a huge piece of shrapnel smashed through one of our bedroom windows and struck the bed where my brother Ralph had lain just a short time before. There was a reason for us being herded down into the cold cellar after all.

It was a requisite of the war years that we all carried our gas masks with us wherever we went in case of aerial gas attacks. So what if my gas mask was of the 'Mickey Mouse' variety in bright red with funny ears attached (junior issue), rather than the standard plain black masks carried by the adults and older children. Just carrying my little brown cardboard gas mask box made me feel part of the great conflict that was being waged around the world.

I also well remember watching the thousand bomber raids towards the end of the war as we went out into the streets to cheer at the sky filled from horizon to horizon with allied bombers on their way to the Ruhr and the German heartland.

Even as a peace-loving quiet child, I felt we owed them something for Coventry, Plymouth, and the East End of London.

Our little school at St Luke's was at this time also invaded by an influx of refugee children from London. I recall the amusement occasioned by their southern accents, which were new to our young untravelled ears, and the reciprocal difficulty that our guests found with the harsher Northern dialects of their hosts.

My brother Ralph was something of a sporting hero at St Luke's school, starring at both soccer and cricket. He was frequently held out by the teachers as an example for me to follow, and he went on to star with the Leeds United Stormcocks and Colts junior football teams of the time.

My two elder brothers had also 'made the grade' in the sporting and wider world. The eldest had a spell with Lincoln City Football Club, and he had served with the Parachute Regiment in the Second World War being involved in the conflict at Monte Cassino in Italy amongst others.

My brother Bernard, who was later to be a tower of strength in supporting me through a difficult period of transition, was playing regularly in the Hunslet Rugby League first team where he starred as a flying winger.

To a quiet youngster, it was quite daunting to face up to matching up to my three big brothers. I was, however, to achieve some measure of personal sporting success, largely through a desire to do well in all I attempted, stemming from an inner drive which said I needed to conform and achieve.

In early 1947, I ventured down to the nearby Parkside Rugby League ground, at that time the home of Hunslet Rugby League Club, to see what the strange game which my brother Bernard enjoyed was all about. My eldest brother when he heard where I had been said he wasn't having me develop a taste for the oval ball game and began to take me with him to see the Leeds United soccer games.

I gradually developed a love for the game of soccer, and I carried along with the massed emotion of the crowd, the collective delight at the team's successes, and the spectacle of the occasion. I began to take part in a modest way in the football games at school, but I dreaded the summer season.

The summer brought cricket. Cricket at St Luke's was played a stone's throw from Leeds United's football ground, on a grassless cinder strewn outfield on Holbeck Moor, with an exceptionally hard cork ball which was propelled at you with a serious risk of injury, on an unpredictable concrete strip wicket.

Avoiding this projectile seemed of more importance than laying bat to it! I was therefore seen as something of a disappointment to the masters who were expecting me to emulate the cricketing successes of my brother Ralph.

I was also something of a disappointment at athletics (a fact that was to have a strange twist in my late teens). So what if someone was a half-second faster than I was over 100 yards (the pre-metric running distance), I still got there!

This lack of athletic achievement was set against the feats of my brothers and sisters (even my younger sister was developing into an accomplished sprinter).

Fortunately, I was more than holding my own on the scholastic front, which maintained a certain amount of consolation for the teaching staff.

Our primary school soccer games were also played on Holbeck Moor, which is nowadays bisected by the M621 Motorway. In the late 1940s, the Moor was a grassless cinder-covered wasteland. Skinned knees and grazed thighs were a certainty, and I carried these as red badges of courage on many occasions.

I played a few games in the school team, which was frequently humiliated by the teams of the larger schools, and the team's shirt, which was red and black in my brother's days, had faded to pink and grey, but I still wore it with pride.

Our form teacher at St Luke's was Mr Rudge, a huge, brusque, chauvinistic man who played Rugby Union for one of the local clubs and had little time not only for the girls in his form but also for the quieter boys, including me. At the same time, he developed an affinity with the 'bully boys' of the form.

During playtime breaks, the boys and girls played in separate playgrounds, and the boys usually played cricket with a tennis ball and wickets chalked on to one of the brick buttresses that supported the playground walls.

On one particular day, having waited patiently for my turn with the bat, as my turn finally arrived, Mr Rudge came striding across the playground.

'Here, young Wardle, let me have a go,' he bellowed as he snatched the bat away from me.

What followed filled me with a delicious sense of satisfaction. Taking a huge swing at his first ball, he connected and the ball took off in a huge arc. The huge smirk of smug satisfaction on his face was suddenly replaced by a look of horror as the ball crashed through the window of the headmaster's office, leaving a neat round hole in the glass.

Exit one red-faced school teacher as he trudged off to offer his explanations accompanied by the cheers of a highly amused group of pupils, and a big satisfied smile from one particular pupil who was busy regaining the rapidly discarded bat.

St Luke's, being a mixed-sex school (more so than they appreciated!) with only a single small hall had obvious problems with joint physical exercise lessons, so country dancing became the accepted solution as an exercise where both the boys and the girls could participate in a joint activity.

I enjoyed these periods immensely, and I became a regular in the country dancing team that became good enough to perform demonstration sessions at other schools.

This love for dancing was to manifest itself again during my twenties.

My social time in these days usually involved solitary visits to the local cinemas, where I could escape for a while into the make-believe world of movie land. It was here that I developed a fondness for the musicals of the time. This fondness I have maintained by having a modern collection of over 500 films on videotapes and DVDs. My reading at the time consisted primarily of the popular boys' magazines of the time, the Hotspur, Wizard, Adventure, Rover, and Champion. These magazines were purchased regularly by my brother Bernard and passed on to me. These provided late-night reading by means of candlelight in my little bedroom as this particular room was not equipped with electricity.

It was in the late 1940s that I had my first aeroplane flight, but I had to sing in public for the first time for the privilege. My eldest sister and her husband took me with them, and two of their friends, who had a son of my age called Donald, to Filey on the Yorkshire coast for a few days.

One evening, we were in the lounge of the Three Tuns Hotel, where one of the guests was playing the piano whilst making arrangements with a friend of his to go flying the next day. Donald and I were near the piano at the time, and we were told that they would take us with them on the flight if we would give a vocal accompaniment to the pianist. Donald declined, but I stepped up to solo render 'Mighty Like a Rose' for my vocal debut. Singing was to be another of my lifetime loves, and this would be not the last time that I sang on stage.

True to their word, we were taken next day on a fifteen-minute flight over Bridlington Bay in a high-wing Auster light aircraft. I had an affinity for aircraft, which would result in my later attempts to join RAF aircrew as a career.

In 1950, our school was chosen to lead off the massed schools' physical training display before over 100,000 spectators gathered in the huge Roundhay Park arena for Leeds Children's Day, which in those early post-war pre-television days was a major spectator event for the city. Nowadays, this giant natural amphitheatre is only used for the occasional pop concert.

As lead school, we were sited at the front left-hand corner of the display immediately below the vast bulk of Hill 60, the huge slope which housed most of the spectators. Our position was the one from which all the other schools took their reference. For my own part, I was positioned at the front left-hand corner of our block and had the job of leading our school and, thereby, the whole massed groups out on to the arena. A fleeting moment of fame relished and savoured by the then diminutive blonde thirteen-year-old.

In 1950, I was to start growing quite speedily, adding over a foot to my height in the subsequent five years. It was also in 1950 that I passed my scholarship to Leeds Central High School, an all-male school (or so they thought!) in the centre of the city. So it was that I said goodbye not only to St Luke's School but also to my childhood.

As to my feelings of difference, yes they still nagged deep down. Something about me didn't seem right, but I was determined to overcome the feelings, to show the world that I could defeat and overcome them and that I could succeed with the deal that nature had given me.

CHAPTER THREE

Puberty and Teenage Confusion

Childhood gone, a passing glimpse
Of things one day to be
Through teenage years of wonderment
And contentment now set free

—Faye Helen Wardle

The educational transition from primary school to high school was quite traumatic. St Luke's was only a small mixed school, and I was suddenly plunged into a world of over 600 mainly older boys, many of whom had already reached the early stages of manhood. The determination to make a go of things again surfaced, and I gradually settled down and began to make some new friends.

In particular, I was very proud of my new school uniform, especially as my royal blue blazer bore the gold coat of arms of the City of Leeds, complete with gold owls. Little did I realise at the time that the next time I would wear royal blue with the city's coat of arms in gold would be as I was trotting out for the Leeds United Football Club, but this was eight years into the future. It is ironic that the third wearing of royal blue with a gold owl was in more recent times at a social function where I adorned my full-length blue evening gown with a small gold owl brooch to the shoulder—three very diverse exhibitions of the civic colours and coat of arms.

I was, of necessity, adapting to the male role in life, burying deep any inner feelings of difference and trying to make the most of what nature had apparently decreed I must be.

I did however during my early teens begin to experiment with cross-dressing in private, and I was confused by the deep feelings of contentment which resulted from these clandestine experiments.

I definitely had something odd about me which I could neither understand nor explain, and my feelings of contentment were tinged with a deep sense of guilt as I didn't feel I should have been expressing such tendencies. I also found difficulty in sharing the deep fascination which my male friends obviously showed towards girls. At the cinema whilst the other boys were ogling the female forms, I found myself studying the female fashions, female mannerisms, and deportment. I was however still convinced that these 'differences' were merely a phase, a transition through which I would pass or which would fade away with time.

I was around this time also drawn towards newspaper articles about Christine Jorgensen (who was formerly George, an American GI) and later articles on April Ashley. I found these early stories of transsexuality fascinating and disturbing. Were such things really possible? I was jealous of their transitional state, and yet I sensed this couldn't be for me, and I must get on and live my own life. But now, there were early rumblings of just what my problem was. It was in a way horrifying and beyond contemplation, and yet . . .

I continued to enjoy playing soccer at school, turning out regularly for my house team and occasionally for the school team. In particular, I enjoyed the sheer luxury of grass pitches and unfaded kit. I think my early games on the cinder patches of South Leeds were now standing me in good stead.

Cross-country running occasionally interrupted the soccer season. This particular activity was mandatory, and I could never understand the need to run off through clinging mud, stinging hail, driving snow, freezing sleet, cold streams, dark forbidding woods, and ploughed fields just to finish up where you had started.

This cross-country running took place when the weather was too bad for football just to compound the madness! We were led to believe it was character building, and some of the boys seemed to enjoy it however (usually the ones who didn't like football!).

It was during 1953 that I made my debut in open-age soccer. One of the masters at Central High was a lovely, rotund character called Mr

Marshall, who was to become a good friend in my immediate post-school days. He was involved with the Centralians, the school's old boys soccer team in the Yorkshire Old Boys League (or West Riding Old Boys League as it was in those days). On one particular Saturday, one of their teams was due to play a friendly match against a team called Bramley Wanderers, and Mr Marshall saw this as an opportunity to 'blood' one or two of the youngsters from school, so I was invited.

I was positioned out on the wing, supposedly one of the easier positions from which to ease me into the game. Every time I received the ball, I was met with a crashing tackle from the opposing fullback, and I received little joy from the game and contributed little to our cause.

At the end, I trooped off the field feeling somewhat dejected and thinking I could never play open-age soccer on the evidence of this game. One of the opposition came over, put his arm around me, and said, 'Don't worry, son, your opponent today is playing for the Northern Command against the Football Association XI at Elland Road on Wednesday. He's just come home on leave and asked if he could have a run out with us.'

What a baptism! I went down to Leeds United's ground at Elland Road on the Wednesday to watch the game, and there was the same fullback turning out against the country's finest!

Summer sports became passable. Cricket at Leeds Central High School was played on grass pitches with a conventional leather-covered ball and was much more enjoyable than the concrete wicket with cinder outfield, together with the hard cork ball that I had endured at St Luke's. I was still something of a spare part on athletics days, being not quite quick enough for a sprinter (although my take-off speed over ten yards or so surprised many on the football field) and not having the necessary endurance for a distance runner.

On one athletics day, in desperation one of the masters gave me a discus and told me to have a go with it. Entering the discus circle, I gave a quick twirl and promptly hurled the discus twenty feet beyond the existing school record, a hidden talent that was as much a surprise to myself as it was to the bemused onlookers.

So it was that I was groomed for special tuition in the event and elevated from athletic obscurity to the exclusive ranks of the school athletics team, competing with them against many schools around the region. My record-breaking early throw I repeated at the School's Athletics Day at Templenewsam arena in 1955, setting a new official school record that stood for several years.

For this feat, I was to be one of a select band of only four from the school, and the only one from my house, who were awarded their school athletics colours that year, and all this from a position of sporting obscurity just a short time before!

I remember my days at Leeds Central High School with fondness. In particular, I enjoyed the all-male environment (except for a strange embarrassed feeling in the changing rooms) as I had started to find female company somewhat disturbing. I was never sure just what was expected of me in female company, and I didn't share the lust that was obviously displayed by the other males towards the girls.

My scholastic achievements were average, but I did obtain ten passes at General Certificate O level.

I was fortunate with my holidays in the 1950s, as my eldest sister and her husband took me with them on their car journeys around Europe.

I developed through them a love for travel and the continent. In particular, I loved the countryside in Germany, a country that was to be entwined with the next episode of my life.

CHAPTER FOUR

Per Ardua Ad Astra

So buried deep the differences
In uniform of blue
From English Moors to Baltic shores
To find first love so new

—Faye Helen Wardle

During the early 1950s, I had to give some thought to my future career when my school days were over. The drive to prove myself in a male-macho world drove me towards thoughts of a career in the Fleet Air Arm or the Royal Air Force (RAF).

There was a certain appeal to having an aircrew commission. I had obtained a sufficient number of passes in the General Certificate of Education for entry to the RAF and applied for aircrew entry early in 1955 whilst still at school. After an initial test and medical at the RAF Careers Centre in Leeds, I was sent down to the Aircrew Selection Centre at Hornchurch in Essex. Here, I was one of fifty-odd applicants who were subjected to a rigorous series of medical tests and tests of dexterity and ability. I passed A1 G1 and moved on to become one of the final fifteen.

We were divided into three teams of five and were thereafter referred to by letter and number, Team A being A1 to A5, Team B being B1 to B5, etc. We had to take turns in leading our team through a series of reliability and initiative tests and various verbal tests and inquisitions.

Having come through the initial tests to the final fifteen, we had already shown our aircrew capabilities. These later tests were to determine our potential as commissioned officers and to test our leadership qualities. From these fifteen, they chose one pilot and one navigator. I was asked if I was interested in an air signallers post, but as this didn't carry a commission, only a senior NCO ranking, I declined and returned home to Leeds.

One interesting aspect of the interviews we were subject to at Hornchurch was that of the final fifteen, the other fourteen wanted to be fighter pilots, whereas I was the only one who wanted to be a bomber pilot. My stated reason for this was that after my spell with the RAF was over, I wanted experience on heavy aircraft to become a Civil Airlines pilot. I don't think this helped my case somehow. I think they were looking for more of a gung-ho, devil-may-care attitude rather than someone who was already looking to the post-RAF period. I also don't think my thick Yorkshire accent helped in those days of elitist attitudes.

So it was that I was to simply serve my two years' National Service in the RAF, after having been prepared to sign on for twenty-two years if I had secured an aircrew commission.

I left Central High in July 1955, and to earn a bit of keep before my National Service started in late September, I took a temporary job as Goods Porter at Leeds Central Station (now long demolished). This was quite an experience; working in teams of three, we were allocated various railway wagons in the goods yard to unload. Bonus was paid to each team on the total weight moved over and above a certain minimum limit.

It was pot luck on your assignments. Sometimes, there were a few metal bars in the wagon which were speedily dispatched, and you moved straight into the bonus weight. Other times, you would open a wagon to find it stacked floor to ceiling with large boxes of corn flakes, and you would be working away for some time with little chance of approaching bonus weight.

To enter the RAF for National Service, I had to once again report at the Careers Office in Leeds for an initial written intelligence test. I explained I had already passed this paper before being sent to Hornchurch earlier that year. Upon hearing that I had been to Hornchurch, they immediately shepherded me through for medical tests without the further written test (just where were their records?).

The medical consisted of visiting a series of doctors, in a line of cubicles, who each carried out individual tests. All went well until I came upon one particular cubicle.

'Just give me a sample in that jar over there.' I was instructed.

I resisted the temptation to come out with the golden oldie of 'what from here' and instead announced that I couldn't at that time.

'Don't worry about it' was the reply. 'Have a drink of water and sit down for a while.' After several drinks of water and watching the procession as all the other candidates, having finished their written papers, dutifully produced their samples, I, last but not least, finally produced a tiny measure for sampling. I was first into the medical section and the last one out!

It was 26 September 1955 that I was to report to RAF Cardington in Bedfordshire to start my two years' National Service. After a few days of more medicals (no problems with samples this time!), haircuts, and kitting out, I was posted to RAF West Kirby on the Wirral peninsula in Cheshire for the eight-week recruit training (more commonly referred to as 'square bashing').

At West Kirby, I was assigned to Trenchard Flight, and I proudly fixed my pale blue disc, which denoted our flight, behind my RAF cap badges. Our drill instructor, or DI, was a tartar of a regular serviceman by the name of 'Tiger' Smith, with a barrel chest, ramrod back, broken nose, and a voice like a delivery of limestone road stone. He was a living caricature of every recruit's nightmare.

There was some rivalry between the three flights in the intake, and this was reflected in the drill test which was carried out just before 'passing out' from recruit training. In this test, each flight in turn performed set drill routines on the square and was marked on their performance by a group of watching officers.

'Tiger' announced to us that his last Trenchard intake had come third, and he was going to make sure that we did better. True to his word, he worked us hard and made our lives hell.

Came the day of the drill test. We were first on the square and pulled out all the stops to impress with our well-rehearsed routine. We were marked at 77, a higher mark than the previous intake's winners, who had scored 75. Tiger Smith's satisfied smirk said it all and confirmed our united effort. Then came the second flight, who were awarded 80 after a near-faultless performance, and to make matters worse, Churchill Flight, who were last on the square, scored 82!

We had come last, but not even the hardened 'Tiger' could condemn our position of third in what was obviously an intake of some standing.

We had what were known as 'Bull' nights, where all in the billet had to work hard, getting everything to shine like a new pin. We were also given a 'six-week task' to carry out. Our billet's six-week task was to build a model of the camp's gymnasium.

No one in our team fancied doing this job except me, so the others agreed to do my share of work on Bull night if I built the model. So when the whole billet was busy shining, polishing, dusting, and washing, I lay on my bed playing with cardboard and plastic fashioning our model. It's not often a female can get a group of men to do the housework while she lies on the bed playing with models! But none of us realised that this was the case at the time!

Another experience at West Kirby was a series of kit inspections. All the kit for each airman had to be laid out on the bed, in a prescribed fashion and form, for the inspection of the duty officer and NCOs. If there were any deficiencies, you would be in trouble. It was not unusual to have odd deficiencies, and we soon realised that the inspection always went down the same side of the billet and back up the other. So we made sure the first side was complete in all respects by 'mucking in', and as the inspection entourage was proceeding down that side, behind their backs, various items were being thrown across to complete the second side from those on the first side that had been inspected. As one of the objects of recruit training is to build up team spirit, then it had certainly succeeded in our billet.

One major outdoor task we had to perform was the reliability and initiative test. For this, we were transported out to the sand dunes of Formby beach just up the coast and deposited there to survive on our own for a few days, camping on the dunes. We were divided into teams of eleven, and I was put in charge of our team. On our second day, we were transported some ten miles inland towards Ormskirk, with the instruction to find our way back to Formby beach within a set time. We were also instructed that we could not use any public or private transport and that we could not call at any shops etc.

As I set off with my team, I took them into the first shop we came upon, to stock up with drinks and food, and then I organised for us to have a lift on a farm transporter to within a couple of miles of our target. Here, we hid under a bridge, allowing an appropriate time to pass to turn up on time according to instructions. Perhaps I would not have scored high on reliability, having violated some instructions, but I would have expected full marks for initiative. Anyway, as suspected, no one was any the wiser, and we had completed our task. Perhaps if anyone was aware of my 'rule bending', then it may have accounted for my ultimate remote posting in the Western World's last outpost on the chilly Baltic shore!

It was at West Kirby that I gave my first blood donation. Dear old 'Tiger' in his regular morning pronouncements told us that a mobile blood transfusion unit was visiting the camp that day and that donations were voluntary. He then added that all volunteers would get the rest of the afternoon off and that anyone who didn't volunteer without good reason would spend the afternoon on the square with him, and he would make their lives hell! Needless to say everyone who could volunteered, including me.

Fortunately, recruitment to blood donations is a little more subtle nowadays. The experience wasn't unpleasant, and it led me to donate blood throughout the rest of my life until reaching the age of seventy when I had to cease donating.

We were worked hard at West Kirby, and during the training, I frequently glanced enviously at the civilians who passed on the other side of the camp fence. I vowed to return someday to look from the outside at someone else being put through it.

However, as National Service ended shortly after I came out, when I went back to the camp a few years later, there was nothing on the site but ploughed fields. The only remaining signs of the huge complex that used to be RAF West Kirby were the two original gateposts now set in the field hedging.

Upon completion of recruit training at West Kirby, we were given a choice of RAF career, which in theory they tried to meet. The 'choice' consisted of placing six preferences from a long list in order of personal preference. The third on my list was radar operator, and this was the post I was allocated.

I was duly assigned to Radar Training School at RAF Compton Basset in Wiltshire, for a ten-week training course. The training was on the somewhat antiquated plan position indicator radar of wartime vintage, but this provided the basic grounding, and got me used to working in dark restricted conditions, which I adapted to despite my claustrophobic tendencies. Why did it give me a warm feeling when I thought that in the war it was the Women's RAF who worked the radar? I didn't know that it was yet again a relationship and association with my feminine side at that time.

Luckily, for my own part, our instructor also was charged with organising the section's soccer team, a task in which he had little interest.

He was therefore happy to pass on the duty to me, as I was brave enough to say yes when he asked if any in our group played soccer.

Most of my time at Compton Basset was therefore spent as football player manager, organising team, strip, etc., rather than on radar training, a real labour of love. A spin-off from this was that I became one of the most popular members of the intake, particularly as the team started to win games and rose rapidly up the camp's league table from the parlous lowly position when I took over. In particular, our instructor was delighted as our on-field success reflected kindly on him.

I was fortunate in having a collection of decent players available in our intake, and I was able to weigh in with several goals, which boosted my on-field confidence and was good for my off-field 'street credibility'.

We had to do a spell of guard duty while we were at Compton Bassett, and on one of these duties, I was placed on the main gate, keeping a check on the comings and goings. During my spell on the gate, the commanding officer's car complete with appropriate pennant approached, and the sergeant, who was with me on the gate, raised the barrier to allow him easy entrance. I stepped out and stopped the vehicle. Going around to the commanding officer, I said, 'Excuse me, sir, can I see your identity please.'

This brought a tirade of abuse aimed at me from the sergeant.

'Just a minute, Sergeant,' the CO snapped. 'This airman is perfectly entitled to stop anyone at this gate, including me, and I would not have expected anything else.' He produced his identity card for me to check and muttered quietly to me, 'You cheeky young pup', as I returned his smile and stepped back to salute his entry. Some day, my mischievous side will get me into trouble!

Despite my preoccupation in attending to sporting matters, I nevertheless managed to pass my radar trade test with flying colours, largely because of a rapid developing affinity to using the necessary electronic equipment. I therefore awaited a permanent posting. I was rather saddened to be leaving Wiltshire, but I looked forward to new challenges.

Yes, I was becoming more self-confident and adventurous.

As the possibilities for postings were worldwide, I expressed a preference for Yorkshire or Germany, on the basis that I wanted to be close enough to home to get home at odd times, or to be far enough away as to not worry about the home visits. Sure enough, I was posted to the Second Tactical Air Force in Germany.

The route to Germany involved a train journey to London and then a station exchange across to Liverpool Street for the journey across Essex and East Anglia to Parkeston Quay, Harwich. At Parkeston Quay, before embarkation, we were given a meal of stew followed by rhubarb and custard.

'No sharp corners for the foods return journey to follow!' I joked. It was to be no joke.

Our sea-bound transportation was an allegedly flat-bottomed antiquated troop ship by the name of the Empire Wansbeck. What was to follow was to prove to be one of the worst nights of my life.

We set off across the North Sea, heading for the Hook of Holland in a force nine gale. The ship bounced around like a cork. We were crammed into overheated conditions below decks in five deep bunks and were denied access to the decks for fresh air because of the storm conditions. Needless to say amongst companions of obvious fragile constitutions, I succumbed for the only time in my life to the 'mal-de-mer' and involuntarily joined in the redistribution of our earlier meal! Yes, there were no sharp corners!

What a night, and despite our on-board efforts to tidy ourselves up immediately prior to docking, what a sight we must have looked as we staggered on to the snow covered dock in Holland! The train journey across Holland was in blessed contrast to our ocean-bound experience, and we gradually regained our composure. One curious fact from our sea trip was that there was every facet of the British armed forces on board except navy! No doubt they flew the fragile mariners abroad!

My first port of call in Germany was to RAF Goch near the Dutch border, which was the transit camp where permanent postings were allocated. We all anxiously scanned the postings board. There alongside my name was 646 Signals Unit RAF Obernkirchen.

I had heard of Obernkirchen from their world famous Children's Choir (older readers may remember their version of 'The Happy Wanderer'), but I had no idea where this was in Germany. I finally located it, a small village near the town of Buckeburg in Lower Saxony, just west of Hannover.

It was quite a long train journey across Germany to our main unit, through the Ruhr and the country's industrial heartland and out into the open farmland of central Germany.

Upon arrival at the camp, which was on a hillside surrounded by lovely pine woods, my companion Johnny Tobin from Northamptonshire and I scanned the hillside location for signs of our radar installation. An NCO from the military police at the camp gates met us.

'Where's the radar?' I asked, anxious to see our new workplace,

'You will find it is not advisable to ask too many questions here.' I was brusquely told by the NCO.

It transpired that the radar sites were on a series of detachments across Germany and that we would ultimately be posted on one of the detachments. In the interim, we were given additional training on the new sophisticated state-of-the art equipment we would be using, and we awaited posting.

While we were waiting for a posting, we were used as odd job men around the camp. After numerous odd jobs, including helping to collect the commanding officer's yacht on a low-loader from Steinudermeer, a nearby large lake, we spent most of our time in the camp's paint shop, painting the various vehicles. I became something of an expert at vehicular sign writing, and I well remember I had to meticulously apply to several vehicles the sign 'Wagen Wird Eingefahren', which was the German signage for 'Running In'.

One detachment which we were advised to try to avoid if at all possible was No 6 way up north on the chilly Baltic coastline at Putlos. Sure enough came our postings. LACs Wardle and Tobin to No 6 Signals Detachment, Putlos, Schleswig Holstein. The 300-mile journey to Putlos involved truck to Buckeburg Station, local train to Hannover, then express train northwards to Hamburg, past Celle, and across Luneberg Heath. From Hamburg, we took a further train to Lubeck, a delightful Hanseatic town on the Travemunde estuary, a bit like Germany's answer to Chester or York. From Lubeck, we had to catch a local train (quaintly called a Personnenzug) along the coast to Oldenburg Holstein, a small town. From Oldenburg, a further truck journey conveyed us to our destination at Putlos right on the Baltic coast, and only five miles from the Iron Curtain border with East Germany. Quite a journey taking several hours in all.

Far from being an isolated desolate spot, as we had been led to believe, we found Putlos idyllic. Whilst the winters could be extreme, the summers were almost Mediterranean, and we were blessed with miles of golden sands ringed by sheltering dunes, and days of golden sunshine in the two summers I was there.

It was in the placid, shallow, tideless Baltic waters that, left to my own devices, I finally learned to swim.

The Official Secrets Act does not allow me to dwell too much on the nature of our work there, but provided we fulfilled our duties, which we did with some diligence; we were given pretty much a free hand for the rest of the time. It was here that I was to meet my first love.

On our visits down to the beach, we were frequently joined by some of the locals from a nearby displaced persons camp (a relic of the Second World War).

The local inhabitants were extremely grateful that they just fell on the western side of the Iron Curtain, rather than within the nearby Soviet zone of East Germany as it was then. We were therefore treated like kings and made to feel very welcome.

Needless to say the local girls were attracted to the visiting airmen and were pleased to join us on our beach expeditions. Being one of the more shy males, I gravitated to an equally shy attractive auburn-haired local girl called Margit, who was of Austrian descent, and we struck up an immediate friendship.

These were halcyon days that passed all too soon. I rose through the ranks rapidly and was soon supervising one of the watches. The comparatively small increases in pay were most welcome and enabled me to send more home to my mum.

When the time came near for my demobilisation, I was asked if I had thought about signing on. I, in turn, asked if it could be guaranteed that I could stay at Putlos. In the absence of such a guarantee, I opted to go.

It was whilst at Putlos that we formed a football team that was to become something of a legend. Although we were only a small unit in numbers, we had the nucleus of a team with some fine players. We also had a fine home stadium for our games. Our camp had been the main German Panzer training ground during the Second World War, and the attached sports facilities must have been excellent when at their best. Unfortunately, they had remained neglected for some ten years.

We set to clearing the soccer pitch of all the mole hills and generally tidying up the facilities. I took charge of team matters (that born organiser coming out again!).

The main problem was opposition; the local Putlos village team had quite a local reputation, so we asked them to provide our first opponents. They obviously had some doubts about the quality of our small band and turned out most of their second team for the game. This team we duly dispatched 7-1, and yours truly managed to score a couple of them.

This result stung the locals into asking for a return game against their full squad. This was duly arranged, and we sailed through 4-2, and the margin could have been even larger.

It was during this game that an accidental collision between me and the opposing goalkeeper resulted in the player being laid out and requiring medical attention. At this time, challenges on the goalkeeper were frowned upon on the continent. I was awarded the dubious nickname of the 'Blond Swine' by the local Germans, who read more into the incident than there actually was. Both my teammates and I found this quite amusing as I was normally the least aggressive in our squad.

We saw off several other local sides, and we were asked if we would like a game against the local town team at Oldenburg Holstein. This was arranged for a balmy Saturday evening in May 1957, just a few hours after the F.A. Cup Final in England between Manchester United and Aston Villa had been shown on Eurovision Television.

As this televised F.A. Cup Final, which had been watched by many of the locals, had involved an unsavoury collision between an Aston Villa player and the Manchester goalkeeper, I was advised by my teammates to try to avoid the opposing keeper that evening in view of my track record!

What we hadn't expected were the public notices around the town advertising the game as Oldenburg vs. RAF XI. If the locals thought we were the RAF representative team, then we had quite a reputation to live up to.

As it turned out we lost 6-3, but we certainly were not disgraced, and the game attracted over 3,000 spectators, who seemed to enjoy it. The opposition were delighted and asked for a return game at our own modest ground. This time, we rose to the occasion and were good value for our one-all draw. I had the honour of scoring our goal.

The successes of our modest little team were a source of pride to our warrant officer, who in a rash moment presented us with a mammoth task.

From time to time, army regiments arrived at our camp for a short stay to use the coastal firing ranges, and our chief, Warrant Officer Marfleet, in his off-duty hours, was in the habit of imbibing alcoholic beverages with the visiting senior NCOs. On one particular occasion, the visiting regiment was from one of the guards (the exact name I forgot), and their claim to fame was that they contained the BAOR soccer champions (i.e. the best forces soccer team in Germany). The visiting colour sergeant was boasting of this fact when our chief stepped in and said his team could see them off! So the wager was made with a crate of beer resting on the outcome (and a lot of inter-service pride). We had no option other than to go out there and give of our best.

I think secretly we were hoping that we wouldn't be disgraced too much, as despite our local successes, to take on the BAOR Champions, who were playing for the honour of their regiment, was quite a daunting task.

Roared on by a horde of their fellow squaddies, the guards team (every one over six feet tall) tore into us from the first whistle. We were swept back by a red-shirted tide and were soon two goals down. The hiding we had feared was in the offing. Our effort was not helped when we had a player stretchered off in the opening minutes. This was in the days before substitutes, and we had to face the rest of the game with only ten men and a rearranged team, as I dropped back into defence.

As is usually the case, this adversity helped our determination, and we came more into the game and made the score 2-1 just before half-time. Despite conceding a silly third goal just after the restart, we again came back to make it 3-2 and had the vaunted champs hanging on desperately until the end as we sought in vain for the equaliser.

We had given them some game, and we had certainly not been disgraced. The after-match celebrations were far better in our camp than theirs, and despite it costing him a crate of beer, we could tell that our chief was proud of his small band. Even the guards admitted we had been the hardest team they had faced.

What of my hidden self during these macho forces days?

I had thrown myself into my new life with gusto and enjoyment, and the hidden female side had obviously decided it was time to take a back seat. With no opportunities to express my feminine side and little time to even think about any 'differences', I was for a while content that I had finally settled into some degree of normality. I was attracted to a lovely girl, was popular amongst my colleagues, and was as happy as I had been for some time. The thoughts of 'what should have been' did indeed seem to have been a passing phase. I was unaware that this condition would not go away.

However, the time to depart from Germany came, and in September 1957, I said my farewells to Margit and my many friends at Putlos. Margit and I vowed to keep in touch and to visit each other whenever possible. She was due to move with her family to Bad Godesberg near the

Federal Capital of Bonn in the Rhine Valley. This was far more accessible from England than the distant Baltic shores.

The journey back to England was less eventful than our outward journey, the North Sea deciding to give us a more peaceful overnight crossing, despite being on the Empire Wansbeck again. The only event of any note was that my friend Johnny Tobin and I missed our demobilisation train at Paddington.

Having been deposited at Liverpool Street Station at lunchtime, we had some four hours before connecting with the train which would take us to Gloucester and the demobilisation camp at Innsworth. So I took Johnny with me to visit my sister Barbara, who at that time lived at Loughton, some twelve miles north-east of London but on the Central Line underground. Sure enough on our return, we did not allow sufficient time to get across to Paddington, and our connection had departed on time (unusual for British Railways!). This turned out to be not too serious an occurrence, and a later train made sure we arrived at Innsworth that evening, albeit a little late.

On 26 September 1957, I therefore left the RAF, two years to the day since enlistment, as a much more confident and wiser person than the one who had arrived at Cardington in 1955.

If only I had known at this time what the future held! If only the opportunities that I had found so late in life had been available then, if only . . . if only.

But life is full of 'if onlys', and none of us is Solomon.

So it was back to Civvy Street and the next phase of my journey.

CHAPTER FIVE

This Sporting Life

On field of green in gold and blue
A chance to star, a dream come true
A lesson learned as doubts hold sway
A time when first love fades away

—Faye Helen Wardle

Back in Civvy Street, I had the initial problem of finding employment. I must confess that I had given little thought to exactly what I saw as a suitable career for myself during my days in the forces, and my experience with operating radar equipment offered little scope back in Leeds. I applied for numerous office and drawing office jobs and secured a few interviews but no offers of employment. Eventually, I was interviewed for the job of surveying assistant in the estates management section of a firm of estate agents in Leeds. They decided to give me a try, and I started in early November 1957 at the salary of £3.10s (£3.50) per week. This was something of a pittance, even in those days, but it was a start.

The firm handled the day-to-day management of a large number of residential and commercial premises in and around the city, and I quickly became involved in a multitude of tasks.

My Saturday afternoons were spent playing football with the Centralians (the Old Boys team of my former school), but much of my social life was spent in isolation, as I seemed by and large to have little in common with the male social groups. I spent my time doing a bit of oil painting and sketching or visiting the cinema. I also spent a lot of time at my eldest sister's house at weekends.

I threw myself into my work in estates management, as I had started to really enjoy the job. I wrote to Margit frequently, mixing my English with my limited grasp of German, and she replied in her attractive broken English. I visited her in Bad Godesberg in Germany, but I sensed a resistance from her parents to her having an English boyfriend. She also visited England, and I was able to show her much of my beloved Yorkshire. She found much amusement in my referring to the dales and fells as mountains.

Some of the magic however had gone from our early togetherness in the Baltic sunshine, and the differences in our cultures and backgrounds were brought home on our respective visits. I also had not overcome the strange resistance I felt to developing a relationship with a female. The correspondence became less and more formal, and we gradually lost touch. I was alone again.

Margit did keep in touch with Peggy, one of my workmates whom I had introduced her to, and through Peggy, I learned that Margit had met and married a German boy. My relationship with her however belonged to another time, another place, and what seemed like another age.

I looked forward with eager anticipation to my games of Winter Saturday afternoon soccer. It was after one match at nearby Dewsbury, when I felt I had acquitted myself reasonably well, that I was approached by one of the spectators (in fact one of a very few spectators). He gave me his name and said that he was a scout with Leeds United and that if I fancied a trial with the club, then would I report at the practice ground at Fullerton Park on the following Tuesday evening.

I was stunned and surprised. One always considers that they would like a try at a higher level, and my experiences with our great team in Germany had whetted my appetite for higher-grade soccer, as I was of a type that played better amongst better players, but this was an offer at a level I hadn't dreamed of. To be involved with the local professional team that I had religiously followed since 1947 was mind-boggling to say the least.

It was with some trepidation that I turned up at the practice ground for training with the part-time professionals. The coaches were Ernie Taylor, Ivor Powell, and Willis Edwards, and the manager at this time was no less than Raich Carter—four great legends and all former internationals.

I introduced myself, and I was told that they would get me fit before giving me a game. I thought I was fit—how wrong I was! To say the programme was gruelling was putting it mildly. What the hell! I wanted to play football, not to be a marine commando!

However, whilst at first I struggled (manfully?) to keep pace with the others, I gradually got to the stage where I could just about hold my own in the sprints and various other endurance tests.

I still couldn't understand why I felt strangely embarrassed in the changing rooms and communal baths. It wasn't that I myself had anything to hide; indeed, my male body was at this time one that most young men would have been proud of. I also took a back seat during the ribald male humour and loud-mouthed cursing which pervaded the dressing rooms and training. I put my reluctance to join in the ultra-macho side of things down to a natural shyness (it was but I didn't realise why at the time) and the fact that I was a newcomer in a strange new world.

Practice games were organised from time to time, and in one game in early March 1958, I had one of those games that sometimes occur when everything went just right. I scored twice, narrowly missed a hat trick, and had a hand in the two other goals as the blues (colour, not mood!) beat the golds 4-2. Ernie Taylor told me after the game that they were including me in the A team to meet Notts County A in the cup tie on the following Saturday.

My elation at this news was tinged with some self-doubt. I had hoped for a baptism in their Yorkshire League team, not plunging straight into a North Midlands Combination Cup semi-final.

While I had developed friendships with the part-timers on Tuesday evening training, most of the A team that Saturday were full-time professionals (many with first team football league experience) whom I was meeting for the first time. It was an awesome experience donning the famous blue and gold strip (it was to be 1962 before the club switched to the even more famous all-white strip that they still use at present), alongside players that I had watched from the terraces.

I kept trying to tell myself that I shouldn't be so nervous. If they hadn't considered me up to it, then I wouldn't have been chosen. My nervousness even overcame my usual shyness in the changing room.

My mind drifted back to the games for St Luke's School only a few short years before on the cinder-strewn Holbeck Moor, just a few hundred yards from Leeds United's ground, and I started to wish I was back there as the butterflies took off in my stomach.

We trotted out and soon were surrounded by several youngsters seeking autographs, and while they obviously didn't know the blonde newcomer, I had one or two books thrust at me for signature. It gives me some amusement now to think that perhaps out there, there are some males, now well into adulthood, who may have a particular signature in a long-cherished autograph book that will now present a certain curiosity value! Even if only as a signature of an early female footballer!

My start to the game was to be disastrous. In the first couple of minutes, I found myself with the ball at my feet in front of an open goal for my first touch of the ball, an ideal opportunity for a dream start. I knocked it towards the goal in an effort that would have beaten most of the amateur goalkeepers whom I was used to facing, not so the agile professional in the Notts goal. He was leaping to block my effort almost before I had made contact. I could sense the disappointment from my new colleagues, and I was never to recover from this early miss. Being the type of person who thrives on success, I am sure that had that early touch resulted in a goal, then with confidence sky-high, my game, and possibly my future, would probably have been very different.

Tackles were flying in hard and fast, and I seemed to be singled out for some particularly harsh treatment. I began to realise that my success in the practice games was largely due to the lack of serious tackling from the opposition.

The game at this level did not seem any more skilful than I was used to, but it seemed to be played at a breakneck pace, which gave little time for dwelling on the ball. Thought and reaction had to be instantaneous. The need for the extra training I had been subject to became obvious. I was black and blue by half-time, and we trailed off two goals to nil down. The last thing I needed was a telling-off, but I was with some justification singled out for a verbal lashing from Ernie Taylor, our coach, as I sipped my half-time beverage.

'You're like a bloody big docile dog, when are you going to get stuck in and give them something back instead of just taking it all?'

I had no reply. The rougher side of the game I abhorred. I didn't consider myself a coward, but I had the old built-in resistance against hurting anyone else. Looking back, this deep-rooted female trait was to be a hindrance throughout my male existence. Anyway as far as soccer is concerned, I believe the ball is the thing to be kicked, not the opposition.

The second half, which was goal-less, wasn't much better than the first, but I learned to avoid most of the bone-crunching tackling, which seemed to be such a feature of the game at this level. It was certainly a man's game, and I consequently didn't survive too long with the professionals.

It was after the Notts County game that I was to witness a first-hand example of how hostile the world could be towards someone who is different in some way. In our team, alongside me that day, was Gerry Francis who had been brought over from Johannesburg and was one of the first coloured players to appear in the football league. He changed quietly, detached from the rest of us, and wouldn't go into the bath until all the rest of us had finished. This brought home just how he was used to being treated in South Africa and how it was carrying forward to his life in England.

I was to experience this 'difference' and 'isolation' in my own recent new lifestyle. Fortunately, we now live in a multi-racial society, where skin colour is hopefully immaterial. Even in South Africa, tolerance is now prevailing. One can only hope that society will learn with time to show similar tolerance to those with gender identity problems. I like to think it is all an evolutionary learning curve for all mankind.

I was glad to return to the local leagues after sampling the professional game. It isn't a glamorous lifestyle that it may appear to be. There is a requirement for a lot of hard work and dedication, and there is little time for enjoyment in the serious commercialised business of modern day professional soccer.

After my spell with Leeds United, however, some of the magic had gone out of the game for me. The injuries began to mount, and I was to eventually retire from the game at the early age of twenty-seven. I still carry some of the scars on my legs from my on-field encounters, clearly visible through their new nylon covering.

I'm glad that I was involved in the game when I was. Of late, sadly the game has been hijacked by the cheats, thugs, profiteers, and commercialism. Even on the local parks' pitches, the cynicism of the professional game has its imitators. I can recall when the object of the game was simply to score more goals than the opposition. Now the principle is you stop the opposition at all costs and you can't lose. As a spectator sport, it has deteriorated into something approaching the amphitheatres of the Roman coliseums with the crowds baying on the lions to consume the visiting Christians.

However, I have many happy memories of my playing days, and they went some way towards my attempts to establish myself in a macho male world that I continued increasingly to find disturbingly alien. Looking back from my newly developed and constructed female form, I like to think that I didn't do too badly in the male world of Association Football. I can but wonder just how successful I would have been with the Doncaster Belles or the Leeds Vixens in the gentler (more skilful?) world of female soccer?

CHAPTER SIX

Discovering the Dales and a Little of Myself

Often rebuked, yet always back returning
To those first feelings that were born with me,
And leaving busy chase of wealth and learning
For idle dreams of things which cannot be,
I'll walk where my own nature would be leading;
It vexes me to choose another guide;
Where the grey flocks in ferny glens are feeding,
Where the wild wind blows on the mountain side

—Emily Jane Bronte,1818-1848

During the late 1950s and early 1960s, I continued, by and large, to prefer my own company. At the firm of estate agents, where I worked, the switchboard operator Peggy, a charming, gentle, middle-aged lady, with female concern sensed my isolation and tried hard to do some match-making for me with Olive, an attractive, ebullient young girl from Castleford, who worked in the downstairs property sales office.

I liked Olive, and we got along well, spending many happy lunchtimes together, usually at the Cookridge Street swimming baths, (now a council car park). I did, for a while, hold out hopes that something more permanent might come from the relationship, but she had a long-standing boyfriend in Castleford, who eventually won her undivided attentions. She was however for a while undecided and stated that she wished she could split herself in two.

The fact that I could consider a long-standing relationship with a girl was however encouraging as my general lack of interest in the female of the species was making me question my sexuality. I knew I definitely wasn't gay, as I certainly had no inclination towards males at this time. Perhaps I was one of those asexual people with a low sex drive who wasn't particularly interested in either sex?

Lovely Olive helped me to allay some of these fears. I remember being deeply saddened when I lost the lass from Castleford when she departed to get married. I think even the bosses at our workplace were relying on me to get her to change her mind and stay with us, as we were given several jobs to do together, but it was not to be. It was not to be the only time in my life when I was to miss out on the love stakes and see someone I held very dear go off with someone else. Indeed, over thirty years later, I was to feel the even deeper sense of loss as a female watching the male whom I thought to be my world departing with another female. Either way, it really hurts!

Peggy was determined (bless her heart) to take me under her wing. I think she sensed, with deep female intuition, a kindred spirit in need of help and guidance. She asked me if I would like to join the Rambling Club, which she and her husband belonged to. As I was mostly at a loose end on Sundays, the day of their activities, I decided to give it a try.

On a wet miserable August day in 1958, I therefore packed my sandwiches and set off for Leeds City Station to meet the Allerton Rambling Club en route to the high Yorkshire Pennine hills. Without waterproof clothing, I was ill prepared for what was to follow.

We arrived at Clapham Station close to Three Peaks Country, to be greeted by a steady dampening drizzle. Our trek from the station took us along the trail to Ingleborough Cave. Here, we were conducted by the cave guide along narrow paths through the cave system, and it was at least nice to be out of the rain. I did have some reservations about entering the cave as my claustrophobia, fear of confined spaces, made me wonder about the wisdom of this subterranean journey.

My fears were not helped by the fact that the only illumination to the cave was the individual lighted candle on a small board that we each carried. However, the cave was not too confined. Then, just as I was settling down to enjoy the experience, I stepped off the path into the knee-deep freezing-cold subterranean mountain stream. Ah well, I was soaking wet anyway!

After our detour in the cave, we followed the steadily climbing track to Gaping Ghyll pothole, an enormous fissure on the shoulder of Ingleborough mountain. Gaping Ghyll is deeper than York Minster is high.

Ingleborough mountain loomed large to the west. I have seen it likened to a huge brooding monster and with its flattened head wreathed in swirling dark clouds; this description seemed particularly apt. Even in such adverse weather, there was a special majesty about the high Pennines.

It was here that there was to be a parting of the ways for our group.

Most of the adventurous males wanted to journey to the top of Ingleborough, while the remainder of the group, mostly female, followed the leveller trail around the mountain's shoulder over the limestone clints. Again the only reason for this division of our group seemed to be some testosterone-driven desire of the macho members to outperform the rest of us or, as these males would put it, a greater sense of adventure. I'll give them the benefit of the doubt in this respect!

The polished limestone clints, which normally shine out with pristine whiteness, were this day dull grey against the darker grey of the surrounding landscape and the sombre grey skies. The whole scene was monochrome, like an old black-and-white photograph. The penetrating drizzle was incessant. I was seeing the dales at their most uninviting and inhospitable worst. By now, the rain had penetrated into my skin.

As a 'beginner', I was expected to remain with the girls, while the men went off to the gruelling summit ascent. In my fast tiring, saturated, bedraggled state, I didn't argue; one time when my own desire to keep proving myself seemed of little importance. This presented me with the opportunity to chat to the girls socially. In this wild Pennine unisex environment, I felt that little more than a social relationship was expected of me. I was readily accepted into their group, partly, I suspect, out of a desire to get to know the new member of their club. I found myself relaxed, strangely in tune, and at ease in their company.

This was great. I was enjoying myself in female company, and they weren't really such frightening creatures after all. In fact, they were easier to talk to than the males.

The girls seemed to enjoy having a male in their company, who could chat about the more mundane things in life, and not be wanting to pursue purely macho pursuits.

How was I to know at this time that I was finally fulfilling a deep-seated need to relate to members of my true gender and share the natural friendliness and bonding that women normally find in each other's company?

I was later to find in my new female form that this communal female friendliness is of a type unknown between the more hostile and untrusting males, who do not bond as easily.

We eventually met up with our mountain-hopping colleagues, who wasted no time in telling me of the adventures that I had missed by not going over the mountain. I didn't tell them that I had been more than happy where I was (they just wouldn't have understood anyway).

Through the continuing, steady downpour of rain, we made our way back to Clapham Station for the train home (via a local hostelry for a very welcome drink and a partial drying out).

Once on the train, in my saturated state, I was escorted by the males of the party to the guards van, where they gave me an energetic towelling down (I am sure that this would have been far more mutually enjoyable nowadays!), while they rummaged through their spare gear to find me some dry clothing. I was asked if I had enjoyed my day. I assured them that I really had.

'Well, if you can enjoy yourself today in these conditions, then you'll enjoy yourself anytime' seemed to be the popular opinion.

I stayed with the male group for the journey home, but I would have preferred the company of the girls who were laughing and chatting in the next compartment.

So it was that I became a regular member of their club. I had learned my lesson with the equipment and made sure I was henceforth appropriately 'kitted out' with appropriate boots, waterproofs, and rucksack. My virtually constant preference to walk with the girls was getting me something of a reputation as a Romeo, a reputation that I didn't discourage, even though I was simply enjoying the company of their group.

As part of the club's walks' syllabus, we were all asked to submit walks that we would be prepared to lead, for consideration towards the following year's syllabus. I submitted several for consideration, and some were chosen for inclusion. One of them was listed as Romeo's ramble on, would you believe, February 14, Valentines Day!

Our walks were not restricted to the high Pennines but were more often closer to our home base. In particular, I enjoyed the frequent visits to the Washburn valley off Wharfedale. This particular well-wooded valley contains the long string of reservoirs that supply drinking water to the City of Leeds. Lindley Wood, Fewston, Swinsty, and Thruscross reservoirs give the area its own mini Lake District. When Thruscross Reservoir was formed in the 1960s; it was unfortunately necessary to submerge the beautiful little village of West End, and the huge concrete dam which now holds back its waters stands in stark contrast to the wooded valley and moorland backdrop.

Wharfedale itself became another favourite haunt, from Ilkley up to Bolton Abbey, past the Strid, where the river's waters funnel through a narrow fissure. Then on to Burnsall, Kilnsey Crag, Buckden with the charming Buck Inn through to the head waters of Oughtershaw Beck with its riverside plateau—ideal for picnics, up to Fleet Moss and the wild-open high heather-covered moorland. Sundays became a day of tranquil retreat to these beautiful parts of my home county.

I tried hard to strike up more meaningful relationships with individual girls in the group. There was Audrey, who I thought I was keen on, and who eventually married Derrick, a great big gentle bear of a man from the club, and there was Barbara.

Barbara was several years older than me. She had obviously had one or two bad experiences with the male of the species and possibly saw me as not presenting a particular threat. Anyway, we struck up an ill-fated friendship, which was to endure for a couple of years. This was to lead to us eventually detaching from the club as it gradually disintegrated, and we took to going off walking on our own.

Apart from the walks, the club also had some pot-holing sorties from time to time. At the times when they chose to take themselves off to the bowels of the earth, I was the most popular member of the club, as I always volunteered to stay on the surface and look after the pile of gear and clothing that they left behind.

Even allowing for my claustrophobic tendencies, I couldn't see the point, or the enjoyment, of grovelling around some damp restricted subterranean passage in virtually total darkness.

The others obviously got something from it, as they used to emerge saturated and covered in mud, eager to tell me about all I had missed. I was happy to take their word for it for like cross-country running, it must appeal to some, but not to me.

The walking I did enjoy, however, and I well remember one particular weekend when I was one of the few in our party who conquered the famous Three Peaks Walk, and in atrocious conditions too. This was in

1960. We stayed at the Hill Inn at Chapel-le-Dale, and some twenty-four of us set out at the crack of dawn to scale the steep sides of Whernside, the highest of the three giant fells.

From the summit cairn of Whernside, we rested and watched an old war department goods locomotive pull a lengthy train of open wagons northwards across the Ribblehead viaduct way below our lofty perch, the chug-chug of its laboured progress echoing eerily down the valleys. This was to prove the last of our views for the day as the mist closed in.

From Whernside, we turned our attention to Ingleborough, the scene of my earlier drenching looming large across the valley.

Sure enough, the mist descended and the drizzle started. Just what did this particular mountain have against me? As the mist thickened our party got split up into several groups, and we were quickly completely segregated and lost.

Visibility was down to about twenty-five yards, and there were no landmarks in view for guidance, just the immediately visible world of the nearby peat bogs and the enveloping grey misty shroud.

Our small group of five was fortunate. We came across the northern ridge, known as the Swine's Tail, and followed this up to the summit plateau, the huge flat-top that is such a feature of this mountain. From here, it was easy to find the summit cairn even in the thick mist.

Our group now numbered only five, and we waited for three-quarters of an hour huddled on the damp, misty summit for the remainder of the party. No one else arrived, so we set off down the eastern slopes, across foot-grabbing peat bogs filled with jet-black waters and the long haul across the valley to distant Pen-y-ghent, the last of the Three Peaks.

Once we were away from the heights of eternally wet Ingleborough, the rain eased, and the mist lifted a little. Tiredness was beginning to set in, however, and my leg joints were beginning to seize up. I had got to the stage where cross-country running and pot-holing no longer seemed so mad!

We had reached Horton-in-Ribblesdale, a point of civilisation, and I wondered if it would be best for me to call it a day there and then, especially as the daunting towering bulk of Pen-y-ghent, our final target, was now faintly visible through the mist to the east.

No! I wasn't going to give up now. I needed to do this for myself, and I might never again get the opportunity to complete this circuit. Again, the desire to succeed was taking over, and I laboured onwards.

I came down from Pen-y-ghent summit throwing one foot in front of the other and just longing for the end of the road. The five of us were the only ones to finish the long walk that day. The remainder, having got lost on the slopes of Ingleborough, had finished way round on the south-eastern slopes and had headed for Clapham village and the train home, abandoning their Three Peaks target.

The Rambling Club was not restricted to outdoor pursuits, and various other social events were organised. The regular photographic slide shows and lectures were particularly enjoyable and were to lead to my developing an interest in colour photography. There were also the dances. These usually comprised Scottish and country dancing interspersed with modern ballroom dancing.

Based on my earlier country dance experience at primary school and the comparative straightforward simplicity of the particular dances, I developed certain proficiency with the reels and barn dances. However, I was completely at a loss with the steps of the ballroom dances. As I was a bit of an odd one out (yet again!), most of the others being ballroom proficient, I decided I ought to do something to remedy this social gap. This was to lead to a very important chapter in my life, which would result in my finally finding a partner and the establishment of my wonderful family.

CHAPTER SEVEN

The Dancing Years

A new love found, a bride-to-be
To compete anew by Yorkshire's sea
A major turn on my journey's roads
With music sweet and ballroom boards

—Faye Helen Wardle

In September 1963, my mother passed away, her smoking habits (one of her ways of finding relief from her heavy everyday tasks) undoubtedly being the root cause of the lung cancer that finally claimed her. I was the last one of her children remaining at home, all of my brothers and sisters having married and departed from home.

I well remember the last words that I heard her speak as the ambulance crew took her off to hospital: 'Who will look after Roy?' It was the plaintive question I overheard from her. Contrary to the subsequent opinion of my eldest sister, I think my mother sensed that I was different from the rest in some way. I had not been in a position to do as much as I would have liked for her. She had deserved some reward for her lifetime devotion to her family duties.

Ironically, my eldest sister was at this time to take me under her wing and allowed me to move in with her and her husband in the affluent suburbs of North Leeds.

On the social front there remained the deficiency in my dancing abilities.

Looking through the local classified section of the Yorkshire Evening Post, I found an advertisement for the Central School of Dance in Leeds, and I decided that this was a good starting point. I could widen my social circle and learn to dance at the same time.

My early impressions of the Central School of Dance were mixed.

The crowd was generally restricted to a series of small unsociable groups, so loners were generally left just that. However, I liked Walter and Jeanette Ferrand, the main professional teachers.

During my first few visits to the school, the communal lessons were in the cha-cha. So while I became reasonably proficient at this Latin American novelty dance, I still couldn't do even the most basic of steps for the remaining dances. I therefore sought pastures new.

My next port of call was the De Grey Firth Dance School, again in central Leeds. This was the opposite of the Central School. The crowd was great and very sociable, but the teachers were generally apathetic. As I enjoyed the company, I continued to attend the De Grey Firth School, and by trial and error, I gradually mastered the basics of the waltz, foxtrot, and quickstep.

Rumour circulated that the business was being sold on, and lo and behold, it was purchased by Walter and Jeanette Ferrand from the Central School. I was now getting the best of both worlds.

I was really enjoying my dancing now and frequently asked one particular tall blonde girl up for what became known as our 'zoom' dance, a particularly frenetic version of the quickstep that we developed.

This particular blonde was to eventually prove my bride-to-be, my regular dance partner, mother of my children, and someone whom I was to ultimately, very regrettably, unavoidably hurt very deeply. I have avoided any mention of her Christian name in this autobiography to avoid any continuing hurt.

I have also avoided mentioning the names of my three lovely children as I wish to try to spare them the barbs of a hostile world.

Under Walter and Jeanette Ferrand, the standard of the dancing of their pupils improved considerably, except for yours truly. As the chairman of my football club said (I was still playing at this time), I played football like a dancer and danced like a footballer! So I decided that private lessons were necessary and made a booking with Jeanette. I was embarking upon what was to prove a lengthy amateur dance career.

There was little purpose in private dance tuition without set goals. I therefore aimed for the Bronze Award of the Ballroom Branch of the

International Dance Masters Association. This I attained in April 1961. There followed the Silver Award (October 1961), the Gold (May 1962), then in turn the first, second, third, fourth, fifth, and sixth Gold Bars between July 1962 and August 1965. I had reached the pinnacle of medal achievement.

My tall blonde had moved (as it turned out temporarily) to pastures new, working in South Yorkshire, and I moved on, encouraged by Jeanette, to the Latin American awards, reaching the sixth Gold Bar in November 1968.

I, even for novelty, took the Bronze Medal in Old Time Dancing in November 1966. I had finally found a pastime that did not involve an excess of machismo, although it was very physically demanding.

My dancing interests were instrumental in my decision to quit the football scene, after one particularly bad injury tore the ligaments in the side of my right foot and left me having to use a walking stick for several months.

I didn't enjoy being just a spectator at the dancing sessions. The gentler ballroom scene therefore took over from the green soccer fields in my affections.

Walter and Jeanette had formed the Leeds Formation Dance Team. I had no regular or particular dance partner at this time, and no competition experience, even though I was well qualified medal-wise.

These facts coupled with my willingness to learn resulted in my being trained in all the roles of the male team members so that I could step in at short notice if any member was ill or absent. While this role demanded a heavy amount of versatility, it left me as a permanent travelling understudy (a jack of all trades, master of none, or Jill of all trades, mistress of none as it was to turn out!). I envied the girls their more flamboyant dance routines and their lovely colourful costumes, although I didn't allow this to show.

Often, the dance team would split socially into male and female groups, and my heart told me that I would rather have gone off with the girls as I so often did with the Rambling Club. Again, there was this inner regret nagging away. Why wouldn't it go away and stop haunting me? I didn't want these feelings; I didn't ask for nor enjoy them.

My social life was very settled in the mid-1960s without much progress in personal relationships. I had dance lessons and practice during the week, and I watched football on Saturday afternoons (the great Leeds team of the 1960s and 1970s was coming to prominence at this time, and I had a season ticket at their games for several years).

Sundays were spent walking with the Rambling Club. I had a widening circle of friends, but no particular girlfriends.

I had moved on for personal sporting activities to tenpin bowling, where I was moderately successful in the Excel Headingley Bowling League. However, even here, I was to be shot to unexpected temporary stardom.

During one of the evening bowling games, one of the Brady brothers, a well-known local bowling family, was having a flying start to his evening on one of the other lanes. The spectators who were originally spread across the centre gravitated to his lane in anticipation of a record score.

No one noticed my own flying start, which even I put down to a flash in the pan, as I ran up a first game personal best of 228. I continued to do no wrong and passed this with a 236 in the second game.

Word gradually spread around the centre that despite the efforts of the more illustrious player on the nearby lane, there were even bigger things afoot amongst one of the lesser teams, and I started to draw some of the spectators to my own lane. The growing band gave me much vocal encouragement as I completed the third game with a 233 for a new centre record series of 697 for the three games. Indeed, had I not missed a simple pin in my final frame, I would have passed 700.

For this feat, I was awarded a gold statuette for best individual performance at the end of season awards.

Needless to say I never again came close to these scores, and the occasional scores over 200 were henceforth few and far between.

It's funny though that throughout all my efforts in life, from the mediocrity, there were just the odd glimpses of occasional stardom, nothing consistent, but enough to keep me going. This has usually resulted in my being able to compete with the best without really being one of the best, not a bad attribute however for my later and forthcoming lifestyle!

Another strange twist to my tenpin bowling activities was that shortly after going full time as Faye, many years hence, I was invited to bowl with an all girls team. Strangely though, I found my new anatomy ill suited for this particular game, and my new firm bosoms were suddenly a major hindrance, necessitating a whole new approach to the game!

I was gradually becoming resigned to bachelorhood. While I found it easy to establish friendships with both sexes at this time, none of the girls whom I was currently acquainted with seemed to be interested in more serious relationships. Again, I had the feelings of being different without knowing how—perhaps the girls could sense this difference?

On the employment front, I had been doing the job of office manager unofficially for some time without the benefits of appropriate salary or formal recognition.

The reluctance of my employers to formally give me the job stemmed from my lack of a formal chartered surveying qualification, which carried more weight than my building qualification, which I had obtained from part-time studies at the College of Building.

However, doing this work did give me a certain amount of autonomy, and I brought my own style to the job.

Rather than being an authoritarian figure, like previous occupants of the post, I introduced a more human dimension, choosing to meet the various building contractors and caretakers at 'level' (usually in their local public house), thereby creating social relationships and working relationships, which resulted in a job that virtually ran itself.

Everyone was kept happy, and no one let me down, in working relationships based largely on trust. This was not to say I was too easy-going, and everyone was aware that they let me down at their peril.

I was to try to carry this humanitarian approach (where was it coming from?) through life, and it was to lead to my later involvement in the fields of trade union activities.

In 1966, my tall blonde returned to my life, and we began to be regular dance partners at the club. Eventually, I plucked up courage and invited her to go with me to the Wednesday night dance at the spa ballroom in Bridlington, and to my delight, she accepted. She was easy to get along with, being fun-loving and easy-going.

I now had my first car, a ten-year-old Morris Minor in British racing green, with the registration of WWT 666. This became known amongst my friends as 'Willie Wardle's Tank'.

I did not appreciate, at the time, the significance of the 666, devil's number, which would bring a small fortune as a personalised plate for someone nowadays, particularly as the Department of Transport has stopped issuing this particular number triumvirate because of the demonic connotations.

At the Wednesday night dance sessions at the Bridlington Spa, there were heats of the Miss Yorkshire bathing beauty competition.

More importantly, there were also heats of the Yorkshire Evening Post ballroom dancing competition, where the first six couples went through to the Grand Finals in September. We had gone along to watch these competitions and enjoy the public dancing with Edwin Harpers Orchestra.

However, fate was about to give my life another important twist. One dance competition couple who knew me and my partner rather disparagingly stated that surely we weren't there to compete. This stung me into action.

'Do you fancy having a go?' I asked my companion.

She was ready to rise to the challenge, and as the dress for the heats was everyday wear, we entered the competition. We finished seventh, just outside the qualifiers, but we had tasted success.

We returned to try again in the heat the following week, came sixth, and so qualified for the Grand Final.

My tall blond and I therefore started having regular dance lessons together and entered various competitions around the country with a small degree of success. We grew closer.

In September's Grand Final at Bridlington, we certainly weren't disgraced, and we were almost awarded enough points to make the second round of the finals, not bad for a couple who had only just started out.

My partner looked absolutely delightful in a pale blue, very full competition dress decorated with a diagonal line of peach roses, and her long blonde hair piled high and set with a profusion of fresh pale peach roses that we had collected from a rose garden on the way to Bridlington, for it was after all in the late 1960s the time of flower power.

For my part, I felt uncomfortable, constrained, and very warm in a tail suit and stiff white shirt with a high starched collar. I did not enjoy wearing a collar and tie at the best of times. The lack of this male necessity I have found to be one of the major advantages of female attire.

In 1967, we yet again entered the Bridlington competition and once again qualified for the Grand Final by coming fourth in our preliminary qualifying heat.

We established a rapport with Jimmy Baron, the compere, and Edwin Harper, the orchestral conductor. Edwin always included in the general dancing a Viennese waltz, especially for us as we particularly enjoyed this dance, and we were able to give full reign to our size, which was suited to movement rather than more static intricate dance steps.

We continued to attend the Wednesday nights at the spa to enjoy the public dancing, even after we had qualified for the finals. Life now seemed more settled and less meaningless.

One of our other dancing successes was that we actually represented the county of Hampshire! This representative appearance actually came about when we entered a competition at Constance Grants Ballroom in South Yorkshire, which was to determine the team to represent Yorkshire in the Butlins Dancing Stars of Tomorrow competition at Blackpool.

The first three couples were destined to represent the county. We made it through to the final six. In the final, the five adjudicators placed us first, second, third, fifth, and sixth, respectively, and on the sliding scale, we were placed fourth overall and just missed out on a place for the county—a case of so near and yet so far.

Shortly after the qualifying event, we were contacted by the organisers of the dancing event. They said that the entry standard in Yorkshire had been so high whereas the entry in Hampshire had been so poor and asked us if we were prepared to represent the southern county? We of course agreed and were granted accommodation at the Butlins Metropole Hotel in Blackpool and a place in the competition at the Blackpool Winter Gardens.

In late 1967, I became engaged to my Viking blonde, and the date of the wedding was set to coincide with her birthday in April 1969. I was overjoyed; at last, I had found myself a partner. My desire for normality was surely now finding fulfilment. If only I knew at this time what life had in store, how my inner self would eventually assert itself and claim its time. And yet if I had been blessed with foresight and avoided the marriage, I would not have had my three wonderful children. They are and always will be, despite their absence from my life, a major comfort and consolation.

During 1968, we attended every single Wednesday night dancing session at the Bridlington Spa. A remarkable achievement as this involved a 140-mile round trip every Wednesday throughout the summer. We had no problems with early qualification for our third successive Yorkshire Evening Post Grand Final.

My inner doubts and feelings had faded during the halcyon days of the late 1960s, and I at last seemed at ease with the gender nature had bestowed on me. I could not know or foresee what was lying dormant and subdued within. It must have been a question of mind over matter as my efforts to get by as male overcame my inner feelings for long spells.

At this time, I was still living with my eldest sister in North Leeds, but as the date for the wedding approached, we gradually accumulated a modest amount of furniture and possessions. To keep these in store was costing us £1.00 per week, a very modest sum nowadays, but an appreciable consideration in the 1960s.

Given my employment with one of the largest landlords in Leeds, we considered renting one of the small properties that they managed so that I could move in with the furniture. I opted for a little back-to-back terrace house in the Armley area of Leeds, which cost the princely sum of twenty-eight shillings (£1.40) per week and so was only eight shillings more than the cost of storage for the furniture.

I moved in with the furniture in late 1968. I therefore experienced, for the first time, living on my own, albeit for just a few short months. This was to be the last time I was to be on my own until, as a confused and emergent Faye, I left our home twenty-five years later in the summer of 1993.

The winter of 1968-1969 was a real bind, particularly as the toilet for the small terrace house was not only shared with some of the neighbours, but was also detached from the house in a separate small toilet block down the street, a design feature of residential lifestyles from Victorian times, which fortunately became discontinued in the latter half of the twentieth century. This detached facility meant that a toilet visit usually entailed donning overcoat (and sometimes scarf and gloves) to venture out in freezing conditions and clutching torch, toilet roll, and toilet key. Needless to say the conditions meant that visits were short-lived as the sub-zero temperatures didn't encourage en-facility dawdling!

However, the economies attached to living in the terrace house at Armley made the odd discomfort worthwhile. The reasonableness of the rental charges made us decide to live in this property for a short time subsequent to our marriage.

The previous summer (1968) had seen a significant change in my employment.

My entreaties with my estate agent employers to pay the going rate for the work I was doing had met with procrastination and a succession of excuses. In exasperation, I sought alternative employment, particularly as I now had to consider my future as a married man.

In my work with the estate agents, I had frequent dealings with the local planning authority and submitted many applications for property alterations for their consideration.

One particular job advertisement caught my eye. It was for the position of planning technician with the local planning authority. I applied, received an interview, and to my surprise was offered the post.

The reaction of my old employers to my imminent departure was to immediately offer me a four-pounds-per-week increase, quite a salary rise in those days, but the die was cast. I welcomed the challenge of new employment and the broader horizons of local government. So it was that I moved into the Leeds Civic Hall on 1 June 1968, into a sphere of work that was to continue for twenty-seven years and would eventually encompass a confused and emergent Faye.

We were married in April 1969 at the beautiful little Norman church of Adel in north Leeds. This little church dates back to the twelfth Century and is the oldest in Leeds. The capacity of this tiny church is only around the hundred mark, so some of our guests had to stand at the rear.

The service certainly had its moments. The vicar had an affliction in one eye and was winking at us all through the ceremony, and as we were walking back down the aisle together, I suddenly found myself walking on my own as my wife's young nephew, who was acting as pageboy and carrying her long veil, had started to walk along her train, thereby pulling her backwards. The wind outside was freezing, and most of my brothers and sisters were missing from the post-ceremony photographs as they absconded to my brother's nearby house for a warm cuppa.

The evening reception was some thirty miles away near Doncaster at a country hotel where my wife used to be manageress. There was to be a minor revolution from my brothers who saw the need to drive so far as restrictive to their celebrations. This we overcame by hiring a private coach to convey them to and from the reception. Apparently, this went down very well, and the party atmosphere went on all the way back to Leeds.

After the very enjoyable evening's celebrations, we bade goodbye to our guests as we departed from the hotel. We had kept the fact that we were staying at that very hotel for the night a secret to avoid any wedding night hanky-panky from our guests. We therefore parked in a lay-by out of sight near the hotel and watched them all depart before we returned to the hotel.

So at the ripe old age of thirty-two, I finally lost my male virginity. The experience however I did not find easy, and the whole experience, whilst wonderful in itself, did not seem to be all that people made it out to be. I couldn't be aware at the time that I was labouring against nature's dictates. Though I was physically capable, there was something holding me back. Something wasn't quite right, and I knew it was this deep-rooted inner oddity and no fault of my lovely patient and caring wife.

For our honeymoon, we had scraped our pennies together and booked the cheapest cabin on a thirteen-day cruise on the P & O liner Oronsay.

After a long train journey down to Southampton and an overnight stay at the Dolphin Hotel, we boarded our ship, which was anchored just in front of the liner The United States. The pristine brand new Cunard liner QE 2 occupied the nearby Ocean Terminal. We set sail to the strains of 'A life on the ocean wave' played by the Band of the Royal Marines on the dockside.

The honeymoon was idyllic, although our bunks, separate and overhung by small wall shelves, were hardly conducive for togetherness. When booking the cabin, I had asked to be placed as far as possible away from the ship's engines, which were midship, to avoid any noise and vibration problems.

We were therefore given a cabin close to the stern. Because of its 'end of the road' location and tapering shape, it had the advantage of being one of the largest cabins available. However, while taking account of the problems associated with the engines, I had neglected one small point.

We were located directly over the propellers, or screws to use their nautical name. While this normally only resulted in an acceptable vibration level, when we crossed the Bay of Biscay in a force eight gale, the screws were leaving the water, and the intense vibration shook everything off the shelves and meant sleep was impossible. During the gale, 75 per cent of the passengers were confined to their bunks with seasickness, but the intrepid Wardle soldiering on determined not to miss a moment of the cruise.

We docked at Lisbon, the Portuguese capital, after sailing up the River Tagus and under the impressive Salazar Bridge. A quick tour of the city, including seeing the white peacocks, and then a taxi ride to Sintra, accompanied by a new-found friend, Paula, a small ebullient girl from Hackney in east London, who was travelling on her own.

At Sintra Castle, the guide went to great lengths to tell us about the wonderful views of the surrounding countryside and across to the Atlantic from the dizzy heights of the castle. However, as the surrounding mist cut visibility to a few yards, it was all a bit irrelevant.

We arrived back at the Oronsay, which we had nicknamed 'Pepper Pot' because of the unusual shape of its single funnel. We were loaded down with armfuls of fragrant mimosa flowers which we had gathered en route.

We were to travel on the cruise almost cheek to cheek with the pristine QE2, which was going through its final trial run prior to its maiden voyage.

We left the storm, mists, and Lisbon behind and headed for the Canary Islands. On the day when we were due to arrive at Tenerife, which was our next port of call, I awoke at the crack of dawn to go on deck to see the island emerging from the light morning mist. It was a peaceful, unreal experience as the palm-fringed shoreline emerged and the warmth of the early morning sun began to penetrate. On Tenerife, we visited a banana plantation, discovering that the bananas are fit for eating when their skins are green!

We took an excursion across the island to Los Americanos, where we walked the full length of the seafront and decided to ride a camel back to where our bus was waiting. We explained to our camel guide that we wanted to go to the other end of the seafront, but despite our on-board protests he insisted on the round-trip and took us back to where we had mounted the beast. Despite our entreaties, we had paid for the round trip, and we were going to get it! Ah well, the ride was certainly an experience, and the bus did wait for us, although I'm sure no one believed our reason for being late.

Next stop was Las Palmas, and here, we found time to relax on the lovely Las Canteras beach and visit an extinct volcano. The weather was warm with a balmy breeze, all very idyllic. No camels this time!

The island of Madeira followed with a hectic dry sleigh ride down steep streets overhung with flowers of Bougainvillea and Jacaranda in the capital Funchal. We were impressed with the lush vegetation that shrouded the island.

It was while in Madeira that we were paid rather a nice compliment. The ship was divided into first-class and tourist sections. We of course were in the tourist class. The professional dance couple who were performing on the ship spent most of their time in the first-class section. At the nightclub we visited in Madeira however, both classes were together.

My wife and I took to the floor for a slow rumba, a lovely sensuous dance that we both enjoyed, to be greeted by table-wide smiles from our friends when we returned to our table. Our companions informed us that some of the first-class passengers had commented to them that they preferred the tourist class dance couple to the ones that they had in first class!

Casablanca was the next port of call, with a coach trip to Rabat and an abysmal meal at the Rabat Hilton. I didn't like Morocco and for some reason felt annoyed at the way the locals treated their womenfolk. I understand that the only time the womenfolk are allowed to walk in front of the males is if there is a suspected minefield ahead!

It was at Casablanca that we almost missed the ship. Whilst my wife was haggling with a group of dockside Arabs for the purchase of a kaftan (the done thing is to bargain with them), I turned to find that a dockside crane had removed our gangplank to the tourist section. We had to race the crane along the dock as it headed for the first to board at the first-class section and make our way back through the ship to our 'home' base.

Of all the ports in all the countries in all the world, I would certainly have chosen anywhere except Casablanca to be stranded, and I can sympathise with Humphrey Bogart and Ingrid Bergman in their desire in the 1940s to leave this particular port.

From Casablanca, we sailed past Gibraltar into the Mediterranean and the Spanish port of Malaga. My wife and I were becoming more and more involved with organising the shipboard entertainments, and she actually never saw Gibraltar as she was busy organising the sweep on the ship's daily mileage at the time, a job that the resident ship's entertainment manager was happy to leave to us.

It was while we were in Malaga that I was to experience just how cold the Mediterranean can be. Taking the local bus (an experience in itself as it was full to bursting) along the coast to Torremolinos, I gleefully sped down the beach straight into the sea. The shock was sharp and breathtaking: the water was freezing. I did a rapid about-turn. Only then, I noticed that despite a busy beach, no one else was in the water. It was colder than anything I had been used to in the distant Baltic and North Sea waters. This temperature phenomenon was probably due to the resort's proximity to the chilly waters of the North Atlantic just beyond Gibraltar's nearby rocky crags. For the Gulf Stream which warms our shores in Britain on its journey North is doing a return journey from the cold Northern Waters when it passes the Straits of Gibraltar.

We approached our homeward journey with some trepidation as we had to recross the Bay of Biscay, the scene of our rough outward journey.

As it turned out Biscay was like a millpond for the return trip with barely a ripple. We had to spend time idling in the English Channel while the QE2, which had docked in Southampton some hours before us, cleared the Ocean Terminal at the start of its official maiden voyage. We in turn docked at the Ocean Terminal which was bedecked with streamers and bunting remaining from the departure of our illustrious predecessor. The hangover celebratory atmosphere from the 'Queen's' departure was in sharp contrast to our regretful end to our own wonderful cruise.

Not to be outdone however, we organised a communal singalong and impromptu conger chain on the boat train back to London from Southampton.

So we arrived back in Leeds at our little back-to-back terrace house in Armley, loaded down with souvenirs, with just a few shillings in our pockets, but some memorable honeymoon experiences.

Accommodation for me and my wife was proving something of a problem. Using the toilet down the street wasn't too bad during the summer of 1969, but neither of us relished using this detached exposed facility during the imminent winter.

House hunting during the summer of 1969 became a necessary regular pastime. We had to miss out on a charming little cottage in the village of Woodlesford that had formerly been the smithy and included a large attached blacksmith barn, due to the fact that we had trouble raising a mortgage. We did however finally secure our own property, a large through terrace house in a secluded part of outer east Leeds, ripe for improvement and with a sixty-yard-long front garden.

In August 1969, we moved from Armley in west Leeds across the city to our new home. For the first few months, the house resembled a building site, but it was ours, and the luxury of internal self-contained toilet facilities was most welcome.

During 1968, I had been troubled by recurring sharp stomach pains that had usually subsided by the time the GP arrived. These continued through 1969 and into 1970. During one particularly bad night-time attack, the emergency GP arrived in time to diagnose that my appendix required immediate removal, so I was rushed into Leeds General Infirmary to experience surgery for the first, but certainly not the last time.

CHAPTER EIGHT

Family Life and the Study Years

A settled life with family new
With studies deep to face
All thoughts of difference buried deep
Neath Fatherhoods pride of place

—Faye Helen Wardle

Meanwhile at my new employment with Leeds City Council, although my main duties were intended to be technical, drafting plans, and graphic documentation to support planning appeal evidence, I was becoming more and more involved in professional duties and the processing of the actual planning applications. Again however, the bar to my progress in this direction was once more my lack of an appropriate professional qualification.

As I did not have a degree, which would have given me an easy route to the Planning School of Leeds Polytechnic, I faced the prospect of a lengthy part-time study qualification route via the Ordinary and Higher National Certificate in Surveying, Cartography, and Town Planning.

In 1970, I therefore embarked on a study course that was to last until the summer of 1979. The ONC was a two-year course with a further two-year course for the HNC. This brought us to 1974. Four years of intense study and examinations. Most of what little spare time this left me was taken up in working on house improvements, and I was becoming a dab hand at 'Do it yourself'.

On the social front in the late 1960s and early 1970s, we continued to enjoy our dancing, but more and more at a social rather than a competitive level. In 1971, we took a late summer holiday on the Spanish Island of Ibiza, a resort which was to become something of a second home, and where we were to make many friends amongst the local populace.

In between 1971 and 1976, we were to visit the island on no fewer than nine occasions to be greeted each time as long-lost friends.

I maintained some contact with the game of soccer around this time by managing various local teams. I also helped to organise what at the time was one of the best events of its kind in the north of England, the day-long Rawdon six-a-side tournament. I was responsible for organising the entries, and at the suggestion of my wife, I made out an entry for a team with the name of Golden Wonders.

There was much speculation as to just who was in our mystery team, and a favourite suggestion was that I had entered a team from Leeds United. The team however were to prove even more popular than the local professional team! As the time came for them to put in an appearance for their game in the ongoing knockout tournament, out they trotted from their minibus, six lovely lasses dressed in an all-gold strip.

At the time of all male tournaments, there were roars of approval, and the large crowd, which had been watching the games, spread over the four pitches, all gravitated to the pitch where the girls were playing. Although they made an early exit, the seeds were sown, and in the following year, we included a female soccer tournament to run in conjunction with the males—my first blow for women's liberation!

As neither my wife nor I were exactly in the first flush of youth, we were keen to start a family as soon as we could afford to. My wife in particular longed for an offspring, and despite my continuing to find love making difficult, she finally fell pregnant in early 1974. Unfortunately, my wife miscarried, and to her eternal credit, although she was obviously deeply distressed, her strength of character showed through, and we battled on.

To our joint delight, she again fell pregnant in early 1975 and gave birth to a beautiful baby boy, our first son (7 lbs 11 ozs) in October 1975. I was thirty-eight at the time but was delighted at what I saw as confirmation of my manhood by becoming a father.

It was during her pregnancy that Leeds United reached the final of the European Cup against the German side Bayern Munich. The final was held at the Parc de Princes in Paris, and securing two tickets for the game, we had a week's holiday in the French capital staying with friends prior to the game. The final itself was infamous for its crowd riots, compounded by the actions of the French Riot Police, whose reactions to a comparatively minor incident in the crowd was to baton thrash as many of the crowd, innocent and guilty, as they could reach as they waded in. Needless to say, this only inflamed a very ugly situation. We therefore left the game twenty minutes before the end, mainly to protect my pregnant wife.

This game and its attendant events were to deeply sour my love for the game of soccer. A sport, which in my humble opinion has since deteriorated into its win-at-all-costs heavily, commercialised present-day state.

I consider that I was, by and large, blessed with playing, watching, and being involved in the game when it was at its best in the 1950s, 1960s, and early 1970s.

For my continuing studies, I was now undertaking a year's planning part-time bridging course at Sheffield Polytechnic, in preparation for taking the First Professional examination of the Royal Town Planning Institute. This examination I duly passed and was finally accepted for the three-year part-time postgraduate diploma course at Leeds Polytechnic, commencing in the summer of 1976.

My wife had given up her own job to concentrate on raising our son. Our competitive dancing had ceased, and even our social dances were now few and far between. I do however recall one particular dinner dance at the Norfolk Gardens Hotel in Bradford when we took to the crowded dance floor to attempt to do the cha-cha, a special favourite dance of ours to which we normally gave full reign.

The bandleader stopped the dance halfway through and announced that there was a couple on the floor who obviously knew what they were doing and would everyone clear the floor for a while to leave them to it.

I suddenly realised that he was referring to us, and we were left on the floor to give a demonstration dance before over 200 guests. It seemed to go down quite well, and we enjoyed the freedom of unrestricted dance space on the floor.

Late in 1976, my wife again fell pregnant in furtherance of our desire to increase our family, and our second son, again a lovely healthy baby (8 lbs 9 ozs), was born in July (just missing out on being born on 7.7.77).

With only the one income and a growing family, our trips to Ibiza and much of our social life had to cease. My spare time was therefore devoted to my family and doing jobs around the house, although I did for a while manage the Leeds United Supporters Club Football team in the Leeds Sunday League.

I settled into normal domestic life, and thoughts of any 'difference' seemed a long way away. Occasionally however, thoughts of what might have been did return to haunt me and send me into moods of depression, which my family must have found difficult to understand. Why, oh why did I get these feelings of inappropriateness, and why wouldn't they leave me alone? I was happy with my life. Why did these pervasive moods keep rising to the surface? Was I the only one in the world with these feelings?

My studies were not all hard work, and we had a delightful field course at Whernside Manor near Dent (a welcome return to Three Peaks Country). Here, my task was to examine the tourist potential of the area, a real labour of love for this dales lover.

We also had an equally delightful week-long field course in Paris, where we studied the French planning systems and consumed copious amounts of French wine.

I completed my course of studies in the summer of 1979 after nine long years and gained the postgraduate diploma in town and regional planning. This diploma made me eligible for membership of the Royal Town Planning Institute and gave me a professional qualification, the absence of which had barred my progress so many times in my life.

In April 1980, we were to complete our family with the birth of our beautiful little girl, the daughter we had both wanted so much.

The 1980s were to be very much the family years.

Increasing restrictions on local government finances resulted in tightening of council budgets, very little opportunity for personal advancement, and a succession of National Local Government wage settlements below both the rate of inflation and the general 'going rates'. This in turn resulted in a steady decline in my real earnings.

Life was one long succession of trying to balance the books and at the same time trying to ensure that my growing family lacked for little. Financial worries were frequent, but by and large, I bottled these up and tried to find my own means, usually by short or long-term loans, to keep the wolf from the door. These worries however usually occasioned the old feelings of unease deep inside where something beyond my comprehension was awaiting its opportunity.

Relationships with my wife became more strained, as not unnaturally the children demanded the bulk of her attentions, and my sexual inadequacies obviously caused her some grief. Our restricted finances also meant that at times I couldn't do as much as I would have liked for her and the family. This in turn increased my feelings of general inadequacy, although my handyman and DIY duties in and around the house were improving all the time.

I tried very hard not to let any problems show, and I like to think that by and large the children had a happy childhood and family life, as they were by now developing into three lovely, intelligent children, who were a constant source of pride to both of us.

For holidays, we had bought a Raclet trailer tent, and for a trial run, we booked a short break at Flamingoland Holiday Park near Malton in North Yorkshire. This turned out to be a catalogue of disasters, which we nevertheless thoroughly enjoyed!

Driving along the A64 to Malton, with our brand new trailer tent in tow, we lost the wheel off the trailer, which became detached and careered off down the dual carriageway. The sprung suspension arm hitting the highway smashed through the floor of the trailer into the pannier compartment.

Regaining the wheel, I had to jack up the trailer and take two bolts from the good wheel to secure the loose wheel. Not a very good start to our camping exploits.

Worse was to follow: the heavy persistent rain had flooded the campsite, and we had to erect our trailer tent in the static caravan field, where all the best sites were already taken. Our ground sheet base resembled a giant waterbed as we spread it on the saturated ground.

From the camp site, we had free rein of the Zoo Park and Amusement Park, but the constant downpour made these dubious pleasures. After three days of continuous monsoon-like rain, I was ready to cut things short and head for home, but the protest from the rest of the family to this suggestion convinced me that if they could enjoy these conditions, then they would enjoy anything (shades of my first rambling experience!).

Ah well, I was born under Aquarius, the Water Bearer, I could bear with the water!

The camping store where I had purchased the trailer accepted responsibility for the loose wheel and to their credit replaced the whole trailer tent with a new model.

Encouraged by the children's obvious enjoyment of the camping life, we took the trailer down to Cornwall for the first of several visits to this lovely county. Our favourite campsite was at Perranporth, close to what must be the best beach in the country.

A casual remark from my wife during one visit about how nice it would be to live in the West Country set me thinking about applying for a job in the county whilst the children were still young.

An appropriate job opportunity did arise as North Cornwall District Council advertised for a development control town planner. I applied, was shortlisted, and invited to attend for interview at Camelford for the post, which was based in Bodmin.

On the strength of this interview, we booked the trailer tent into a caravan site near Wadebridge for two weeks, one week before the interview and one after. We reasoned that we could house-hunt the week before and finalise things the week after if I got the job, or if I failed to get the job, we could have a week's holiday whilst we were down there.

Our journey down to Cornwall was in gale force winds, and I had to pull into a lay-by for a rest in the hope that they might subside. They didn't, and erecting the trailer tent was quite an experience, and not to be recommended in such conditions.

We had obtained lists of properties for sale in and around Bodmin, but upon inspection, these were generally very disappointing. We obtained further particulars from a local estate agent and studied them over lunch on our day of arrival. One property in particular stood out and was just a short walk from the town centre.

We visited this house, a lovely detached house at the head of a cul-de-sac, with a large garden overlooking the school playing fields and dotted with palm trees. The occupants made us most welcome, and an inspection of the interior confirmed that this was ideal for our purposes with four bedrooms and a loft play space. We confirmed that if I got the post with the local council, we would buy this house, and they agreed to hold it for us until after the interview the following Thursday.

It was at this point that I began to get a strange sinking feeling. Everything had gone too perfectly. We had a friend waiting to buy our house in Leeds, we liked the town of Bodmin, and we had found a lovely house right next to the school that the children would attend and which was only five minutes walk from what would be my new office. It was all too perfect. My portents of doom were not misplaced.

The day of the interview dawned, grey and damp. Funny, how even the beautiful Cornish landscape can look depressing on a dark overcast day and the brooding Cornish Moors took me back to my walks in the Yorkshire Dales! We drove the short distance to Camelford, and my wife took off with the children while I attended the interview.

It transpired that I was the last of seven planners being interviewed that day. Last because they were taken in alphabetical order.

I entered the interview room and had to sit in the middle of a horseshoe of councillors. Questions were placed from all sides. The most recurring concerned why I wanted to move for less money (the new post being one step down from my job in Leeds). I had some difficulty explaining about the environmental benefits for living and working, such as how can you compare working on the back streets of Leeds with working on fifty miles of Atlantic coastline?

There were also other financial benefits that would more than compensate for the small reduction in pay such as saving on travel to work expenses and increased travel allowances at work. But I did not want to dwell too much on the financial considerations as I considered the quality of life aspects more important.

An amusing moment occurred when one councillor told me I would have difficulty understanding some of the Cornish people, to which I replied that I had trouble understanding some of the people in Yorkshire!

After being grilled for three-quarters of an hour, I was told that the seven applicants had been shortlisted from an original list of eighty-seven, and that if I waited outside they would give me their decision almost immediately. Outside, the other six had arrived for the decision. We were kept waiting for a further three-quarters of an hour.

Eventually, the administration head emerged and called one of the candidates back inside. We were then informed that they had offered him the job and he had verbally accepted.

As I dejectedly gathered up my things, the administration head came over to me and said, 'Hard lines, it's just taken them three-quarters of an hour to decide between you and him.'

This didn't help. Out of eighty-seven, I might as well have come eighty-seventh as second.

My family was waiting outside as I left the council offices and shared my disappointment. We had to visit our new-found friends in Bodmin and tell them that we wouldn't be able to buy their house after all. The bottle of champagne I had with me in the hope of a celebration we consumed in a more restrained atmosphere, before making our goodbyes and taking another week in Cornwall as holiday.

A particularly unusual twist to this episode of my life was the first telephone call I received upon my return to work in Leeds was from the chairman of North Cornwall Planning Committee. He said he had been trying to get hold of me for a week to apologise as he felt I should have been given the job but a narrow majority had outvoted him.

With hindsight, I could but wonder just what turn my life would have taken if this borderline decision had gone in my favour? I would also have loved to have been at their decisive talks to see just how they arrived at their decision and what criteria were used.

Further interviews followed job attempts at Taunton Deane in Devon, Wimborne Minster in Dorset, and Shepton Mallet in Somerset, but these didn't present as ideal a situation as the Cornish post, and I wasn't offered the posts; indeed given the respective situations, it is doubtful if I would have accepted any offer.

Any further ideas of possible moves faded as the children started school, made friends locally, and settled into their education. I busied myself when the opportunities arose in working on the house.

We had already extended into the roof space to give five bedrooms in total and modernised all the facilities with the benefit of an improvement grant. We had also replaced the old timber garage with a large modern precast concrete garage.

The garden, which was a jungle when we bought the house, was now taking shape. In addition to all these improvements, I also built a utility extension on the back of the house and installed fitted furniture into the kitchen and bedroom. All-in-all years of work and effort that I was later to regrettably leave and lose.

At work, one aspect of my character was to land me in a sphere of activity that was to expand my experiences and occupy a fair percentage of my leisure time.

I have never been slow to make my views known when I perceive any form of injustice. Perhaps this stems from the inner feeling of injustice that I have felt from nature's joke at my own expense.

However, my inclination to speak up at work landed me with the job of what was at that time (in the early 1970s) known as the departmental representative (later to be known as departmental steward) with the local government union NALGO.

Being a non-political animal, I was able to apply a fair-minded approach to my union dealings, something which was fairly unique in a world of largely political dealings and self-interest. As a result of this apparent neutrality, I was seen as something of a friend to all, and I rose rapidly through the union ranks. My organisation and leadership qualities that had been thwarted by my lack of progress within the department therefore found outlet through the union.

My main union activities however were on the sporting and social side, occupying all officer posts during my years with both the Branch Sub-Committee and on the Yorkshire and Humberside District Sports Committees.

I was branch chair (it is politically correct not to use the term chairman, and I hate the terminology chairperson, as whatever else I've been, I've never been neutral in gender terms!) for two years in the early 1980s and was honoured with the branch presidency in 1985, the ultimate honour for service recognition in the branch.

My union involvement earned me many friends and a few enemies, particularly amongst the local politicians. It has been my experience however that friends have short memories and enemies long ones.

In particular, I recall after the union had found it necessary to take industrial action at a time when I was leading the branch as chair, the then leader of the city council seemed to think that I was personally responsible for standing up to him, and he openly vowed that I would never get on while I was working with the council.

This attitude was totally unjustified as I was personally opposed to the action, but I was only pursuing the job that the branch had bestowed on me by helping to resolve matters. I don't think it is coincidental that I was constantly overlooked for promotion and was still doing the same job some fourteen years later despite many opinions that I deserved better from both inside and outside the council.

Additionally, many former colleagues that I have helped in some way as they climbed the ladder of success now don't wish to know the new me, but this is part of the price for the path that I have taken.

Conversely however, there are some people whom I have stood up to in the past as Roy who do not forget that it is the same old character behind the new persona and do not waste an opportunity to put me down.

My trade union activities continued until the time of my imminent changes in 1993. Whilst not exactly expecting a golden handshake, my many years of dedicated service in many capacities did not even merit a letter of appreciation when I resigned from office from the by-now (1993) new union of unison.

The passing did not go unnoticed by the Planning Stewards Committee however, and I received a lovely letter which brought a tear or two to my eyes, stating amongst other things that my efforts over the years had made the department a far better place to work than may have otherwise have been the case.

My three children were now growing fast and moved in turn from nursery school to the local primary school. My eldest boy in particular was maintaining the Wardle family tradition of athletic achievement, becoming a fine distance runner even at a very tender age.

The other two also enjoyed and were very capable at running events, and all three featured in many local fun runs and athletic events.

They even seemed to enjoy the adverse weather conditions, an attribute that they didn't get from me as I think back to my dislike of cross-country running at school. The two boys joined a local athletic club and represented it at many sports meetings around the North of England.

Another tradition the boys were to maintain was my love of the game of football. This may have stemmed from my taking them down to Temple Newsam Park from a very early age to kick a ball about with their dad.

To help them further their interest in the game, when they were eight and ten, respectively, I took them down to Pool-in-Wharfedale, where a friend of mine organised a series of junior football teams for the village.

My youngest boy was to play for his age group with the club for several years, gaining a cup runner-up medal in the process. The oldest boy was to last even longer, playing with the club through to the age of almost eighteen and winning both league and cup medals in what was to turn out to be one of the best junior teams the Harrogate and District League had seen.

For my part for the first couple of years of my boys' time at Pool Juniors, I took on management and training of the under 10s, the youngest team. This was a very satisfying job as the youngsters were full of enthusiasm and attention and had not yet developed the more cynical aspects of the game. In conjunction with this, I also managed the Leeds NALGO representative football team through to several triumphs in the Yorkshire and Humberside Cup. In fact, I gained more awards as a manager than I did as a player.

With the Pool Juniors however, my activities were becoming too time consuming. Midweek training was followed by the Sunday games that usually meant I had to virtually be in three places at once! I had to make sure my two boys were delivered to their games or departure points and then attend to my own team before dashing off to collect my two sons again. However, their obvious enjoyment of the game was ample compensation, and it also furthered their sporting progress at school.

I was conscious of the fact that I wasn't in a position to do as much for my daughter as I was for the boys, and this is one of my continuing regrets as she not unnaturally gravitated more to her mother. I loved, and still love, all my children deeply and equally and wish I could have shown this more to my daughter. It also hurts very deeply that one of my daughter's parting remarks, made to her mother shortly before I left home, was that she didn't want two mothers. I didn't want to be a second mother to any of my children, just their old dad in a new, more contented format.

In order to broaden my own personal social circles, I sought admittance to one of the local Masonic Lodges and was accepted as one of the junior brethren.

The Masonic Order suffers unjustifiably from a bad press, mainly occasioned by their self-imposed cloak of secrecy. However, their activities are chiefly designed to ensure a high code of moral behaviour from their members, and indeed I often thought of their activities as being likened to adult boy scouts, and the harmless ceremonies that they jealously guard do go back to time immemorial.

What often goes unnoticed and unheralded is the vast amount of good work that they do in the community at large and the large amount of fund raising for charities.

Certainly, I could not have wished to meet a more sincere and friendly group of people. There is much that I now miss about being involved with them, as my new persona as female meant I had to tender my resignation to this all male preserve prior to my emergence as Faye. Even then the mischievous feminist in me resulted in my contemplating donning my smart cream two-piece suit and high heels and going to a lodge meeting as Faye prior to my resignation!

I decided however to subjugate my temptation to strike out for women's lib and retire gracefully to leave them to their worthy and harmless activities.

However, in the interim I had enjoyed three years of mainly very happy times in the Masonic Order. It was well worth the experience.

At home, I was again beginning to have periods of deep depression and unease. I knew despite a lovely home and family, something was wrong. The same something that had haunted and dogged my life was waiting to emerge; my twin personality was claiming its time. I was again confused and felt very much alone. It had to be fought and suppressed; it shouldn't and couldn't be allowed to manifest itself. The question that had shadowed my life still remained: Why wouldn't it go away and leave me alone?

CHAPTER NINE

A Time of Change

Just remember in the winter
Far beneath the bitter snows
Lies the seed that with the Sun's love
In the Spring becomes the Rose

—Amanda McBroom, *The Rose*

It was now late 1991. The moods deepened, and I spent long hours on my own in our front room, accompanied by my thoughts and a stream of television programmes, which were generally of little interest. My wife and children must have worried about my need for isolation and my general gloom. My wife was obviously unhappy herself, and this added to my depression. My strange inner feelings had not gone away, and it seemed they never would. My life was passing, and the miracle that would relieve or dispose of these feelings was not happening.

Efforts to snap out of it worked for a while, and the progress of my children was a big consolation and was also a big incentive to keep things going as normal as possible, but the unease returned. I recognised deep down what the problem was but felt that in my circumstances, nothing could be done to alleviate the situation. I knew things should have been different and time was slipping away. I hated myself, and I hated whatever it was that had played this trick of nature.

The boys developed an interest in computing, and I welcomed the opportunity to join them in this pursuit. My youngest son in particular soon outstripped me in computing ability. My pride in my three children did an awful lot to ease my way through a life that was becoming increasingly fraught with thoughts of what should have been.

Wading through the evening and Sunday papers became regular highlights of my routine, and in one sojourn through the News of the World, I found an advertisement for Stephanie Anne Lloyd's Transformation Shops, which catered for the transvestite community. 'Come and spend four hours with us being pampered as only a woman can be with our Changeaway' ran the byline.

Perhaps a journey to the nearest shop at Prestwich near Manchester would provide the outlet and relief that I desperately sought? I had no knowledge of the transvestite world and indeed to some extent, at this time, shared the common aversion to being involved in this world. But nevertheless, I had to seek some resolution to the nagging doubts that haunted me.

I therefore took the plunge and travelled the M62 to Manchester.

On my first visit, my nerve broke; after a quick look around the shop, I beat a hasty retreat and returned home. This didn't seem my scene at all.

Self-chastisement followed, just what was I afraid of? Here was a heaven-sent opportunity to express my feminine side with no apparent harm to anyone else. So a second visit followed shortly afterwards. We have all, transsexuals and transvestites alike, hesitated and been wracked with guilt at this first tentative step into a different world.

Looking back from my new format, my heart goes out to all those who have hesitated and given up at this point. It was no less a person than William Shakespeare, who said, 'To thine own self be true'.

We all therefore have to find our own way as individuals, wherever that way lies or leads. We must all if we have any desire for contentment seek out where our paths lie; otherwise, we will never be complete within ourselves.

As I self-consciously entered the shop on my second visit, Laura, one of the assistants, obviously sensed my unease and offered her assistance.

'I've come to give you a challenge,' I said quietly. 'I'd like to try your Changeaway.'

At six feet one inch height and over 18 stone in weight at this time, this certainly presented them with a mighty challenge. How could they possibly feminise this giant figure of masculinity?

The lovely Laura set to with a will. First problem was the clothing. The size 24s, which it was decided was my size, were limited, and many proved inadequate. Eventually after heatedly struggling in and out of a multitude of garments, we arrived at a long plain black dress with a certain amount of inbuilt elasticity and a shawl collar (ideal for covering the double chin!).

I looked at the effect in the mirror. The sight from the neck down, whilst large, nevertheless looked quite pleasing, assisted by strategically placed padding.

Above the neck however, the incongruous sight of a middle-aged male head destroyed any illusions.

Again, Laura rose to the occasion. I was told to put my change, etc. into one of the handbags provided (my first use of such an accessory). Then downstairs to the make-up salon, Laura set to work living up to the shop's Transformation title and applying my first serious makeover.

The expert application of make-up certainly drastically altered the features, but the bald pate still glistened in the salon lights. This is where the final coup-de-grace took place. Laura studied my natural colouring and produced a long, wavy auburn wig. After a few deft touches from her styling brush, she stepped away from between me and the mirror for me to see the end product.

To say I was totally amazed is putting it mildly. Staring back at me from the salon mirror was an attractive, albeit overweight, female. The change was sensational.

'How's that?' Laura asked.

I felt something stir deep inside, and I was close to tears. This was an image I could recognise and warm to, a new congruent self-identity. I was confused. Could it . . . no; I instantly dismissed the passing thought that sprang from my seeing my new format.

'It's wonderful,' I mumbled in reply.

'You can stay down in the shop with us or go upstairs to the private lounge,' Laura announced.

I took the easy option, not feeling confident enough to meet anyone else, and I retreated to hide away in the upstairs lounge.

I was the only customer for the Changeaway that morning, and I settled down to read the magazines and watch some videos on make-up and deportment techniques—all very feminine and surprisingly enjoyable.

It was working; the deep contentment at just being female for a short time made it all so worthwhile.

All too soon it was time to clean up, divest, and, as I liked to call it, turn back into a pumpkin.

The 'change back' was sad, but I felt I now had an outlet to express myself once in a while for four short hours. The effect on my outlook was instant. I was much happier at home and at work, and to avoid the clothes problem at Manchester, I started to lose weight—I now had an incentive.

My next visit to Manchester was some four or five weeks later, and this time, I was greeted by Lesley, who was later to prove a great friend and helper. I asked if Laura was there, for, to slightly misquote a well-known saying, 'Better the angel you know'.

Despite the fact that I had made only one previous visit, and that some weeks before, Laura greeted me like a long-lost friend and whisked me upstairs to once more start the conversion.

It was back to the same black dress as my reductions still weren't sufficient to present any options. The major change came with Laura's choice of wig for me. She worked the options. Looking back, I suppose this was the first step in my establishing an identity. After trying the blondes (too pale) and the brunettes (too dark), she produced a gorgeous light ginger strawberry blonde. This seemed perfect, and the result was stunning.

It was at this point that a major milestone in my life occurred, as Laura stood back to admire her handiwork.

'Well, I certainly can't call you Roy looking like that,' she said. 'We must find you a femme name to use.'

Oh dear! I hadn't even considered this as being necessary, but she was right: I certainly didn't feel like Roy when I was 'en-femme'.

So what was it to be? I certainly didn't see myself as a Jennifer, Stephanie, Josephine, or any of the fancier names.

'It must be something short and similar to my own name,' I announced.

'How about Joy?' Laura asked.

This suggestion snapped me out of my mood of euphoria as I thought of my daughter, who had Joy as one of her names.

What was I doing? And yet these sojourns to Manchester were not harming the family. On the contrary, they were greatly helping my overall moods and well-being.

'No, definitely not Joy,' I said with feeling.

She thought for a minute, and I was happy to leave the suggestions to her at this stage, as I had no particular preferences myself.

'Then how about Kay?'

'Kay . . . Hmm? A possibility, but a bit harsh sounding,' I added, thinking also that it would always remind me of a certain catalogue company!

I hoped I wasn't going to be impossible to please.

'OK, how about Fay?' was her next suggestion.

I studied carefully. I could not think of any objections to this suggestion.

'Yes, with an "e",' I decided, as it was feminine without being too fancy, short, and similar to my male name.

So that was it, 'Faye'. Little did either of us know, or envisage, but we were actually making decisions on the name which would be with me for life eventually.

I decided that my middle name of Harry should be feminised as well. Helen seemed a good, suitable approximation and appeased my love of Greek mythology. So Faye Helen it became, being not too far removed from Roy Harry yet feminine without being too flowery. I was pleased with the outcome of the name search.

One aspect of my feminisation that surprised me was the ease that I had in wearing a three-inch high-heel shoe, and on this only my second appearance, I emerged from the make-up room into the shop at almost six feet four inches in my heels—a giant red-haired Amazon, like a figure from Norse or Teutonic legend.

Lesley was appropriately impressed at the transformation, and her surprise and admiration were genuine.

'I like the ginger,' she said. 'Definitely you.'

I again retreated to the lounge, but after a while, encouraged by the attitude of Laura and Lesley, I ventured down into the shop for a chat to the girls.

The state of my 'well-being' increased, and I eagerly awaited my visits to Manchester and the chance to release Faye.

So this was it (or so it seemed): I was a transvestite, enjoying dressing and being female for a while. The only thing was something that still nagged deep inside—a something that was still unappeased. Faye was battling grimly with Roy, and now that she had been released, there was to be only one winner.

I had opened her cage after all these years, and she was screaming to be recognised. Her days of quietly nagging were over. This would normally have been quite a shock to me, but I had always known she was there and I was weary of the battle to keep her suppressed. I was beginning to find my true self.

On subsequent visits to the salon at Manchester, Lesley took over from Laura (who left for pastures new) as my personal beautician, and I became a 'regular' getting to know Julie and Gaynor, two more of the Transformation beauticians. I spaced my visits so as not to drain the finances too much, consoling myself that as I didn't drink (only socially and very infrequently) and abhorred smoking (something I had never done), my monthly visit was by way of my 'spending' money.

The use of the ginger wig became regular, and it was becoming something of a trademark, until one visit when I was quietly watching television in the lounge when Julie breezed in from the downstairs shop.

'Sorry, Faye, but I've got a customer wanting to buy the ginger wig. Here, try this one.'

So my beloved wig was whisked away to be replaced by a chestnut brown one, which wasn't really me. This would never do, so I placed an order to buy a ginger replacement (the first step towards my own personal female wardrobe).

The next milestone occurred while I was enjoying a coffee one day in the shop. Lesley announced that she was going to the shop around the corner for the lunchtime sandwiches, so I placed my order. Then she dropped the bombshell.

'Why don't you come with me, Faye?'

I felt myself going cold. While I had become accustomed to transvestites and transsexuals coming and going to and from the shop, the thought of venturing beyond the doors of the salon as Faye I hadn't contemplated, and the thought filled me with dread.

'Come on,' Lesley chided.

'But it's cold outside, and I haven't got a coat,' I protested.

'We'll lend you a coat.' No escape with that excuse.

'But what if there are people about?' I continued.

'I'll check first.' Lesley wouldn't be deterred.

She had a quick look outside. 'Come on, there's no one about.'

So Faye took her first steps into the big, wide world.

Sure enough, turning the corner, going to the sandwich shop, we were confronted by a horde of school children. I froze.

'Come on, head up and shoulders back,' whispered my companion.

So onward and into the sandwich shop. The staff in the shop didn't give me a second glance. I then dutifully followed Lesley back to the salon, where I flopped on to a settee.

'There you are,' Lesley smiled. 'That wasn't too bad, was it?'

I felt too weak to reply.

So it was that I began going out on short walks, usually during the hours of darkness in the early evening. Released from the safety of the salon, this was a whole new ball game. On one such stroll around the neighbourhood, a policeman coming in the opposite direction confronted me. My heart sank, and I waited for 'Hello, sir, what are we up to?' But all I got was a polite smile and a salutary 'Good evening'. I smiled back, not daring to venture a vocal acknowledgement.

The confidence was growing, but not enough for the next culture shock.

During my visits to the salon, I became friendly with several transsexuals (TSs) and transvestites (TVs) who called in (why was it I felt more comfortable with the TSs than I did with the TVs, and found myself envious of their TS condition?).

On one occasion, I was chatting in the shop when in breezed Amanda (a TV from East Anglia) with her 'real girl' friend Julie. I struck up an immediate friendship with the two of them and envied Amanda's devil-may-care confidence. I was invited to join them for lunch in one of the local restaurants. My reluctance was quietened by Amanda's assurances about my appearance, and off the three of us went for a delightful meal. By now, I had built up a small personal wardrobe and felt reasonably smart in a quiet way.

Then again came the unexpected. Amanda announced that 'she' had things to do and instructed Julie to take me with her shopping down to central Manchester!

Horror of horrors! No way!

The thought of being in Manchester's busy shopping streets as Faye started me out in a cold sweat of panic. They were not to be put off and couldn't understand my reluctance. It was mischievously pointed out to me (I wasn't sure if they were serious or not) that it was a long walk back to the salon (they had given me a lift to the restaurant). So with some trepidation, and a little excitement on my part, Julie and I set off for the shops.

We parked in the Arndale Centre car park, close to the scene of the later IRA bomb blast that was to decimate this area of the city, and we walked out into the busy Arndale shopping centre.

I should point out at this stage that to create a female breast form, I had purchased in a recent sale, a pair of silicone prosthesis. Being in the sale, I had no choice as to size and had to accept a somewhat larger pair than I would have liked. These not unnaturally became known as my 'Dolly Partons'. On this particular day, I was also wearing three-inch-heel court shoes.

'How are you doing?' Julie enquired after a while, obviously noting my unease at this public exposure.

'I feel as though everybody is looking at me,' I whispered in reply.

'Obviously,' she said. 'If you passed a six foot four inch flame-haired female with boobs that size, wouldn't you have a second look?'

We both had a good laugh, and a lot of my tension passed away. I was becoming strangely at ease with this 'girls-out' afternoon shopping trip.

So it was that I tentatively introduced myself as female to the world at large. My feelings at this were a strange mixture of apprehension and excitement together with an even stranger underlying contentment—all new and all very confusing. I began to wonder with trepidation where all this was leading.

CHAPTER TEN

Faye Emergent at Long Last

All my life I have not known who I am
or where I was going
Now I am like the arrow sprung from the bow
My path is clear

(Babylon 5, Channel 4 TV, August 1996)

For a while, my monthly visits to Manchester seemed to be the answer, although they were becoming more and more adventurous. Yet why did I feel so happy and at peace as Faye, and so at odds with myself as Roy?

I dreaded my return to Roy. Although I loved all my family deeply, I was conscious of my inadequacies as a husband, a fact that obviously caused my wife deep grief and me recriminating concern. She pleaded with me to take medical advice for my inadequacies, but I dreaded what the findings might be.

I told myself that the visits to Manchester were pure escapism, to a new and exciting world without the problems and pressures of Roy's world. But yet again, that something deep inside, where I kept Faye hidden, nagged to have its existence acknowledged.

When I phoned Manchester to make an appointment one day late in 1992, Julie, the Transformation beautician, greeted me with the news that she had been hoping I would call.

She was wanting to invite me to appear on Radio 5 with Stephanie Anne Lloyd and a preoperation transsexual who was under treatment in Manchester. Radio 5 wanted to interview an established transsexual (Stephanie), a TS going through the process of change, and a transvestite. Julie asked me if I would appear as the TV as I was one of their more confident clients (a statement which made me realise just how far I had come in such a short space of time).

I agreed to appear given that it was the anonymity of radio and not television.

I turned up nice and early and donned my best taffeta outfit for the interview (what a mistake this choice of clothing was to prove to be!). I was introduced to Stephanie and Natasha (the young transsexual); yet again, it was funny how I could readily strike up a rapport with the TSs. Stephanie was interviewed in private, and then Natasha and I were called in.

An immediate problem was my taffeta skirt, which interfered with the microphone reception as it rustled. So I had to sit as frozen and immobile as possible while verbally expounding on the problems associated with time requirements for make-up and dressing (that's why women take so much time!). I also was quizzed on the inadequate capacities of handbags (no longer wondering just what they put in there) and on the general problems of just being female.

All in all, the Radio 5 people seemed satisfied, and it was all done with the maximum respect for my privacy being only referred to as Faye.

A spin-off from this interview was my friendship with Natasha, who was from the south-east, and I tried, whenever possible, to get over to Manchester when she was on her visits to the clinic every six weeks.

After her clinic treatment, we would go out for a drive in her lovely Jaguar sports car like two excited long-lost sisters.

It was during one of these journeys along the M66 Motorway to the north of Manchester that I was saying how lucky I thought she was being transsexual, when she said, 'It strikes me that you're transsexual rather than transvestite. You are so happy and natural as a female, not at all like the other TVs.'

I went quiet for a while.

So there it was the fact that I had tried so hard not to face, acknowledged and stated by someone else.

'That may well be so, but there is no possible way it could work out' was all I could think of saying. My thoughts were confused; there was a feeling of horror and pending doom mingled with relief that long withheld feelings were being aired at long last.

The ironical twist to this particular episode is that shortly afterwards, I have gone on to pursue my destiny as a female, whilst lovely feminine Natasha has been forced by personal domestic pressures to revert to her former male persona.

I am sure she will find, like me, that it is not something that will go away, and that eventually she will find her true way. Unfortunately, we have now lost touch since her return to her male existence, but my heart and deep wishes go out to this kindred spirit who helped me to face myself at last.

It was in October 1992 that I took myself off to the Showcase Cinema near Leeds to see the film *Just Like a Woman*.

This film was about a transvestite who made good, so it held a certain attraction. I was of course in male role at the time.

The ticket girl gave me a big knowing smile and said, 'I'm sure you'll enjoy this film, sir.'

This took me aback slightly, and I checked to see if I'd left my earrings in!

I recounted my experiences in Manchester a few days later, and I said that as I had been in RAF uniform when I saw *The Dam Busters* for the first time, I might as well have gone as Faye to see *Just Like a Woman*! Sure enough, Shirley, one of the extrovert Manchester Concord members, suggested that we go back to the cinema 'en-femme'.

So it was that we returned to see the film again, and Faye went to the cinema for the first time. I chickened out at the cash desk as the same girl was on duty. I didn't want her saying, 'Hello, I told you you'd enjoy it', so Shirley got the tickets.

My sports and social duties in Leeds were still going strong, and I organised a trip to the newly opened Euro Disney just outside Paris. What I hadn't anticipated was the interest this would generate. I had to organise six coaches to take the 256 people who booked for the four-day trip.

Amongst them was Lesley from Transformation at Manchester, who, when I was talking about the trip, had asked if she could come and bring her family.

Despite one or two hiccups, unavoidable with a party of this size, we had a wonderful few days, and my three children had the time of their lives being set loose in Euro Disney.

On our final day in Paris, we went to Montmarte, and on the way down from the Sacre Coeur Cathedral, we passed Tattys Ladies Departmental Store.

At this store, all the girls took themselves off to look inside while the men waited outside. As Lesley passed me as they came out, she whispered to me, 'You would have enjoyed it in there, kid.' Too true, and no doubt when I now visit Paris next, I will avail myself of the facility!

The journey home was not without incident, as I couldn't find my passport. Fortunately, I didn't need to produce it at Dover as our coach was waved straight through. Otherwise, as organiser, it would have dented my credibility. It later turned up tucked inside my toilet bag. Yes, 'just like a woman'!

I had started to take more of a pride in my physical condition and appearance. I had slimmed over two stones off my previous bulk and had started to safeguard my fingernails and allow them to grow longer.

One of my few long-standing feminine attributes are my hands and nails, which despite my masculine expansions had remained relatively soft and slender. I encouraged this aspect by hand creams and regular manicures. It created an additional source of annoyance for my wife, who frequently complained at the length of my nails and couldn't understand my reluctance to cut them.

I compounded this hand care by attending a nail-care salon near to the Transformation shop. Rachel, who had worked at Transformation for a while (a young bubbly girl who could be brutally honest at times, which ensured you respected her opinions), had left Transformation to work in the nearby 'Nail File' salon and had invited me around for a manicure.

I breezed into the salon past a line of females who were waiting patiently and confidently approached the smiling Rachel at the reception counter.

'How am I doing?' I asked her quietly,

'Great!' was her reply. 'You sailed in like a stately galleon, and no one gave you a second glance until you got to the counter, then you plonked one elbow on the counter, and crossed one leg over the other just like a bloke standing at a bar.'

This was an early lesson in feminine deportment and brought home the importance of body language.

As for the nail treatment, this was great. A careful massage of the hands and fingers with hand cream, a careful clean, and a manicure of the nails were then followed by fifteen minutes of pampered bliss. The hands were swathed in thick cream lotion and then placed in electrically heated mittens for a full quarter of an hour. For completion, the cream having by then melted into the skin, the nails are again cleansed and finished with a base coat and topcoat. All in all, a wonderful introduction to being pampered as a female. It all felt so right and so wonderful. I felt a little bit like a child being given a pass to the chocolate factory.

It was at the Nail Care salon that I was introduced to a clear matt nail polish that could be worn undetectably to protect the nails whilst I was my male self. This ongoing link with Faye while pursuing Roy's life I found deeply comforting.

It was now late 1992, only twelve short months since my first nervous, tentative steps into the world of femininity. It was at this time that I was to meet someone who was to both hinder and help my progress.

I first met Rachael one afternoon in late 1992 in the Transformation shop. She presented an unlikely picture of a male to female transsexual (even if preoperative) in male working clothes, smoking a pipe and with several days growth of facial stubble!

She seemed to take to me however, and initially, we got along fine. Again, I was finding this affinity with the TS world.

Rachael invited me to go with her to the Northern Concord (a Manchester-based self-help group for transgenderists—both TS and TV).

The Northern Concord at this time met at the Rembrandt Hotel in central Manchester on Wednesday evenings. I was also invited to change at her digs in Rochdale en route. By this time, I had become reasonably proficient with my own make-up, so changing away from the salon was no longer a problem.

The Northern Concord meetings are like meetings of the Women's Institute, mainly sedate and very friendly. I continued to attend their meetings whenever possible, and I made many friends there.

Rachael moved from Rochdale to share a terrace house in Urmston in West Manchester with little Gina, a quiet male to female transsexual. I was invited to change there when necessary. This was a great saving on my stretched finances, and it enabled me to grow away from Transformation, although I have maintained friendship with the girls there and call in from time to time for a chat. After all in a way, it was Faye's place of birth! I smile inwardly sometimes when I visit there nowadays as I recall how impressed I used to be when in the shop and an established TS called in. I never used to dream at the time that someday it would be myself in that position.

My confidence as Faye was increasing all the time, and my time spent 'en-femme' was becoming more and more perfectly natural. Gina, Rachael, and Faye were becoming very much a threesome, and we were to visit most of the Northern Concord's social events together.

The comments about how relaxed and happy I seemed as a female were being made more and more, particularly by my friends at Northern Concord. Not for the first time I began to wonder where this was all leading and how it equated with my life back in Leeds.

My enjoyment of my time as Faye was becoming increasingly invaded by a growing confirmation of my condition. This was no transvestite voyage of cross-gender exploration, but an outward expression of something that had haunted me since the days of my early childhood, my need to be female.

The truth, the doubts, and the horror of the consequences began to weigh heavy and began to turn Faye from a gentle happy person into a sad, resentful, and confused individual. Life now seemed to present a series of culs-de-sac, and my whole world seemed to be crumbling into uncertainty. What had been a relief was becoming a burden of worry. I feared for my family, and I feared for myself.

The culmination came at one of the Northern Concord meetings early in 1993. I felt a real need to talk to a female about my problems. I had the opportunity to have a long chat with the wife of one of the Concord members who provided just the type of understanding and sympathetic ear I needed. She expressed no surprise at the revelation of my feelings, and the chance to unload my problems was a great help, albeit temporary.

Leaving the Northern Concord, I wept uncontrollably. Rachael drove me back to Urmston, and we talked for most of the night. The outcome was inevitable: I had to have expert advice urgently. I could no longer go on in the half-and-half limbo that I found myself in.

Rachael and Gina were under treatment at the Portland Gender Identity Clinic in Manchester, and I made an appointment to see their consultant. This was in March 1993.

I attended the clinic as Faye as I didn't think I could have gone through with it as Roy. After a quick journey to Urmston to change, it was another dash over to Didsbury and the clinic.

While I was nervously waiting in the clinic's reception lounge, I thumbed through a copy of one of that month's women's magazines. I arrived at the horoscope page and out of curiosity consulted the current prediction for Aquarius, my birth sign. It read as follows:

Aquarius, 21 January-19 February

You might have kept it secret and bottled up. You may even have hidden it from yourself. But the urge to make a revolutionary change in your life has been bubbling away deep inside—and you must acknowledge it. This month's ruler Uranus aligns with Neptune in practical and ambitious Capricorn, and the effects of this alliance are earth-shaking. What's more, it could be you causing shock waves. So remember, you're at the height of your powers, with great depth of insight. If you trust your inner voice, and avoid the pitfalls of confusion or self-doubt, you can go far. It's time to break out of your rut and soar away to a better world.

I read through it several times. I've got an open mind on the powers of prophecy, but I just couldn't believe this particular prediction given what I was contemplating. I tore out the relevant section of the magazine to keep for future reference.

The first consultation that day was with Barbara, the consultant's assistant, who whilst trying to do her best to put me at my ease nevertheless asked some very pointed questions, particularly about my childhood years.

After the lengthy session with Barbara, I was taken through to see Dr Joe. Dr Joe was charming. After studying Barbara's notes, he asked me his own questions, studying me closely all the time.

I felt my soul was being laid bare. After what seemed like an eternity, he announced that it was a textbook case of gender dysphoria or transsexuality.

While deep down I had always known that this was the case, I felt an overwhelming feeling of relief at his confirmation. He went on to say that it was an unusual symptom of the condition that the life experiences were so similar from TS to TS. While I was obviously greatly relieved that it was a genetic rather than a mental condition, I was suddenly filled with horror and foreboding at the consequences of what this really meant. I did suffer from gender dysphoria, and I should have been female from birth. The truth that I struggled all my life to hide was being aired and confirmed.

Joe carried out a full medical examination, which included sending a blood sample off for analysis. It would therefore be a couple of weeks before I could be considered for any treatment. His only comment on my health inspection was that my blood pressure was up a bit. I pointed out that this was hardly surprising as I had dashed over from Leeds on the busy M62, dashed to change from male to female, dashed over from Urmston to Didsbury, and then been subjected to two stressful interviews after which I had been given a thorough medical examination, all with a view to one of the most important and far-reaching changes of life that could be imagined. It would have been a miracle if these events hadn't raised the blood pressure somewhat. This caused him to smile, and he said he was prepared to accept that.

The next few days I spent in something of a daze, caught in what seemed an unreal world between Roy struggling for his existence and the emergent Faye who was taking over like a genii escaping from a long captivity in a bottle.

How could I deny myself the opportunity of spending what remained of my life as it should have been from the outset?

CHAPTER ELEVEN

The Problems at Home and at Work

Life is largely froth and bubble
Two things stand like stone
Kindness in another's troubles
Courage in your own

—Diana, Princess of Wales, New York,
24 September 1996)

The consequences of what was happening to me finally caught up with me on a further visit to the Concord meetings one Wednesday. There was to follow the most traumatic night of my life, as the value I placed on my life plunged to zero.

Changing back from Faye to Roy always filled me with a deep sadness, but on this particular occasion, the impossibility of my circumstances and what was necessary really began to register. As I drove home, the tears began to surge, and the sobbing was deep and uncontrollable. I had to pull into Birch Services car park on the M62 Motorway to the north of Manchester as I was in no fit state to drive. It was to be a long night of soul-searching.

How could I confront my family with my earth-shattering problem? It would almost certainly involve my having to leave my home and family.

How could I possibly be accepted at work, and how could I possibly break the news there?

What about all my friends?

Was I capable of coping with being regarded as a freak, a pervert (the usual misconceived accusations towards transsexuals), or an object of ridicule and facing all the other problems that went with the general widespread lack of understanding?

No, I could not see any possible way forward.

I considered the alternative. I couldn't kill Faye off or hide her away now that I had at long last found my true way. I'd had a taste of how my life should have been—there was no possible way back.

No way forward and no way back, my life had reached an impossible impasse. When I was in my teens, if someone had said we could change you into how you should be, I would have been in my seventh heaven. Now here, I was with the opportunity finally within my grasp, and I just couldn't write off my existence so far. The third alternative then crept surreptitiously into my thinking.

If there was no way forward or back, then there was the third and obvious solution. It had to all end there.

The tears stopped. Why hadn't the solution occurred to me before? Surely, this would be the kindest thing for myself and all concerned, and no one need know why. I had had enough of this unjust mortal coil. I couldn't face the future, and I couldn't change the past. Perhaps next time around, Mother Nature will get it right, if there is such a thing as reincarnation, or maybe I had served my penance in this world and it was time to go, but how could I just end it all?

Any obvious suicide would negate my insurance policies and present the family with severe financial problems. A car accident seemed the obvious answer, but how? I couldn't consider anything that would involve another vehicle and possible injury to another person.

How could I be certain that any accident would finish me? Having Faye trapped in a maimed deformed male body was a scenario too horrific to contemplate.

Oh dear, what seemed an easy option was proving very difficult. I couldn't face a lingering death in any form, and there's no easy undetectable suicide.

Funny thing, when it comes to the crunch, it isn't as easy as it might appear, or it may be that I didn't have the bravery to see it through and was really seeking excuses not to. It was all so confusing.

What was I contemplating? I shook myself away from such thoughts. I needed a breath of fresh air.

I walked over to the Services' toilets, thankful for the chill, fresh night air and the refreshing wash in the toilets, and then back to the car for the process to start all over again.

I remember little else of that night at Birch Services. I had an odd fitful nap in the car and long tearful sessions until my eyes and face ached with the effort. At about 5.30 a.m., I finally decided that there was nothing for it but to face what needed to be done and the consequences. I think deep down that I knew what the outcome was going to be. I didn't have the stomach to face death, and my whole being was yearning towards the inevitability of finding my true self at last. I was tired of being haunted with doubts about how my life should have been. I must face the consequences and all the attendant problems and go for it.

I should have been delighted at the prospect, but I was deeply saddened by the likely costs. I must pay the price and take both the punishments and the rewards.

I drove, somewhat drained and very tired, straight down into central Leeds ready for work, arriving at the work's car park before the office opened at 7 a.m., and I was outside the office when the doors opened. I flopped into the chair at my desk; I was near to exhaustion. Shortly after my arrival, Lynne, one of my colleagues who usually arrived early and regularly shared an early morning cuppa with me, came through the door.

'You look awful,' she said. 'What on earth's the matter?'

I needed to tell someone at work, and this seemed as good a time as any. Lynne was a quiet, sensible girl, and I knew that I could depend on her discretion and trust her to keep the secret for as long as was necessary.

'I've got the option of becoming a very unhappy old man or a very lonely old woman,' I announced.

Poor Lynne looked bemused. I produced a photograph of Faye, taken at Manchester.

'That's what Manchester wants to turn me into,' I offered by way of explanation.

A confused look of disbelief appeared on her face, and I briefly explained about my situation. To her credit, her reaction was a mixture of sympathy and understanding.

'Sit down, and I'll make us a drink. You look as though you could do with one' was her first reply, and we had a long chat before anyone else entered.

The mere fact that one of my colleagues had some idea of what I was going through was a tremendous help over the next few weeks.

The fact that Lynne was aware also had its amusing side at times.

There was one occasion when one of my male colleagues, having had a hard time from one of the female members of staff, upon passing my desk, exclaimed to me, 'I don't know, Roy, bloody women!'

I think he was expecting some male words of support and comfort from me, but I just kept quiet and caught Lynne's eye nearby. She was obviously very amused.

'He picked on the wrong one there, didn't he?' she whispered across to me with a broad grin as he vanished down the office.

Meanwhile back in Manchester, the idea had been mooted for a week-long canal trip involving TVs and TSs for August 1993. As my wife enjoyed an odd week abroad on her own or with our children, she could hardly object to me having a week away on my own, so I asked the Manchester crowd to include me in the arrangements. Rachael and Gina were already booked together with Lucy from Rochdale. Then came the surprise: Rachael had found a couple from Wales, Chris and Eileen, who were keen to make the trip with us. I was therefore introduced to them when they were in Manchester and when I was on my way to the Portland Clinic for the results of my medical.

The time was now early March 1993, a landmark month in my life.

Eileen and Chris were to prove real friends. Eileen in particular was to become a tremendous help and female guide during my transitional period. Eileen was therefore present when I returned from the clinic with the news that my medical condition was all right, and I was proudly clutching my first batch of Premarin female hormone tablets, albeit the small trial dosage of 0.6 Mg per day.

The dosage and administration of Premarin must be carefully monitored because of the likelihood of adverse side effects. Eileen also witnessed me taking my first tablet at the start of a long, long road.

I had by now abandoned the use of my 'Dolly Partons' and instead used a pair of 'Melody' prosthesis of more modest proportions. More of the consequences of this boob change later.

After my day at the clinic, it was necessary to change back to travel home to Leeds. Eileen still recounts the tale about that first night when she was staggered by the transformation as the tall redhead she had been introduced to vanished upstairs and a tall male appeared later from upstairs dressed in grey sweater and a pair of slacks. She didn't know it was I at first.

I was still fighting shy of the two apparently insurmountable major obstacles—Informing my family and my employers, although these two necessary steps were looming large.

On the work front, it was gradually emerging that I had some sort of problem. Bev, the other female in the office with Lynne, intuitively suspected something was going on and must have noticed the little asides, which Lynne and I enjoyed.

As females are the easiest to tell and indeed seem to have a greater flexibility of understanding, I realised that the time was approaching when I must let Bev into the secret.

The need to let Bev know came to a head when Chris, one of my friends at work, was having his leaving party upon taking early retirement. My worries and lack of sleep were beginning to have their effect on my facial appearance. Bev thought I was perhaps dying and that I didn't want to broadcast the fact.

'No, it's worse than that,' I replied to her questions.

'Have you seen a doctor?' she quizzed.

I declined at this time to expand further. My reluctance stemmed from a desire for the news not to spread around the office before it needed to.

We enjoyed our lunchtime celebrations at a local hostelry with Chris and the crowd from the office, with Bev's curiosity unanswered. Back at the office for another farewell drink with Chris, Bev's keen eye noticed my hands.

'Are you wearing nail varnish?' she asked with a slight trace of curious amusement.

Oh dear! Only a female would notice the almost invisible clear matt covering. I withdrew my fingers from the desktop and gave her a long hard look without answering her question. She had to be the next to know.

It was now the time of the large Annual Fun Fair on the streets of central Leeds, an event which Bev and I had attended from work in 1992. I took the opportunity in arranging to visit the 1993 event with Bev to let her into the secret while we were alone on the corridor at work.

'I'm having a sex change,' I told her, seeing little point in beating around the bush.

She looked relieved.

'Is that all?' was her rather surprising reply,

'The way you've been acting lately, I thought you had cancer or some terminal illness. Anyway, it will be great to have another woman in the office. There's not enough of us in there.'

No problems therefore with Bev's acceptance. The two girls I worked with now knew. As for my male colleagues, they could wait. They wouldn't understand anyway.

I continued to put off telling my family and employers, afraid of the consequences of these giant steps. Bev kept insisting that I should talk it over with my wife. She was right of course, but how could I approach such earth-shattering news? I had to choose an appropriate opportunity.

As it happened, events took their own course, and my wife took matters into her own hands. It was becoming increasingly obvious that something was wrong, and she suspected the logical occurrence that I had found another woman. I had, but it was one I had known and kept hidden for so long, afraid to subject her to a world devoid of understanding.

My trips away were becoming obvious, and as I returned from one day in Manchester, she enquired where I had been. As I frequently made trips around the country in my capacity as social secretary at work, I used a trip to Gloucester as an excuse on that particular day.

This was not out of a deliberate desire to be untrue, but to protect her from the truth that would only create pain. Unfortunately, in her suspicions, she had checked my departure mileage and the mileage on the car when I returned. It was obvious that I hadn't been as far as Gloucester.

She had also on one occasion followed me to Manchester and had videoed my car parked outside Rachael and Gina's. She had obviously not seen me departing as Faye, or perhaps she hadn't associated the tall redhead with her husband.

I hadn't had any inclination that her suspicions ran so deep. The time to break the news had arrived. I tried to explain the circumstances of the need to change, but the deep hurt and total rejection were obvious. I held out my hand, hoping for some sign of acceptance or understanding.

There was none; her shock and disgust hit me hard. I had hurt her deeply, and the overwhelming feelings of guilt and despair flooded back. What really hurt was when she asked if I no longer loved her. I couldn't answer. I did still love her, but not in the way she wanted or deserved.

When she told the children, they shared her rejection and shock. My eldest son even smacked me in the face. My hurt and rejection were tempered with a little pride for the way he was backing his mother. Only my youngest son seemed reluctant to reject his dad and continued to act as though the inevitable might not happen.

This hurt even more. I think the two of us had always been extra close and his reluctance to lose his dad accentuated all the doubts and worries I was feeling, but the die was cast.

I could not go back now that I had seen a glimpse of how my life should have been, but it was all so difficult and heart-rending. What had I done in this or any past life to justify this impossible situation?

I was relegated to sleeping on the settee downstairs at the insistence of my wife, who declared that she wasn't lesbian and therefore didn't want me near. The atmosphere around the house was unbearable.

A break from home in the emerging circumstances was now regrettably unavoidable. While deep down I had hoped that perhaps we could work something out for co-existence, I think I had also realistically appreciated that a new life entailed a complete break in everybody's interests.

At my wife's insistence however, I made an appointment to see our own GP in Leeds about my condition. For her part, I think she was hoping he could somehow dissuade me from my course of action. For my part, I was hoping his confirmation of my condition might help her to understand what was necessary.

In the event, he satisfied neither.

The whole question was totally beyond his comprehension (an early insight for me into the abysmal depth of the lack of understanding on the subject), and he just sat looking nonplussed as we both had our say.

He decided that the best thing to do was to refer me to the local Gender Identity Clinic at St James Hospital in Leeds for a meeting with the gender identity psychiatrist. This appointment held out promise for me of treatment on the National Health Service if they were also satisfied that the condition of gender dysphoria existed in my case. The psychiatrist at St James was charged with the responsibility of deciding who was accepted for NHS treatment for the whole of West Yorkshire.

Being on home territory in Leeds, and as my wife went with me, I went to the clinic for the interview as Roy rather than as Faye. With hindsight, I think this was a mistake.

During a long interview, in which the psychiatrist covered most of the ground that I had gone over with Dr Costanza in Manchester, he seemed largely unsympathetic and had a manner that I found somewhat out of tune with the type of attitude I would have expected from someone charged with his responsibilities.

At the end of my interview, he called in my wife, who had been talking to his assistant, and announced that he was satisfied that the condition of gender dysphoria existed in my case, but that he wasn't prepared to take me on board because of my age and the fact that in his opinion, he didn't think that I would be convincing enough as a female at the end of the day. He went on to say that I had managed all right so far as male and that there was no reason why I shouldn't remain so.

I found this decision to be somewhat strange and subjective, but although it hadn't done much for me and my wife, I wasn't too downhearted as I was almost certainly moving to Manchester, where I would come under a different specialist and health authority. And from what Gina and Rachael had told me, attitudes, the other side of the Pennines, were a bit more enlightened.

I couldn't know at the time just how the Leeds psychiatrist's decision would have such a profound effect on my life.

Also at the request of my wife (at this time I was prepared to do anything to try to appease her), I agreed to see a hypnotherapist in Leeds. Again, I believe she was hoping he could do something to make me change course.

He told me that he couldn't do anything to help my gender problems (I didn't expect he could) but that he could help me to relax as I was obviously very stressed out.

His treatment did seem to help me to relax more (just being with someone who was not judgemental helped in this respect), but I was not prepared to go along with his suggestion to try past-life regression.

If there is anything in reincarnation, then to find out just who or what I had been previously would not help matters now. If anything, it would probably just add one more area of concern, and I had enough of those to be going on with.

I was however to receive yet one more shattering problem in May 1993. I was involved in a head-on collision on the A58 road at Bardsey, between Wetherby and Leeds, which wrote off my lovely Volkswagen Passat car.

Journeying home from a site visit at Harewood after finishing my planning work, there was a sudden torrential cloudburst that flooded the roads. I turned a sharp bend in Bardsey village to be confronted by a parked bus. Under normal circumstances, this would not have presented any problems as I had sufficient braking distance.

However, as I started to brake, the car aquaplaned on the wet surface straight towards the back of the bus. I instinctively threw the steering wheel over to the right and narrowly missed the bus, but unfortunately, there was a car coming in the opposite direction, and despite my efforts to avoid him, we collided head on.

To compound the incident, the car behind him ran into the rear of his vehicle.

The driver of the car in the middle of the crash, to his credit, quickly checked that both the driver behind and I were all right and announced as long as we all are all right, then never mind the cars (his exact words were a bit stronger than 'never mind!').

I was all right until a lady came out of a nearby house and asked if I would like a cup of tea, then I just burst into tears, I think partly from delayed shock and partly from pent-up emotions.

My car was towed away by a local garage on instructions from the Automobile Association and declared a write-off. For a while therefore, I was without the convenience of personal transport.

As for my friends at this time, I considered that they should be the last to know of my imminent change of lifestyle.

However, circumstance dictated that there was to be one exception. Terry, one of my friends from another Council Department, occasionally joined me for an odd drink on a lunchtime when we talked about our mutual interests in computers. My preoccupation one particular lunchtime must have been obvious.

'What's wrong?' he asked.

I broke down again; things were really starting to get to me.

'Lets get out of here,' I sobbed. 'I've something to tell you.'

We walked around central Leeds as I composed myself, and I explained to Terry what was about to happen. His reaction was that he thought I was making a big mistake but that male or female I would still remain his friend.

Terry kept his word, and we continued to enjoy a drink together on most Monday lunchtimes, including after my change to Faye, although my previous pints of bitter gave way to glasses of lager and lime or gin and tonic.

At home, my eldest sister had phoned to berate me for what I was doing to my wife and children. She too expressed total rejection, saying that there was nothing female about me and that I would look ridiculous. She also said that as far as she was concerned, it was a death in the family, and she wanted nothing more to do with me as a female.

This particular rejection was ironical for when Joe at the clinic had asked me if there were any of the family that I could turn to for support if necessary, I had replied that my eldest sister, who had helped to bring me up and was like a second mother, might understand. It just shows how funny human nature can be.

Could no one understand? How could they possibly think that such a traumatic course was some form of flight of fantasy? It all continued to be very disheartening and did not augur well for future relationships with my brothers and sisters.

I console myself that all this rejection was against Roy, a persona that I too have rejected, as they never got to know the quieter, gentler Faye, so how could they possibly judge her?

It's strange, but I continue to be both surprised and disappointed by those whom I hadn't expected to be accepting and those whom I had.

My close friend Harvey frequently relieved my all-round problems. He had left the Leeds Planning Department, where we worked together, to work in private practice, and his new job took him around the country.

For company on his trips, he often asked me if I could get time off work to go with him on his trips. These outings were a welcome relief from the day-to-day cares that were besetting me and got me away to parts of the country as far afield as Dorchester, Merthyr Tydfil, Edinburgh, and Glasgow.

While he was busy on his duties at these ports of call, I availed myself of looking around the local Ladies Fashion shops to get used to what the future held for me.

He often confided little problems in his life to me, as good friends do, and I often responded, without elaborating, that they paled somewhat compared to my own problems! Harvey at this time had no knowledge of what I was contemplating.

Harvey also enjoyed travelling abroad, and I went with him together with Chris and big Michael, a mutual friend of ours, on several channel-hopping excursions.

Harvey, Chris, and I had also taken ourselves off some little time before for a full week's holiday staying at a gite in central France, not far from the Vosges Mountains. From our gite, we were able to journey both into the Vosges Mountains and also across to the wine regions around Dijon. This was an idyllic week of food, drink, rest, and relaxation, which did much to drive away the tensions that I had carried lately. I have hazy memories of long wine-tasting sessions in the wine cellars of Beaune, just to the south of Dijon.

Sadly, I now see little of my good friend Harvey, as he preferred his friend as male, although we did meet from time to time for a meal.

The change in our friendship is one more victory for the attitudes surrounding gender differences. This is a pity as we had a special sort of friendship which I miss, although I must admit that it is easier for two males to enjoy close friendships rather than male and female and that it is I who has occasioned this barrier. I have also now established friendships with other females, which have helped to fill the void left by the loss of my close friendship with Harvey.

On the work front, breaking the news to my employers was taken out of my hands in an unexpected way.

I was called down to have a word with the personnel section of the department (or human resource section is, I believe, the modern terminology!). I was confronted by David, the personnel boss, who was looking a trifle embarrassed, and Margaret, his next in command, who was looking a bit shocked and was studying me closely. My heart sank; something was wrong.

'We've had a phone call from a David Bird claiming to be from the Manchester Evening News and saying that they've got photos of you dressed as a female entering a gender identity clinic in Manchester and asking for a story. Would you like to have your say?' David asked, continuing to look slightly embarrassed with this particular scenario.

I felt my head begin to swim; the cat was out of the bag in the worst possible way.

'I'm sorry, but it is something that I have had to consider seriously, and yes, I have been attending the clinic, and I am currently having treatment for gender reassignment,' I replied somewhat hesitatingly.

I anxiously searched David's face for signs of disgust or lack of compassion. He seemed to be now taking it all in his stride. I glanced at Margaret and thought I detected a slight smile of acceptance, or was it my imagination?

'OK, leave it with us for the moment. We will have to discuss this with management,' David announced.

I returned upstairs to my desk, stunned and bemused. I was relieved however that something that I had seen as an impossible task had been taken out of my hands and had been done for me.

Bev was waiting for me on my return to my desk. 'What's wrong?' she asked.

'They know downstairs,' I replied, and I recounted what had transpired.

'Good, it's time they knew,' she added.

The next step was that I was called down shortly afterwards to a departmental management meeting, where the full management team was assembled. Not knowing what to expect, I remained quietly submissive, a far cry from the Roy, who had not been afraid to speak out in the past, or was this further evidence of the emergent Faye? I was to be both pleased and surprised by their reaction.

With the exception of the senior assistant director, a typical rugby playing chauvinist (shades of Mr Rudge, my old school master) whom I never saw eye to eye with (what is it that makes Rugby Union players ultra macho and chauvinist?) and who announced that he would rather it went away and happened somewhere else, the overall reaction seemed to be sympathetic and supportive. The pronouncement was short and to the point.

'We are making arrangements to accommodate the changes, and Margaret from personnel will be personally responsible for handling your case. Any problems, then refer them to Margaret.'

So initially, it was as easy as that. All my fears for continuing in my employment were unfounded. I was particularly pleased that a female was to be my 'guardian angel', and I smiled at the mental picture of all the males stepping backwards to avoid any of the responsibility. Funny thing how the male mind has so much difficulty in coming to terms with questions of differences to sexual identification.

I therefore had regular meetings with Margaret from personnel, who presented a sympathetic shoulder during this early traumatic period.

Margaret informed me that they were arranging a series of sectional meetings with the staff to explain to everyone about the changes.

Things were gradually beginning to fall into place as obstacles were gradually being overcome. The impossible dream was becoming more of a reality. My confidence and well-being began to improve at the prospect of what had seemed the impossible becoming possible.

Was all this really happening? Was I really to fulfil the desire that had haunted me for so long? It was still all dream-like and somehow unreal. So much had happened in such a short timescale that I felt the need to take stock and allow things to sink in completely.

The effects of such a radical change of lifestyle are earth-shattering, not only for the individual concerned but all those associated with the individual. I had reached something of a point of no return. The die was really cast, and I was prepared to press forward towards all the further challenges that were lying in wait. I could begin to give full rein to the female within me.

As for my physical development, the effects of the Premarin were virtually instantaneous. My breasts began to itch and ache, and growth was becoming apparent. This increase in breast size led to a painful but amusing incident with Eileen from Wales. On one of her visits to Manchester, we were talking about breast prosthesis, and I was comparing the 'Dolly Partons' with the later 'Melody' prosthesis that I had used, offering her both to examine. Mischievously, I pointed to the emergent buds beneath my blouse.

'How about these then?' I asked, expecting her to accept these as a third prosthesis.

She did, but I didn't expect her reaction. Grabbing a handful of what she took to be silicone, she gave my right breast a sharp playful tweak.

As I almost hit the ceiling with the resultant sharp and unexpected pain, the look of horror on her face showed that she hadn't appreciated that it was all me!

The clinic was acknowledging my development by stepping up my Premarin dosage from 0.6 Mg to 1.2 Mg, then to 2.5 Mg, and on to 5.0 Mg. I was also told that I should be ready to go full-time female in March 1994 after twelve months on the Premarin. However, events were to overtake even this deadline.

I was finding the body changes exciting and wonderful, but embarrassing while living a male lifestyle. I had taken to wearing loose floppy sweaters to hide the changes, but Margaret from personnel said I was going to have to consider moving my date of coming in as Faye forward as I was beginning to look odd, and I couldn't go on much longer going to work in a male suit with boobs!

I warmed to this suggestion, as I was anxious to get underway on the long practical learning curve that lay ahead. So it was over to the clinic at Manchester to see if Dr Joe was happy with this suggestion. His response was that if I felt ready for this major step, and my employers were happy, then why not?

It was therefore agreed that I should go full time after my canal trip holiday in late August 1993. I consequently arranged to take leave from work for a week before and a week after my trip to allow a full three weeks for me to begin to adapt before going back to work as Faye.

My first day back at work would therefore be Monday, 13 September 1993.

The time had consequently arrived for my permanent change of name.

Rachael and Gina had a female solicitor in Rochdale, and I made an appointment to see her to change my name by deed poll. After this initial meeting, which was to provide the necessary details, a further appointment was made for 21 July 1993.

This date was to become my unofficial birthday. I took Chris from Wales with me to witness the document. The deed poll was passed to me for signature, and I penned R. H. Wardle for the last time officially, and F. H. Wardle for the first time officially to the section which read as follows:

I absolutely and entirely renounce, relinquish and abandon the use of my said former name of Roy Harry Wardle and assume, adopt and determine to take and use from the date hereof the name of Faye Helen Wardle in substitution of my former name of Roy Harry Wardle . . .

It was as easy as that, my old and new signatures, paying the princely sum of £30 plus VAT, and the deed was literally done. For purely practical purposes, I continued to use my old name for the following month until the complete changeover.

Back at home, the situation was continuing to be intolerable for all concerned. I had a standing invitation to go stay with Gina and Rachael in Manchester, but commuting daily to Leeds didn't present a financially viable solution.

Bev from work came to the rescue and offered me digs at her house for during the week, and I could return to Manchester at the weekends and use the Manchester address for my place of residence.

Bev was going away in early August on holiday, and she suggested that I moved in for a trial period while she was away to look after her cat and to give me a break from the stresses of my life at home.

My wife seemed relieved at the prospect of my departure and suggested that it would be better if I stayed away permanently from that point.

So it was that I was to leave my family and home, the hardest and most enduringly painful step of all, and yet deep down, I appreciated the necessity of a complete, clean break in the best interests of all concerned.

Only a loving parent can appreciate however just how it felt to leave my three lovely children in such circumstances. They had made clear their desire not to know the new me, and I inwardly resolved to always be available should they wish to see their old dad in new format at some future date.

In truth, I did however share my wife's relief at the break given the emerging stresses and deteriorating atmosphere at home. It was some small consolation that I had experienced the pleasures of seeing my children safely through their childhood to the threshold of independent adulthood. I have not seen my children since this time in the summer of 1993.

I had one aspect as a father that I wanted to carry out before leaving. I wanted to take my two sons, who were emerging as two fine young men, out for a drink with their father.

My friend Terry therefore arranged for the four of us to visit the New Roscoe Public House in Leeds on a Thursday night when the groups performed there.

At the pub, the earlier subdued nature of my two boys was gradually evaporating as they relaxed, and they were obviously beginning to enjoy themselves. Then my friend Terry announced that he had never been for a drink with his father.

I felt myself beginning to fill up as I looked at my two fine sons and realised that this was to be the last and only time for both of them and me.

As I felt the tears starting to well, I made a hurried dash to the exit, to our vehicle in the car park, and the cover of darkness. I sat in the car for a while until I eventually composed myself and then returned to the bar.

It was obvious that something had taken place in my absence. It was afterwards that Terry informed me of what had transpired. Terry had commented to the boys that their dad was a long time, thinking I had left to go to the toilet.

'He's probably varnishing his nails,' retorted my eldest son.

At this, Terry apparently rounded on him and said, 'Look, what your dad has to do, he can neither help nor avoid, and at least, he has the courage to face it. Just remember that!'

'I know. I'm sorry,' said my son.

This poignant tale perhaps holds out some hope of future reconciliation with my children and also illustrates what a good and understanding friend Terry has proven to be.

At work, the staff, intrigued by the notification of a series of staff meetings to 'discuss an important issue', soon realised that I was the only one excluded from these meetings, and I was quizzed as to what they were about as they saw my exclusion to mean that I already knew their content.

I simply told them to wait and see. They were soon to find out why.

I asked personnel to leave these staff meetings until after Malcolm, one of my friends at work, took his early retirement, as he is a lay preacher and I wasn't too sure how he would take the news with his deep religious beliefs. In the event, he was to return to the office for a visit some weeks after I had gone full time as Faye. The office went quiet as he approached my desk and leaned over.

'It must have taken a great deal of courage for you to have continued as you were before,' he said. And this came from someone whom we were worried about in terms of reaction!

Malcolm and his wife continued to be good friends to me and made me very welcome on my visits to their lovely home at Stratford-on-Avon.

One incident from the staff meetings that I heard about concerned Christine, a fellow planner, who was an avid Leeds United fan and who frequently talked over the team's progress with me.

'Will he still want to talk about football?' Christine asked Margaret, who was conducting the meeting.

Margaret replied that it was a sex change and not a brain transplant! The perfect way to deal with that particular question and a good way of getting it across that I was still the same person but in a different format.

By and large, the females in the office took the news far better than the males. One male colleague asked me if I was homosexual (the usual and typical response to the news of this nature).

'Do you mean do I fancy girls?' I coyly replied, and I left him to ponder on that one.

Another male colleague said he couldn't understand why I wanted to leave the elite to join the second-class citizens (another classic case of misplaced male superiority). I responded that as far as I was concerned, I was joining the elite, not leaving them. My subsequent life as a female has only reinforced my opinion in this respect.

The staff meetings meant that another major step was out of the way: now, everyone at work knew of the pending changes.

The next steps were the practical ones of changing my entire documentation, etc., and notifying all others who needed to know of the pending changeover.

I composed a lengthy standard letter stating how and why my name and status would be changing, and I took numerous copies of this letter and an equal number of copies of the deed poll for confirmation. These had to be distributed to banks, credit card companies, National Insurance Office, Department of Transport, Automobile Association, etc.

This led to one amusing incident at my bank, where I had asked for the change of name on the account. Upon receipt of my letter, the bank manager phoned me to say that to effect the changes, he would need to see the original deed poll as he couldn't act upon a copy. I told him that I was reluctant to entrust this to the Royal Mail system and that if he could let me know when he had finished if I brought it in personally, and I would return to the bank to collect it personally.

He duly phoned me at work to say that the deed poll was ready for me to collect together with a form for me to sign, and they would be at the reception desk. I called at the bank and was greeted at reception by a young female bank clerk.

'Yes, Mr Wardle, I have an envelope for you and a form of authorisation for you and Miss Wardle to sign,' she announced, obviously unaware of just why the account name was changing.

'It's all right,' I replied. 'I can sign both halves.'

'No, you misunderstand me, sir. You must sign the top half, and you will have to take it away for Miss Faye Helen Wardle to sign the bottom half,' she insisted with some concern.

I gave her a big smile and said, 'The name on the account isn't the only thing that's changing,' as I signed R. H. Wardle at the top and F. H. Wardle at the bottom.

I collected my envelope and left her with a somewhat incredulous expression on her face.

During the interim period between leaving home and going full time as Faye, I led a confused life of being Roy during the day at work and Faye for most of my spare time. This in turn led to one or two amusing situations. Spending my weekends at Manchester as Faye meant I was able to slowly adjust to my new imminent lifestyle and commence the long haul of adaptation by concentrating on deportment, gestures, and the thousands of other new and exciting aspects that being female entailed. I needed to study and learn aspects that a biological female would have developed naturally over the period of her life.

It meant however that I often returned to my digs at Bev's in Leeds dressed as Faye to emerge for work the following day as Roy. I told Bev that her neighbours would be asking the police to dig up her cellar floor to find out what had happened to the missing female!

There was also an occasion when I dashed home to Bev's from work, had a quick change and make-up, and went out to the car ready to nip over to the Northern Concord meeting at Manchester. Just as I was pulling away, a car drew up alongside me and blocked me in.

Someone playing silly devils was my first reaction, but as I glanced across at the driver, I realised it was my friend Harvey, who had heard that I was staying at Bev's and had decided to call around. I don't know who was the more surprised. Whilst by now, I had told Harvey of the impending changes, the sight of me as a redheaded female made him hesitate, and I'm sure he contemplated driving straight off.

However, I waved him over to my car, and we sat for a while and had a chat. As first impressions count for a lot, I was wishing that I had taken more care with my wig, make-up, and general appearance.

So that meant that two of my friends, Bev and Harvey, had now met Faye. So far so good.

Actually, indirectly it was Harvey who gave me the impetus to pen this autobiography. When I was talking to him shortly after the news broke, I mentioned that maybe I ought to write a book.

'Go for it,' he said with feeling. 'People need to know.'

That's right, I thought. I would make a start and see what transpired. So began this factual account that, at times, must seem stranger than fiction.

CHAPTER TWELVE

Faye's Early Days

The time arrives for the dream to begin
As first steps taken in a world so new
A chance to find what life can bring
With Nature's obstacles and friends so true

—Faye Helen Wardle

August 24 1993 finally arrived, the day when I was to finally say farewell to my male persona and allow full reign to the female who had haunted me for so long.

I finished work at lunchtime as I had arranged to spend my first few days in Wales with Eileen and Chris. It was a strange feeling as I changed at Bev's, taking off my male clothes for the last time and donning my favourite red two-piece ready for my journey.

It was as I was packing my car prior to setting off for Wales that I was to have an experience that brought home to me my new state.

Conscious of someone approaching as I was loading the boot, I turned to be confronted by Big Michael, the friend of Harvey and me. Without hesitation, he grabbed me and gave me a big kiss stating that he supposed that was in order now.

'Well, yes, I suppose so,' I replied, confused by the fact that I found it an enjoyable natural experience. We chatted for a while; he seemed totally relaxed with the new me He said that I looked great and that he wanted to be the first to you know what after the gender reassignment operation!

Good grief! I had only been full time for five minutes! However this was a good confidence booster, and I set off in good spirits.

I called at a fish and chip restaurant near the M1/Denby Dale junction for a delicious meal. There were no problems here, and I warmed to being called madam and miss.

My few days in Wales provided just the right, quiet, easing period before the hectic week that was to follow.

Eileen, Chris, and I left Wales to journey up to Manchester to Rachael and Gina's to prepare together for our canal trip.

One of my first jobs after we arrived there was to have my ears pierced, and I took myself off to a beauty salon in Urmston to have this done, a small mark on each ear followed by a small gold stud being fired into each earlobe. These studs would have to remain in place for several weeks until the hole hardened without healing up.

Given that the date for me to arrive back at work as Faye was looming large, I started to give more thought to my overall appearance.

The main problem with my appearance was my beloved ginger or gold wig. Very long and full, it took years off my apparent age and was a great confidence booster. However, was it the right image for a middle-aged professional businesswoman?

Unfortunately not. So back to the wig shop. Here, helped and guided by the female staff, I arrived at the new look Faye, a shorter, less full, grey and blonde mix, smart and businesslike, and more my age.

I wasn't too displeased with the change, and I had a fortnight to get used to it before my appearance at work.

28 August 1993 was our departure date for the canal trip, and after Lucy's arrival (complete with two dogs), our convoy of three cars, packed solid with luggage, provisions, and passengers, left Manchester for Stoke-on-Trent and the Etruria Boatyard.

The boatyard had been forewarned of the unusual nature of this particular boatload, and the owners had met some of us on an earlier reconnaissance visit. Our reception was friendly, and we were introduced to our narrow boat 'King Arthur'. Little did we know at the time that the next seven days were to be largely ill-fated.

I suppose that when you have six people and three dogs (Gina and Rachael also took their German shepherd dog) in close proximity to each other day after day, it is a recipe for some friction. Couple this with a boat that had a slow leak and a dodgy propeller, and you have some idea of just how things developed.

Our planned seven-day canal journey was to be a 110-mile Midlands circuit with 94 lock gates, quite an undertaking for a largely inexperienced crew.

A member of the boatyard crew took the boat out of the harbour yard on to the Trent and Mersey Canal and turned south towards the first lock gate only some quarter of a mile away. At this lock gate, we were given a practical demonstration of how to operate the canal lock. After this, we were on our own.

In this only my second week as Faye, I was dressed practically in navy blue slacks and sweater. Slacks or tracksuit bottoms were to be the order of the day during the trip. Hardly a very feminine introduction to my new life, and it was ironical that having eagerly awaited going 'full time', I was to spend so much time in trousers!

We moored the first night at stone, having successfully negotiated the first few lock gates. Gina and I were to be the principal 'maids of the locks', and we developed a good working relationship.

Rachael and Chris alternated on the tiller, Eileen was virtually full time in the galley, and Lucy kept the dogs occupied. With the exception of Eileen, these duties alternated a bit as the week wore on, and I was to enjoy spells on the tiller. Believe me, a sixty-four-feet longboat is not the easiest of crafts to control.

It became obvious that not all was well with our craft. Poor old King Arthur developed a list to port, and the cavitating vibrations of the propeller made steering the boat difficult.

Relationships became strained, and arguments developed. However, there were tranquil, peaceful spells aided by the warm days of the late summer sunshine and the walking pace progress of our craft as it chugged along the calm canal waters.

I was given the task of ensuring that our rate of progress was up to date, and my method was to allow four miles per hour of travelling plus fifteen minutes per lock gate. As we had got operation of the locks off to a fine art, we gradually accumulated time. This I didn't mind as it is far easier to lose time than to make it up.

Our journey took us south on the Trent and Mersey Canal to the outskirts of Wolverhampton and then westwards towards the Shropshire Union Canal. Joining the Shropshire Union, we turned north towards Cheshire.

We approached the infamous flight of twenty lock gates at Audlem with some trepidation. Allowing five hours to negotiate this succession of locks (fifteen minutes per lock), we were to decimate this time and come very close to the all-time record for the descent. Our overall time for negotiating the twenty lock gates was one hour thirty minutes, and the all-time record stands at one hour twenty minutes.

We were informed that our descent was the quickest that year, a credit to our joint team effort.

Arriving at the top lock, the start of our descent was delayed by a boat coming up the flight. I was on the tiller, and Chris, Rachael, Gina, and Lucy working in two overlapping teams of two were on the lock gates. Eileen was below decks. The fact that a boat had just come up the flight meant that all the locks were full and there were no delays waiting for the locks to fill on our descent. Our intrepid lock crews ensured that all the gates were open to the locks on my approach, and we set off down.

Handling the large narrowboat through the succession of tight locks and pounds was no easy matter, and I arrived at our mooring point outside the village pub at the bottom of the descent something of a physical wreck. The wig was a mess, and my make-up was virtually non-existent. As I flopped over the tiller, a gentleman who was walking his dog along the towpath and taking an interest in our craft approached me. I was preparing myself for some smart cutting comment when he looked at me and said, 'Have the men left you to do all the work, dear?'

Despite the comments from my companions about not seeing his white stick, it was a nice little boost to my rapidly waning confidence.

The rest of our experiences in the village were not so pleasant. The locals in the pub were far from friendly, and when Gina and I visited the village charity shop with Eileen, we were followed around by one of the assistants like a couple of criminals, much to Eileen's annoyance.

After almost a full day in Audlem (to use up some of the time we had accumulated), we continued northwards past Nantwich and then eastwards to Middlewich past the appropriately named Wardles Corner, before rejoining the Trent and Mersey Canal, and turning south back towards Stoke-on-Trent.

There was one amusing, although at the time painful, incident when we moored at Hassall Green. I had been feeling less feminine than I had for some time, spending all day in trousers and little or no make-up. Not that feminine attire and make-up are essential prerequisites of femininity, but they do boost a girl's confidence.

We decided to call at the local pub in the evening, so I determined that it was a good time to make a special effort with my appearance, a lengthy make-up and dressing session (not easy in the restricted confines of the boat), and there was the Faye I recognised. Off with the trainers and on with the three-inch-heel court shoes and I was ready to face the world.

Seated in the 'Olde Worlde' pub enjoying the local beverages—this was life. Came the time for me to visit the bar. Drawing myself up to my full height, I headed towards the busy bar. Intent on viewing the bar customers, I failed to take note of the low-beamed ceiling and gave the top of my head a resounding whack on one of the timber crossbeams. As I staggered backwards, the concerned landlady dashed out from behind the bar.

'We don't usually get them as big as *him* (!) in here,' she said to my companions. This was literally adding insult to injury, so I retreated back to our boat with pride, confidence, and head badly hurt.

The atmosphere on the boat remained strained, and I was at the stage where I was looking forward to arriving back at Stoke-on-Trent and the chance to be able to concentrate more on adapting to my new life. This trip which had seemed a good idea earlier in the year wasn't proving the type of start I needed.

It was near Sandbach where things came to a head with our ailing boat. I was on the tiller steadily negotiating a lock when I was suddenly enveloped in a cloud of steam. Switching off the engine, we drifted over to the canal bank and moored up. Rachael went off to a nearby hamlet to phone for the engineer from the boatyard.

The engineer duly appeared after a short wait and found that a broken fan belt had caused the overheating. However, we had not appreciated that the bilge pump had been working all the time to compensate for a leaking hull. Seeing no apparent reason for the bilge pump running, the engineer switched it off and went on his way. We too set off not appreciating that the boat was gradually sinking! This fact became obvious as the boat listed more and more to port. We decided to head back for Stoke at full speed to arrive there on Friday instead of Saturday.

There was one further hazard from a personal point of view, the Hardcastle Tunnel. This canal tunnel just to the north of Stoke is two miles long and takes some three-quarters of an hour to negotiate.

Being somewhat claustrophobic, I was deeply worried about such a long journey in a confined black tunnel. I therefore went below decks with Eileen and a pile of magazines and crossword puzzles to take my mind off the journey. While it wasn't as bad as I feared, I was deeply relieved as we broke into the daylight, and I made my way aft onto the deck to do a stint on the tiller.

We limped into Stoke to spend our last night on board back at the base at Etruria.

Our convoy of cars headed back to Manchester up the M6, and I was able to start my 'real life test' in earnest. My first job was to take Eileen and Chris back to Wales, where I could stay overnight. This was a good move. Away from the crowded confines of the canal boat, I felt able to relax at last.

We stopped at a public house at Woodseaves village for a meal, and given my recent experiences in public houses at Audlem and Hassall Green, I was somewhat hesitant as we entered. However, the reactions of the staff and customers, or rather the non-reactions, put me at my ease. This was compounded as I went to the bar to be greeted by 'Yes, miss?'

I was finding that the smallest things can either boost or shatter your confidence, a situation that was to continue for some time, and suddenly mine was back on an even keel. Faye was starting a long, hard, but wonderful journey.

My brief sojourn to Wales was to allow me to unwind a little before my return to Rachael and Gina's in Manchester for a few days.

My return to work with Leeds City Council was now approaching, and I returned to Bev's in Leeds on the night of 12 September 1993.

Dear Bev, as 13 September dawned, she was like a mother hen with a new chick.

My whole appearance, make-up, dress, nails, and hair all came under close scrutiny before I was passed as 'fit for work'. I once again wore my favourite red two piece, comfortable but smart and feminine. Bev took a couple of photographs of me for posterity before we left her house.

The car park attendant greeted us as we pulled into the Civic Hall Car Park. I had been informed that he had been forewarned about the new me, and he was his usual pleasant self, only this time with a huge curious smile as I emerged from Bev's car.

'Good morning, Faye. Big day then?' he chirped pleasantly.

'Morning,' I replied, returning his smile and pleased that he had adapted to my new name.

I felt my heart running fast as Bev and I approached the office doors that I had entered so many times as Roy. I had never in my wildest dreams ever thought that this moment would come and I would be going into work as a female. Just how would my colleagues react to Faye? I recalled that in Stephanie Anne Lloyd's autobiography *A Girl in a Million*, she had been greeted on her first day at work as a female with a bouquet of flowers and everybody offering their best wishes. I had also heard that others elsewhere had been shunned and ignored at their place of work when they entered.

As it happened, I think everyone was so determined to act normally that there was nothing more than the odd cursory 'good morning' as I walked through to my desk. Was it my imagination however, or did rather a large number of staff find some excuse to walk through the office and steal a sideways glance at the 'new girl on the block'?

When the news of my pending change had first broken at work, one of my colleagues, Nick, had said that some of the staff were treating it as a joke, but he would show them I was serious and he would take me out for a drink on my first day in work as Faye. This was a very kind and considerate thought, but on this my first morning, he made no mention of his earlier offer.

I was wondering if he was having second thoughts when actually presented with the new me. However, at five minutes to twelve, he came over to me.

'Where are we going then?' he asked.

'For what?' I feigned surprise.

'For our drink,' he said.

So off we toddled to a local hostelry for a pleasant and welcome drink. He couldn't know what this small measure of acceptance meant to me.

So there it all was; my return to work was something of an anti-climax. The strange mixture of dread and anticipation that I had felt preceding my return had no basis in actual events.

After two weeks of near normality however, I was once more to be given a bit of a confidence jolt.

I was summoned before a management meeting and given a lecture about not visiting certain parts of the office where some people were having difficulty in coming to terms with the new me. Ironically, one of these was the race relations section, where I would have thought tolerance was the order of the day.

Sadly, it has been my experience, with human nature in general, that it is far easier to ask for tolerance than to give it. I was also told not to go flaunting around the office chatting to other members of staff!

I was both hurt and annoyed. I had certainly not sought to offend anyone, far from it. I had not been 'flaunting around the office'. On the contrary, I had sought a low profile.

My new area of work did however necessitate visiting other areas of the office, and any 'chatting' was no more than the casual social exchanges that any members of staff might conduct with each other during the course of the working day.

I think this criticism of 'chatting' in part was down to the male edict which sees nothing wrong with two male members of staff chatting at considerable length about the comparative merits of several pubs or last weekend's soccer or rugby matches, but if I wanted to ask one of the girls where was the best place to buy large-size tights, then this was time-wasting trivia which had to be condemned!

I felt somewhat devastated. Was I to be subjected to undue and unwarranted restrictions and criticism? I was pretty sure that this was not the normal type of treatment for other female members of staff?

I mentally resolved to keep myself totally to myself and just quietly get on with my job so as not to give them the slightest excuse for any further victimisation. As I was about to leave the meeting, however, the assistant director from building control delivered something that was to partially repair my damaged ego and confidence.

'I would like to say however that we have been very impressed with your appearance so far, as none of us knew exactly what to expect,' he announced.

'No,' I replied somewhat subdued, 'I think some people were expecting Kim Basinger to walk through the door, and some were expecting something from the Rocky Horror Show. I hope I've come somewhere in between.'

'I think you have,' he said, smiling.

I left the meeting feeling I had been kicked down and then picked up. This was to be the order of things in so many ways. I didn't want preferential treatment; neither did I expect to be especially singled out for undue criticism. I just wanted to be left to get on with my job as I had been in the past.

I believe my colleagues at work have had the greatest difficulty in coming to terms with the change. They had known Roy so long and so well that they just couldn't see me as anything other than Roy in a dress.

Conversely, Eileen and Chris from Wales and my many friends at Manchester who only knew me as Faye had no problems with calling me by my new name and referring to me as 'her' or 'she'. I was quite simply female as far as they were concerned. They had not known my 'alter ego'.

This difficulty at work with colleagues coming to terms with the change manifested itself in so many ways. In one instance, a memorandum was circulated which contained the text as follows: 'Faye Wardle has requested information on this topic. Please get details to him as soon as possible (!)' Being called Roy, particularly on the telephone, was a regular occurrence, and I could often sense the embarrassment as they sought to rectify this mistake. I was of course prepared to accept that the problems associated with the changes would not resolve themselves overnight and could understand most of their difficulties. However, some made little or no effort to come to terms with my changes.

The problems of my voice, which I was trying hard to soften but which was still very much male, were not only restricted to my employment. When I took a phone call at home one day, the young lady caller asked for Miss Wardle. I had great difficulty in convincing her that it was Miss Wardle speaking. It was the young lady from my insurance company, and I explained that I was undergoing gender reassignment.

'Oh, do you mean a sex change?' she asked.

Weary of this misnomer, I replied, 'No, dear. A sex change is when you sleep with someone different.'

We both had a good laugh after which we got along fine.

I was finding that the ease I felt in the company of females was increasing. I was largely accepted as one of the girls, and I enjoyed being included in the girl talk. Their acceptance of me was brought to a head one day when having a lunchtime chat with a female colleague. She was expounding on her problems with men when she said to me, 'And you know what men are like, Faye,' and she paused, giggled, and said, 'But of course, you do!' She had obviously completely discounted my previous self for a while, purely seeing me as another female.

These tiny unconscious gestures of acceptance always gave me a warm, satisfying glow. I felt I was on my way down the long road to fulfilment.

My relationship with Rachael at Manchester was becoming increasingly strained, particularly when I found out that she had been phoning my wife and had been hindering rather than helping my transition. I therefore had to contemplate ceasing my stays at Urmston.

The parting of the ways came one Friday night in late September 1993. Leaving behind Rachael and Gina's, I was confronted with something of a problem.

My arrangement with Bev in Leeds was that I would stay with her only during the week and not at weekends. I sat in my car at Manchester facing the prospect of sleeping in the car for the weekend, and then I remembered that I had a standing invitation to stay with Eileen and Chris in Wales. I consulted my limited finances and worked out that I could just afford the petrol to Wales and back to Leeds, so I set off for the Principality.

As anticipated, I was made very welcome down in Wales. Eileen was concerned at my downhearted state. The departure from home and family, my changed lifestyle, my accommodation problems, and the parlous state of my finances were all suddenly starting to weigh heavy. Was I really doing the right thing? Roy was still having his say, even in his death throes, but Faye was having none of it. She had waited a long time, and she was here to stay.

I had made the start that was the important thing, so from here, it was onward and upward.

CHAPTER THIRTEEN

The Press and Life on My Own

Freedom can bring loneliness
With prospects of a life alone
Faced only by a hostile Press
With words like spears and hearts of stone

—Faye Helen Wardle

I had taken the precaution, with a degree of foresight, to put my name down on the Leeds Housing Register for my own accommodation some time before my change over to Faye. Events were soon to prove the wisdom of this move.

As I was now stuck for weekend accommodation, my friend Terry suggested that I contact my friend and ex-colleague Chris. Chris lived alone in a large semi-detached house in north Leeds and had been a staunch friend of both me and my family for some years.

'I never thought of Chris. I'll contact him,' I said.

Terry however suggested that I leave it to him as if Chris wanted to say no for any reason, he would find it easier to tell Terry than to refuse me. I gratefully agreed.

Later that day, Terry phoned me to say Chris was totally agreeable with my staying there and was annoyed that I had not contacted him directly (do you ever feel that you just can't win!).

So for a while, I stayed with Chris at weekends and at Bev's during the week.

On one of my first weekends with Chris, he offered to take me in his van to pick up my few personal belongings from Rachael and Gina's at Manchester. This we accomplished, and he announced that it was a bit early to travel back to Leeds. So off we toddled to the West Coast for lunch on the pier at Southport and then on to the Blackpool lights. I found the packed promenade at Blackpool a bit daunting in my early in-between state, but by the time we reached the Tower, I was beginning to relax and enjoy myself.

Chris had never been up the Tower, so this was our first target. We squeezed into the packed Tower lift; the ascent was far from uneventful. Chris said something to me, and unaware of an eagle-eared youngster within earshot, I replied to Chris's statement. The youngster grabbed his mother's arm. 'Mum, it's a man. Mum, Mum, it's a man, it's a man!'

Oh dear, despite his embarrassed mother's pleas for him to be quiet, he was insistent, so by the time we reached the top, all the lift's occupants were aware of my intersex condition. The temptation at the top to squeeze one obnoxious offspring through the Tower's safety bars and out into space was overwhelming!

After our ascent from the dizzy heights of the Tower, we had to pass along the balcony of the Tower Ballroom. Here, an organist was playing for a crowd of ballroom dancers.

At Chris's suggestion we sat down to listen to the organist for a while, and knowing of his affection for organ music, I was happy to agree.

Chris said it was a pity that it wasn't Phil Kelsall playing the organ (a particular favourite of his) when the organist, announcing his departure, said that the rest of the evening's music would alternate between the Night Hawks Dance Band and Phil Kelsall on the organ.

We were therefore hooked for the rest of the evening. For me, it was pure nostalgia as we watched ballroom dancing to an excellent big band and one of the best organists in the business.

As I was gradually easing into my new life, I was to be dealt one more body blow. My telephone rang at work one day. It was a reporter from the Yorkshire Evening Post, the major newspaper for local coverage, asking about my changes and stating that they were to speak to the management of my department about my case. I initially agreed to meet him in the hope that he would not bother anyone else. As I thought about this decision upon putting the phone down, I began to question the wisdom of this arrangement, so I went down to see the personnel section as to the best course of action.

Once more, I was called before a meeting of management. I was berated for having anything to do with the press, and I was told that under no circumstances, should I meet them. I was virtually accused of encouraging such attention, and I was informed that it would be entered on my disciplinary record as a warning as to my future conduct! All this despite the fact that I had considered my actions to be in the best interests of all and had myself reneged on any meeting.

I yet again felt chastised and criticised through no fault of my own. I was left feeling that despite the veneer of acceptance; there was an undercurrent of unacceptability that would have rather not had me in the department. This was not personal paranoia but was based on the way I was being singled out for criticism for the slightest thing.

The Yorkshire Evening Post, getting no joy from me or my employers, made up their own story from what little information they had available. (There is an old journalistic saying that the truth should never stand in the way of a good story!)

It would appear that someone had alerted the Evening Post about my case, and I was in no doubt that it was once more the mysterious Mr Bird.

The story appeared on the front page of the Evening Post edition under the headline 'CALL ME MADAM'. It read as though I had suddenly turned up at work in female attire without any previous announcement or arrangements, thereby completely shocking the staff.

This was completely contrary to the actual course of events and the early counselling approach whereby all the staff were forewarned and given time to get used to the idea before my changeover.

The story was accompanied by placards around the city emblazoned 'City Council Sex Change Shock'. I thought of my family and the impact on my children, especially at school. All my attempts to keep a low profile had failed.

Much is made of the freedom of the press in this country, but there seems to be little protection for the freedom and privacy of the individual. The press really should be made more accountable for the way they are allowed to decimate innocent people's lives for the brief filling of a few lines of news space. I wonder just how many editors and reporters have skeletons in the cupboards of their own lives and how they would feel if these skeletons were dragged out and aired publicly across their home town! I wouldn't mind betting that censorship rather than news space would rule the day in such cases!

The original worthy intent of 'freedom of the press' was intended to ensure that matters that were in the public interest were not kept hidden. I cannot see how my personal problems of sexual identity were 'public domain' to the extent portrayed. This kind of treatment must surely constitute an invasion of privacy.

It took the later hounding by the press of our lovely ill-fated Princess Diana to bring home the question of the behaviour of these media animals.

Like an earthquake, after the initial warning shock, came the main impact. I was made aware at work the following day that the press had laid siege to the office. The National Daily tabloids had latched on to the story and were waiting in force for their own story and photographs. At least this time, management appreciated that this situation was no fault of mine, as was evident from my distress at the evolving situation. I was advised to take some work home and stay away from the office for a few days until things quietened down.

The problem remained however as to how I was to avoid the press on my departure from work that day. My colleague Nick, who had taken me for a drink on my first day at work as Faye, came to my rescue. He arranged for a car to be waiting at our emergency exit at 4 p.m., and I was smuggled out and whisked away up to near the university where my own car was parked.

Prior to leaving work, I had been informed that the press had found out where my digs were with Bev and had been harassing Bev's neighbours and her boyfriend. So I retreated to Chris's home in north Leeds for a period of enforced seclusion. The harassment of Bev and her boyfriend was to result in my having to vacate my digs there. Yet one more senseless victory for the gutter press.

I was left hoping that history wasn't going to repeat itself as I recalled how the uncaring, irresponsible press had been responsible for Stephanie Anne Lloyd and Caroline Cossey, two earlier transsexuals, losing their employment.

As human beings, we take time to take up the case against fox-hunting by hounds, but we seem to care little when the newshounds hunt down their human quarries and leave them battered and wounded.

For the first few days after my return to work, I arrived at 7 a.m., before the arrival of the press who were still laying siege to the office, and

I stayed inside the building until 4 p.m. when I left unnoticed by the rear emergency exit. They therefore gradually gave up and left empty-handed, and my life was to return to normal or as near normal as possible.

I registered as homeless with the council, and Chris agreed that I could stay with him until I found my own place.

It was now late October 1993, and my luck was to turn at last. I was offered a flat in a council high-rise block, and I gratefully accepted it. It was a nice, quiet block in a reasonably pleasant setting not too far from the city centre and was mainly occupied by elderly residents. I now had a place of my own but little or no furnishings. I moved in on 1 November 1993.

On my first night of occupancy, I sat in a bare flat with only a camp bed and two old worn armchairs (which I had salvaged from a flat clearance). Life suddenly seemed a lonely, empty, and friendless place. I thought of what I had left behind and the uncertainty of what lay ahead. I felt drained by recent events and wept uncontrollably. It was the living that was proving hard, not the changes to me that in themselves still held out the major compensation.

Having got the initial despondency out of my system, I set about building a new home for myself. I had taken my music centre, most of my record collection, spare television set, and spare video recorder with me when I left home, so I had some in-home entertainment.

5 November turned out to be a black night for me amongst all the fireworks. It was during bonfire night that some kind character broke into the old Metro car that I had purchased to replace my Passat.

I had left the car on the car park of the flats, and they vandalised the interior, pulling out wiring and bending the steering wheel into a figure of eight. Worst than that they stole my only female coat, my lovely full-length mackintosh from the back seat together with my scarf and gloves. I then discovered that my purse had been in the pocket of my mackintosh coat, so that had gone as well. This contained all the money I had, even the small change. I had no prospect of any more money until pay day on 16 November.

Once again, I was devastated. I was confined to my sparsely furnished flat, without transport, money, or even a coat to go out in. I had reached rock bottom. I must have cried for hours. What else could go wrong? This wasn't at all how I had envisaged my new life.

Yet again, Faye took control. The only way was up, and I began to think positively. My workplace was only two miles away, so I could walk there and back (despite the discomfort of my new high heels). I still had my male mackintosh, so that would have to provide warmth and comfort as a stopgap measure. I had enough food to last until pay day if used sensibly. So what was so bad?

My new female determination to take on the world was showing through. I knew some people were expecting me to fall flat on my face. Well, I would show them!

So it was that for a couple of weeks, I struggled to work on foot through some particularly cold November weather.

Around this time, there was better news from my relatives. My brother Bernard, the ex-rugby player, phoned me to say that he had seen a small follow-up article from the Yorkshire Evening Post expose featured in the Sunday Mirror. This was the first he had heard of my changes, and he wanted me to know that it was all right as far as he was concerned. He asked me to call around and see him at his home at Otley to the north of Leeds. I took up his invitation and was made most welcome.

I asked his wife Jeanne how he had taken the news. She replied that he had been quiet for a while, and then he said sadly that he had lost his brother. After a further quiet spell, he brightened up and said, 'But I've gained a sister.'

My brother Bernard was a consistent support until his sad recent death. His wife Jeanne still keeps in touch and provides me with snippets of family news.

Coinciding with my brother Bernard getting in touch, my sister Barbara in London sent me a card of support to my workplace, as she didn't know my new home address. I got in touch with her and was invited down to visit them for a weekend.

This acceptance and resumption of contact with some of my relatives meant more to me than could be imagined at a time when I was starting to feel very much alone in an apparently hostile world.

I drove down to London in my recently repaired Metro with a mixture of anticipation and apprehension. My brother-in-law Harry was in the army in the Second World War and was a Burma Star veteran. He was very much a man's man, and I wasn't at all sure just how he would react to Faye.

My fears were totally unfounded. He was the first to greet me in their hallway with a big hug and the words 'come on in, gal'. My sister Barbara also seemed pleased to see me and also seemed pleased with my appearance.

The following day, Saturday, they took me shopping around the local shops at Chingford to see if I could pick up a cheap coat to replace the one that had been stolen. While I didn't find a coat, I did manage to pick up one or two odds and ends for my flat.

Upon return to their own flat, Harry said he had been watching me when we were out to see people's reactions to me, and the only time anyone gave me a second glance was when they heard my voice. I told him that I had been watching him as well to see if he had been at all uncomfortable in my presence, and I was delighted that he was completely at ease in the company of the new me.

They later took me to visit the families of their two sons, my nephews Keith and David, and again I was made very welcome. It was lovely to establish contact with some of my relatives again and even more so to be accepted as their new sister or aunty.

CHAPTER FOURTEEN

Love as a Female in a Strange, New, and Wonderful World

First stirrings of a love new found
A brand new year on brand new ground
Hope of fulfilment near at last
To be denied by judgement past

—Faye Helen Wardle

The Portland Clinic in Manchester was continuing to monitor my progress and physical condition. There was a slight problem for a while with my cholesterol levels and weight fluctuations, but by and large, they were happy with my progress to date.

I was more at ease in female attire now, and the early feelings of guilt were fading. It just felt so natural and right. I was, for the first time in my life, totally at ease with my inner self. The deportment and mannerisms were improving, but the voice was still a major problem.

My first Christmas on my own loomed large. However, Barbara and Harry from London were coming up to stay with Bernard and Jeanne from Otley, and they had booked to have their Christmas lunch together at a charming hostelry in Askwith village in Wharfedale near Otley. To my delight, they invited me to go with the four of them, and I jumped at the chance.

However, they discovered that all the places for the lunch had been booked up, so it looked as though I was going to be unlucky. Not to be outdone they phoned back to the hostelry and said they would take the first cancellation to be told that someone had just cancelled, so I was duly booked in.

Christmas Day arrived, and I had the initial problem of what to wear for the luncheon. I was told that it would be party frocks, so I chose a frilly cream blouse and a full-black chiffon evening skirt and set off for Otley. At the hostelry, we were greeted with a glass of hot punch, which was very welcome on a chilly day.

There were one or two quizzical looks at the large blonde from the other guests, but by and large, everything was great, and the meal was lengthy, filling, and very enjoyable. I had more than my fair share of the glasses of punch and white wine, and I felt totally relaxed for the first time in months. Harry, bless his heart, insisted on paying my share of the meal, which was more than welcome on my stretched finances.

On New Year's Eve, 1993, I was invited to go with Bernard and Jeanne, who were babysitting for their daughter (my niece). My niece's children were charming, and Lauren, the youngest, caused some amusement with questions such as 'Aunty Faye, did you have pigtails when you were a little girl?' and 'Aunty Faye, what's wrong with your voice?'

So I was eased through the festive season into 1994, leaving behind a year to remember. I had gone into the year as a male and came out of it as a fledgling female, a year of great contrasts, of extreme lows and highs and of momentous changes. Faye was on her way. Just what would 1994 have in store?

Physically, the hormone treatment was working wonders. Despite having problems controlling my weight, the waistline was reducing while the hips and thighs were widening. My breasts continued to grow steadily, and I was thrilled at the soft mounds of bosoms, these very necessary female appendages.

The overall appearance of my torso was becoming definitely female (with one small exception that I would have attended to in due course).

Emotionally, I frequently cried when I thought of my family and the long months since I last saw any of them. However, my deep satisfaction from my new form and life kept reminding me that despite all the pain, heartaches, and rejection I had endured, the decision to face up to my condition and recognise it had been the right one.

Socially, early 1994 was a quiet period with long lonely hours. This wasn't unexpected as time to adjust was necessary for both me and those who knew me. I was frequently invited over to Jeanne and Bernard's at Otley for a meal, and they helped me a lot in redecorating my flat, which was gradually becoming more like home. I had been given various items of furniture and had purchased a second hand three-piece suite from one of my work colleagues.

My little MG Metro was once again vandalised in the car park. Just what do these mindless morons get from such wanton destruction, especially when it is obvious from the age and condition of the vehicle that it belongs to someone who can ill afford repairs? After a lengthy spell of travelling to work on the bus, I purchased a ten-year-old two-litre Ford Sierra saloon car with the help of a car loan from work. The Metro I sold off for scrap. I was at least fully mobile once more.

I was still under the GP at Manchester for my hormone tablet prescriptions, but he was only prepared to issue these until I found a GP in Leeds.

In March 1994, I passed a small milestone. It was now twelve months since I had taken my first hormone tablet. It was also around this time that I finally received my new driving licence from the Department of Transport, bearing the name Miss Faye Helen Wardle and a female denoting reference number. I had already received my revised NHS card. Things were beginning to fall into place one by one.

Hand in hand with the physical changes were the shifts in emotions and moods. I was beginning to think female more and more. I don't know how much of this was down to the hormone treatment, or whether it was the release of feelings that had been so long subconsciously suppressed and hidden.

One of the main differences I noticed was the removal of one particular millstone that I had carried throughout my existence in the male role: I now no longer felt that I had anything to prove. I could just relax and be myself at last. It was all new and very wonderful. Gone was the need for constant competitiveness. The perpetual need to prove I was something that I wasn't. I could just let things come naturally now.

I realised that I was going to have to build some sort of new social life in and around Leeds. This task is difficult at the best of times but is virtually impossible when you are half-male and half-female as I was physically at this time.

I occasionally returned to the Northern Concord meetings in Manchester to maintain old friendships when the opportunity occurred. On one particular visit, their notice board carried news that the north-east area of the Beaumont Society was organising a canal trip on the Leeds and Liverpool Canal in Leeds.

This offered an opportunity to meet new friends in the Leeds area, albeit in the TV/TS community rather than amongst the general public, but it was a start while I was in my transitional state. Little did I know at this time that it was to be through this source that I was to fall in love for the first time as a female, a love which, though unrequited, was to confirm to me my ultimate arrival as a heterosexual female.

Dr Joe Borg Costanza at the Portland Clinic had decreed that by July 1994, I should be receiving for my medication 10 Mg of Provera progesterone per day in addition to the dosage of Premarin oestrogen, which by now was 7.5 Mg per day. My GP in Manchester refused to prescribe these additional tablets until Dr Joe gave written authorisation. So it was back to the Portland Clinic for the necessary confirmation.

Dr Joe was pleased with my progress so far, especially my deportment, and prepared the necessary letter for my GP confirming my increased dosage. To my surprise and delight, he also confirmed that I was now ready for referral for consideration for the final gender reassignment operation.

I was elated at this prospect of going forward for my operation, but I was unprepared for the next turn of events.

I was becoming accustomed to the side effects of the Premarin tablets, especially the cyclical bouts of depression. However, shortly after starting on the Provera, I began to gain weight quite rapidly. My ankles and legs began to swell and ache, and violent headaches were accompanied by deep depression.

During one particularly bad sleepless night, I arose at 4 a.m. and cleaned off all the nail polish from my fingers and toes as I was convinced that I would need to be hospitalised and that I would be sent to a male ward.

The thought of needing to revert, even if only for a while, did not help my depression. I also decided on this night that I must see my GP urgently, which meant travelling to Manchester.

With the morning post, as if on cue, came the bombshell. A letter arrived from my GP at Manchester, saying that regrettably, he could not keep me on his list as I was now resident in Leeds. So there, I was physically down and had no GP.

I phoned the office to say that I couldn't attend work that morning and then phoned the local Medical Board who gave me the names of several local general practitioners.

On studying these, I found that one of them was a medical practice close to the end of my street. Their receptionist answered my call and promised that one of the doctors would phone me back.

When the call came, it was a young female GP, who seemed unfazed by the fact that I was undergoing gender reassignment treatment and said that as I was within their catchment area, they were obliged to accept me on to their panel of patients.

I duly made an appointment to see her urgently to have my worrying symptoms checked.

My new doctor confirmed that what I was experiencing were the side effects of the medication, and my body should gradually settle down. If it didn't, they would have to review my medication. This news was something of a relief, and I was doubly pleased at finding a pleasant sympathetic female GP so close to my home.

As part of joining the new medical practice, I was required to undergo a medical check by the practice nurse. This proved to be routine, but the nurse seemed amused and intrigued by my half-and-half state.

When she was completing her examination and paperwork, she hesitated, somewhat bemused.

'Problems?' I asked.

'It's this last section here. It says testicular or breast examination, and I'm just wondering how to complete it in your case,' she replied.

'That's easy,' I said. 'You just cross out "or" and put "and" in its place.'

We had a good laugh, and I left thinking that if her report was for a computer entry, then there would be one machine blowing its mind trying to sort out that section of the form!

My new GP also took on board my referral for surgery from Dr Joe at the Portland Clinic. This meant, in turn, a referral back to the gender psychiatrist at St James Hospital in Leeds who had dismissed me some eighteen months earlier. I was not happy at this prospect given his earlier subjective attitude, but I was convinced that he would change his opinions once he saw me as a female and knew the fact that I had been living full time female for over a year.

I was totally unprepared for his response to my GP's request to see me with a view to consideration for gender reassignment treatment on the National Health Service.

This response was to devastate me and indirectly change the course of my life and cost me my employment.

My GP called me into her surgery to say that she had received a reply from the Leeds psychiatrist and that he was refusing to see me. He stated that he had seen me some eighteen months previously, had made up his mind then, and saw no reason to want to change that view. He confirmed that he was satisfied that the condition existed but was not prepared to treat me because of my age and my incongruous appearance as a female (even though he had never seen me as Faye!).

I felt my heart sink, and I was stunned and speechless. My GP seemed subdued and uncertain. She did however say that she thought he owed me the courtesy of seeing me now and that she would write to him again to this effect.

I left the surgery in a daze and close to tears. Just where did this leave me?

Back home at my flat, I stood in front of the mirror. Was I really so incongruous? Perhaps other people saw me that way. I took off my make-up and clothing and looked at my half-and-half body. It looked like a Frankenstein creation made up of spare parts. The upper half was now female with my two new firm breasts, but the lower half still carried my male appendage, society's determinant for sexual identity. Surely, this part of me was what was incongruent, not my overall appearance.

I flopped on to the bed, too devastated to cry. Despite my hitherto determination to go forward to a new life as a female, I had never contemplated being denied in such a way, and a major doubt suddenly began to hold sway.

I arose and found a few items of male clothing that I had left tucked away in a plastic bag at the bottom of my wardrobe. Perhaps I had kept these for just such an occasion? Going back to being Roy seemed to be now a logical option in my confused and devastated state.

When I tried on the male clothing, it not only looked odd and hung funny, but it also felt completely alien and strange.

No way! By now, anger was beginning to seethe. Faye was back and ready to fight again. Just who was this man to deny me my destiny! How dare he so unjustly condemn me out of hand and unseen as a female?

I sat down and composed a letter to my GP. I attacked the opinions of this psychiatrist who had set himself up as God and his rejection of me.

I stated that he seemed to have stereotyped parameters as far as size and appearance are concerned for females, despite the fact that we come in all shapes and sizes, and he was not the type to change his opinions whatever the changing circumstances. Any further attempts to get him to see me now were therefore pointless. I therefore reserved, and requested, the right for a second opinion elsewhere.

Ironically, my GP had already come to the same conclusions and, after consulting with her partners at the Medical Practice, had decided to seek an extra contractual referral for me outside the West Yorkshire Authority. Whilst this held out some hope of treatment outside Leeds, it meant more delays and still left some area of doubt.

Meanwhile on the social front, the time arrived for the Leeds and Liverpool Canal outing from Leeds. This was a big success and enabled me to meet and make friends with several members of the Leeds Group. I therefore started to attend the Group meetings of the Beaumont Society in Leeds. I think the insulated security of the cross-dressing community provided a welcome bolthole during my early transitory days. I also found once again that contrary to popular misconceptions. the transvestite and transsexual community is composed of some of the most gentle and genuine people you could wish to meet. It is a community which transcends all social barriers and is not restricted to just a single strata of society.

It was around this time that I met Jack. We were to strike up an immediate friendship. Jack is one of the kindest and considerate of people. I didn't realise that my attraction to gentle Jack was to unavoidably develop for me into something much deeper, arousing feelings that I had never expected nor anticipated.

He was to prove a very true friend and a great pillar of strength for me through some very difficult times.

My confidence and feminine deportment continued to improve, and I was being accepted as a female more and more. There is a saying that if it looks like a duck and quacks like a duck, then it must be a duck. Well, I was beginning to look like a duck (in analogous terms!), but my quack was unfortunately still more drake than duck. But I did feel I was gradually moving forward.

There were however isolated incidents of bigotry and unacceptability. In particular, I recall one occasion when I was on my way home from work and was walking past my old school, The Central High, which was being converted into offices. One of the workmen on the scaffolding obviously noted something different about the six-foot blonde passing the site and shouted down a particularly crude cutting comment.

I stopped, turned, and said to the offending workman, 'Can I have a word with you?'

'What?' came the gruff reply, as several of the other nearby workmen stopped work to watch events.

'I'm having my problem dealt with. Why don't you do something about yours?' I snapped as ladylike as possible.

His workmates were falling about laughing as he coloured up. I turned and walked off, head held high. This brought home to me just how my confidence had improved, that I could now handle male prejudice even on that bastion of chauvinism, the building site.

I also realised with this incident that the average loudmouth is little more than an insecure coward who will shout abuse from the security of a crowd or from a distance but like most 'bully boys' will back down when confronted. Not that I recommend confrontation. Rather, it is generally better to ignore adverse comments and simply go about your business. The temptation sometimes to verbally strike back can however be overwhelming at times.

I had at least dealt with the situation in a ladylike, dignified manner. A basic behavioural principle, which had been drilled into me at the Portland Clinic, was 'Remember dignity at all times'.

Another basic principle that I carry at the forefront of my mind and which has stood me in good stead is that if you can show people that you are comfortable with your new self, then they will be comfortable with you. This, by and large, has proved to be true, and I never hesitate to poke fun at myself, which can do much to relax other people who might be unsure how to react in my company.

It really was a whole new ball game, so much to learn and so much to unlearn, but I welcomed the challenge.

CHAPTER FIFTEEN

Early Retirement

A time to move to leave behind
The work of yesteryears
To find the means for fulfilments course
Through one more veil of tears

—Faye Helen Wardle

In my employment, things were continuing to prove difficult despite a veneer of acceptability. I had been taken away from my hitherto high public profile duties and moved into a purely internal job, assisting one of the assistant directors with policy formulation.

I was moved out of the office that I had shared with some dozen other members of staff and sited in a small room on my own, where there was a computer terminal for my use. This led to a somewhat isolated, segregated working environment.

Apart from the odd encounters on the corridors, I, therefore, had little social contact with other members of staff, and no contact at all with members of the general public.

Management solved the question of toilet arrangements by removing the Gents sign from one of the small Gents toilets and replacing it with a Unisex sign. I was instructed to use this toilet. This resulted in my having to share toilet facilities with a dozen or so male members of staff who had habitually used this toilet, hardly conducive to assisting my feminisation.

There was not even a mirror to this facility, and the one that I placed on the wall vanished after a few days.

Yet one more hint of unacceptability came when I was informed that I would not be sent on a first-aid course to renew my first-aid certificate despite the fact that I had served successfully as first-aid officer at work for several years.

Initially, the excuse for this was put down to a surfeit of first-aid officers, but when I challenged management on this point, I was told that not everyone would be happy if I had to treat them now.

It really is unreasonable and, to my mind, inexcusable, how some people, even supposedly intelligent, somehow see you as untouchable when undergoing gender reassignment, whereas actually in my neutral state, I was the best equipped to deal with all the staff. I thoroughly expected to be sent for an AIDS test in perpetuation of another baseless, widespread myth about the condition.

Just to add insult to injury, my dismissal as first-aid officer was shortly followed by a memorandum going around the office asking if anyone was interested in going on a first-aid course! So much for being oversubscribed with first aiders.

It was fast becoming obvious that although hidebound by the council's declared equal opportunities policies, there were elements within the department that wished me anywhere but there. At least the senior assistant director had the courage to admit this to my face at the outset.

Whilst these small discriminatory matters were very hurtful at the time, they helped to strengthen a resolve within me to combat these prejudices which occasioned such treatment at every opportunity. This resolve would ultimately lead me to take a higher public profile in my new life than would otherwise have been the case.

My condition did not merit such discriminations. Just what gave these people the right to condemn me simply for being what I am? I was angry. I would show them all. But I could not combat the prejudices engrained within those who had known me for so many years as Roy. Faye was still Roy in a dress as far as most of them were concerned.

I was beginning to appreciate why so many transsexuals found it necessary to break away into a completely new world away from their old life. It is impossible to mould your new life into your old one without extreme difficulties.

At this time however, I was still grateful to have a job, and in my somewhat vulnerable state, I had to be prepared to accept such treatment without complaint. My colleagues on the union side wanted me to pursue through the union the right to continue my duties exactly as they were prior to my changeover, to insist on remaining in the office where I had worked previously and to insist on the right to use the Ladies toilets.

The old battling Roy had gone however; all Faye wanted was a quiet life with as few waves as possible. Injustice had been a lifetime pet hate of mine, and it was now rather ironical that having supported the rights of so many people over the years, I had little or no wish to do the same for myself.

There were times however when I could almost sense what was left of my old male self shaking its head at my lack of fight. But I was weary of such battles; it was better for my new ego to take the feminine way, to take it all on the chin with quiet dignity. I liked myself more this way, and anyway, Faye would find her way. She was stronger than Roy in other more subtle ways.

The way I was regarded and treated at work was however to make my decision to leave the Planning Department that much easier when the time came.

During these early days as Faye, I was socially 'persona non grata' and received few invitations. Bev did take me along to one or two of the girl's nights out, but the age gap was more of a barrier between me and the girls rather than anything to do with my condition, although I enjoyed myself for most of the time.

I was beginning to discover that life holds little social opportunity for unattached females in late middle age. Social circles in my age group tend to cater for couples, and I was finding out what 'being on the shelf' felt like.

With one or two exceptions, the males in the office just didn't want anything to do with me now. This wasn't too much of a blow as I now had little in common with them anyway. Good old Terry remained true to his word to remain friends, and we still had our usual once-a-week lunchtime drink, a tradition that we still continued whenever possible.

My increasing use of the computer at work to prepare reports meant that I often had to visit the typing pool for advice on word processing techniques. I consequently developed a friendship with Marie, the typing supervisor.

Marie, Bev, and I, on one evening, took ourselves off to the Odeon Cinema in Leeds to see *Priscilla, Queen of the Desert*. Would you believe the film was about a transsexual and two drag queens!

On the subject of films, I now found that when I watched a film, usually on television nowadays, I saw the film from a completely different viewpoint.

I noticed this particularly when I watched films that I had seen previously some years before. My viewpoint was now totally feminine. I was able to view the story from a different angle, and I cried readily at all the sad parts.

Christmas 1994 was looming large, and there was still no progress on my GP's attempts to obtain an extra contractual referral for my operation.

This lack of progress for something that I had been decreed ready for some months previously was beginning to weigh heavily. While ever I had the male appendage, the 'Roy in a dress' protagonists had a case. The operation was absolutely vital for my self-identity, yet it seemed as far away as ever.

It is not too bad waiting for this vital stage of the conversion process if you have some idea of just when it will be taking place. The position I was in however was that I seemed to have little chance on the NHS and no means of raising the funds to go private.

In early December, I did have a novel social experience. By chance, I had made friends with June, who ran a chain of homes for people with learning difficulties to the south of Leeds.

At fairly short notice, I was invited to attend her organisation's dinner dance at the Cedar Court Hotel near Wakefield. This presented something of a daunting experience as it meant journeying on my own and meeting a host of people for the first time, a very necessary step for my social advancement.

I wore a black-and-gold evening skirt with a black lace blouse and felt rather conspicuous standing on my own near the bar. However, I was relieved to find one or two people that I recognised, and I began to relax.

In particular, I was pleased to see Pam and Roy. Roy is the brother of my sister-in-law Jeanne in Otley.

After a lovely meal, June enlisted me to video the speeches and presentations with her video camera, and after this, there was general dancing.

I sat at our table, chatting to Pam, and I noticed that I was obviously the topic of conversation amongst the VIPs on the top table. One of the guests on the top table came over to me and asked me for a dance. I declined, sensing some sort of set-up. I was surprised by his reaction.

Leaning over, he whispered, 'Get up please. We stand to make £1,000 for charity.' Intrigued, I warily agreed and enjoyed a dance debut as a female.

As the dance finished, I asked, 'OK, what was this £1,000 all about?'

'Well', my companion replied, 'we were talking about you on the top table, and Sir Michael, the guest of honour, said he would donate £1,000 to charity if I could get you up to dance.'

He went on to say that he had to confess that he had known me before as he had dealt with me on a planning matter in South Leeds and that he thought what I was doing was wonderful.

The whole evening was something of a confidence booster. Faye was on her way into the wider world, and I doubt if even Ginger Rogers had earned £1,000 for her first few minutes on a dance floor! Some weeks later, I was sent a photostat copy of Sir Michael's cheque as proof that he had honoured his wager and charity donation, together with a short thank you note for my part in the proceedings.

Jeanne and Bernard invited me around to their home at Otley for my Christmas lunch, so I was eased through Christmas 1994 and into 1995.

The year 1995 was to prove a momentous year that was once again to see me soar to the heights and plunge to the depths in my quest for fulfilment.

Early 1995 offered little advancement at work. There were still the underlying elements of unacceptability, and there seemed little prospect of the situation improving for me. I was once again denied any status or financial progression, despite my advancement on dealing with policy matters in my new internal role which was dealing more and more with junior management matters. I made an application for consideration for an extra grade when the opportunity arose, but when my case was heard by management, it was fairly obvious from their attitude that I would receive little favourable support.

I did expect that the assistant director to whom I was directly responsible and whom I had helped on many projects in my new duties would speak up in support of my case, but it again was apparent that he didn't want to be seen as going against his colleagues on the management team. I think the decisions on the regrading had been made in advance, and such as were made were to the 'blue-eyed youngsters' in the department, and I was not the only deserving older member of staff who was overlooked.

Having worked in the department for twenty-seven years, I had seen many changes. I used to say that working for planning in Leeds was like playing football for Liverpool (a comment made when Liverpool were at their best). You couldn't work for any better.

Over the years, it had saddened me to see the morale of the department deteriorate, and the current regime was a pale shadow of many of their predecessors.

I could go into the reasons for this decline, but this is my autobiography, not a party political broadcast. It is however a fact that my conclusions in this respect were arrived at before the commencement of my conversion and are not based on sour grapes for the way I was being treated as Faye.

There was also no progress with my extra contractual referral. Frustration was therefore the name of the game both at work and at home.

I was enjoying Jack's friendship on a regular basis, and he frequently invited me over to spend Sunday evenings with him, where we enjoyed a lovely meal that he had prepared and a quiet evening watching videos or just chatting. I found his companionship very comforting during these largely difficult times.

Towards the end of February, I sent a request to personnel at work stating that as I had now been a full-time female for eighteen months, could I now use the Ladies toilet close to my office rather share the distant Unisex toilet with a dozen male colleagues? After deliberation, I was informed that personnel were happy with the existing arrangements, and I was to continue to use the Unisex toilet.

This, to my mind, was a final confirmation that things were unlikely to improve at work for me, and the demeaning situation of sharing a toilet with males was to continue. In some respects, this was the last straw. I had taken much undeserved treatment for eighteen months without complaint; I now had to assess just where this left me.

I spoke to my friend June about the situation and asked if she had any suitable vacancies with her organisation.

I was invited over to see her at work, and she offered me the post of administration officer at her main office. This offered the opportunity to solve several problems.

If I took early retirement from the Planning Department, it would give me a monthly pension and release a sizeable lump sum. This lump sum would enable me to pay off my outstanding debts, and more importantly it would give me the means to fund my operation privately. The new job with June would give me a new start away from the prejudices at my present job in a climate where they only knew me as

Faye. The smaller salary at June's would make up the shortfall between my pension and my salary with the council. It all seemed suddenly so ideal. I therefore took the decision to seek to leave the council.

When my friend Harvey had left the department, he had penned a letter to personnel expressing his concern at the way the department was going and saying there was far more pulling him away than there was holding him there now.

He went on to say it had not always been so. I knew just how he felt, but despite a temptation to set out my own opinions on my old workplace, I was aware that this was a pointless exercise. It would take far more than a few written words to right the wrongs, and anyway, there are none so blind as those that cannot see, or do not want to see.

The department no longer had a human heart but had become a machine guided by automatons. All the machine sought was unthinking acquiescent cogs to keep it rumbling. Sentient human parts were no longer required. There was no place for an emergent Faye in such an organisation, and even Roy had wasted too much of his life trying to steer things away from the inevitable departmental decline.

Neither do I consider this decline unique to my old department, as it is so evident in so many spheres of public service. Our public services are now akin to our empire—once great, now in decline, and virtually non-existent. In Leeds, the Planning Service had become seriously undervalued, and any review awards over the years had gone in favour of the money-producing departments, whereas we were only fulfilling a statutory obligation, which contributed little in financial terms, but a great deal to the social advancement and well-being of the city.

On 7 March 1995, I went in to see Margaret in personnel and put in a formal request to be considered for early retirement effective as soon as possible. Margaret said she would have to put it to management and she would try to put it to their meeting that was then in progress. This was at 8.45 a.m. I returned to my desk. At 9 a.m. (just fifteen minutes later), Margaret phoned me and asked me to call down to see her. She told me that management had agreed to my request and I could leave on Friday, 11 March, the end of the same week.

'Were they doing handstands at the prospect of my departure?' I asked.

'Just about,' Margaret replied.

So that was it. Even one of the bosses said that it was disgusting the way that I was being shunted out of the back door after twenty-seven years of dedicated service. I thought of all the involved leaving 'dos' that I had helped organise for various members of staff over the years, and I was saddened in a way that my departure was to be rushed and unheralded. But by now, I just wanted away. I carried enough bitterness to ease my departure, and I hoped this bitterness could be left behind with all the memories both good and bad.

Quite a few of my colleagues expressed the opinion that I was allowing myself to be driven out by management, and it would have been more in character for me to stay and fight. But that was Roy's character; Faye had enough to worry about, other more important things on her mind.

However, on the Thursday afternoon (the day before my departure), Bev called into my office and asked if I could come through to the office where I used to work. I followed her through to be greeted by a large gathering of my colleagues. Bev announced that they were not letting me go without some sign of appreciation. I was presented with a gold chain bracelet and necklace, a set of earrings, and a voucher for Evans, ladies wear shop. Bev said they had decided not to invite management to the presentation, and I agreed that I would have found that inappropriate in the circumstances.

I felt a lump in my throat and was totally unprepared for making any speech. I did however manage to get my thoughts together and said that it was usual for any departing member of staff to say something to the effect that they had served the department 'man and boy'. Well, I could go one better than that! I also said that while there were many of the staff that I would miss, it was time for Faye's Phase 2.

On the morning of my departure, I called down at Thurstons Bakery Shop, below where I worked, for a buttered currant teacake for Lynne and me. This had become something of a morning routine before I retreated to my isolated office. As I entered the shop, the staff in the shop lined up and presented me with a Parker pen and pencil set and a lovely card that they had all signed. I had a little cry.

There really are a lot of nice people out there, and I was both touched and delighted by this gesture. It left me feeling that overall, I was better thought of in the local shop than I was in my own workplace!

So it was that I turned my back on my work with Leeds City Council. The last message from management was for me to make sure that I handed in my car parking disc for the council car park. It had been over a quarter of a century since I first started work with the Planning

Department. I had gone into it as a young man on the verge of marriage, and I was leaving as a middle-aged female with an uncertain future.

I welcomed the new challenges, and more importantly, I eagerly awaited the lump sum element of my pension, which would enable me to seek private resolution to my delays with the operation and also to clear my burden of debts.

I booked an appointment with Dr Russell Reid in London, one of the country's foremost gender psychiatrists, who had the power to take up my referral for the operation.

It was shortly after leaving my job with the council that I was to be dealt a major body blow to all my hopes and dreams.

I received a letter from solicitors acting for my former wife. She had taken out an injunction laying claim to my lump sum, and the money had therefore been frozen until the matter was resolved through the courts.

All my efforts and the sacrificing of my job had therefore been in vain. On the morning when I received the letter, I just sobbed and sobbed, totally devastated.

Jack called at lunchtime as I had previously invited him around for a meal. It was once again very comforting just to have his presence at a time when I was at something of a new record low. He also had the ideal solution to my initial woes, a short drive in his lovely Audi car to get me out into the fresh air for a while.

I appointed my own solicitor in Leeds and with deep regret cancelled my appointment with Dr Russell Reid.

I had done all in my power for my wife and family. I had left them the house and all possessions, and a nice Fiat Uno car. I had taken all the debts with me, and I was continuing to pay the mortgage on her house. Yet she had seen fit to take action which would mean I could not now afford to continue the mortgage payments and which would decimate the two of us with court costs.

She had created a situation from which neither of us could gain.

This was a measure of the bitterness, which she obviously felt, as I could not help but feel that the object of her actions was to try to obstruct my final operation. If she had been advised to take such action, then it was ill advice, which ultimately she would possibly regret just as much as I.

However, her action was to extinguish many of the feelings for her that I had carried with me. I could understand a lot of her adverse feelings at my actions, but not the depth of this bitterness. Through my solicitor, in an attempt to reach an early solution to the case, I offered half of the lump sum as a full and final settlement, and I also offered to relinquish any claim to the house and any of the possessions that I had left behind.

For my part, I sought simply to shed all future responsibility for mortgage payments on her house, a complete and clean break. The remaining half of the lump sum would pay for the operation and pay off some of the debts, which would mean that I could just about manage thereafter.

This offer was turned down. I couldn't understand this refusal, and I was convinced that if it went to court, they would see how reasonable I was trying to be. After all, legally I was entitled to half of the house and half of all the possessions.

If I had wanted to pursue my entitlements, my ex-wife and my children could have been made homeless. I didn't want that; all I wanted was the minimum for my needs and survival. But it was to drag on and on. The respective solicitors were on to a nice little earner. It was not in their interests to reach an early solution. Such are the vagaries of our legal system.

Socially, I attended the regular transsexuals get-togethers at the Portland Clinic in Manchester, where we compared experiences. We frequently had demonstrations and guest speakers. On one particular evening, we had a visit from Bette, a local speech therapist, who agreed to take five of us for speech tuition on a once-a-week basis.

As these speech therapy sessions were on a Wednesday evening, they coincided with the Northern Concord meetings. Wednesday therefore became a day of enjoyable routine. Jack would collect me from my work at June's, and off we would go to Manchester for a picnic in the car before the therapy class and then on to a pleasant evening at the Northern Concord.

In early June 1995, a large celebratory function for June's fiftieth birthday was held in Wakefield. This was quite a 'do', and I donned an appropriate black full-length evening gown for the occasion, with a black jacket that I had purchased with my Evans vouchers. This evening too was full of positive experiences, and one in particular was to prove quite amusing and was to provide me with the title for this autobiography.

On my jacket that evening, I wore an attractive large gold butterfly brooch, and one of the female guests, who were obviously aware of my transitional state, asked me during an interesting conversation if there was any significance in the butterfly.

'Yes,' I replied, 'but if you're unimpressed by the butterfly, you should have seen the caterpillar.' I'm sure she caught the analogy, and we enjoyed a good laugh together.

Working for June was proving difficult, and the job was obviously more involved than I had at first envisaged. In particular, my time did not permit me to spend the time necessary on developing the computerised side of things that I would have liked to have done. I was therefore moved into the care side of the home's work, but this too didn't work out, and I had to leave her employment in late June. This only added to my financial problems, but it did at least mean that my time was now all my own for the first time in my life.

It did also mean that my Wednesday routine could be stretched through the day. I therefore had my friend Jack around to my flat for lunch, and we would then have a leisurely drive over Woodhead Pass past the reservoirs of the Longdendale Valley to southern Manchester. Here, we would have a picnic which Jack had prepared (usually we picnicked in Wythenshawe Park) before my speech therapy and a visit again to the Northern Concord, a regular day of pleasant routine in what was becoming a stressful period awaiting the resolution of the court case.

I was also around this time troubled again with weight gain. How much of this was attributable to my hormone dosage, and how much a result of my worries with the court case? I do not know, but this could prove a problem if not rectified before any clearance for the operation.

My sister Barbara, sharing my concern at my weight gain, suggested that I go back on to the diet cookies that I had tried some years before and which had greatly reduced my weight at that time.

This suggestion presented a little difficulty as Lorna, the lady who was the local agent for the diet cookies, had only met me as Roy, and that was some years ago.

Only one thing to do, bite the bullet and go around to see her, as I couldn't find her phone number in the phone book.

So I ventured off to her house in Horsforth in West Leeds, only to find no one at home. I penned a quick note which read as follows:

'Do you still do the diet cookies? If so, please phone me at the number below.'

I signed it Faye Wardle with the rider, 'It used to be Roy but that's a long story', in the hope that she might remember me. I posted this through the letterbox.

Later that day, the telephone rang, and a rather nice female voice told me that Lorna didn't live at that address any more but that she could give me Lorna's new telephone number. She went on to say that she had been intrigued by the footnote, and I confirmed that it was quite a story as I thanked her for her help.

After I had put the phone down, I was wishing I had pursued the conversation, as she sounded genuinely interested and very pleasant. However, I phoned Lorna, and while she didn't do the cookies any more, she put me on to an alternative product.

Shortly after my call to Lorna, my telephone rang again. It was the first lady saying she would love to meet me and would I like to call and see her for a coffee and a chat?

I said I would love to and made an appropriate visit.

I therefore found a new best friend in Jackie, or Jackie 2 as I call her, to avoid any confusion with Jack in conversation.

It transpired that Jackie, apart from helping her husband Nick with the family business, also performed as a cabaret singer at clubs around the region.

We got along fine from our first chance meeting, and she has remained a staunch friend, accepting me as a female from the outset. It was through Jackie that I was also to meet Tina, who was also to prove a true friend. These new social contacts were just what I needed at this particular time.

I was still attending the Leeds and Bradford meetings of the Beaumont Society and even wrote a regular column for their magazine under the heading 'Faye's TS Corner'. I had many a pleasant evening out with them on their social trips and well remember one particular trip around Tetley's Wharf Brewery Museum in Leeds.

At this museum, we were conducted in a group, with a crowd of other people, through various sets depicting the history of ale brewing through the ages. It was when we arrived at the Edwardian era that I was once more to be shot to public prominence.

Upon entering the Edwardian public house, we were led through to a section that contained a small music hall set. Here, it was my first reaction to sit at the back while there was a rundown of an Edwardian song and dance routine on the stage. Rosalind, the social organiser for our group, insisted however that we commandeer the middle of the front row. Sure enough when the performing male vocalist came down to the audience to choose a partner, he picked on me, and I was coerced into joining him on the stage for an impromptu song and dance routine.

So much for keeping a low profile! The most difficult part was trying to make the male baritone voice sound as contralto as possible! When we moved on to a Second World War set, I said if they wanted me to do a Vera Lynn impression they could forget it!

Resolution of the court case seemed no nearer, and procrastination seemed to be the name of the game. My solicitor seemed confident that a solution was close and pressed for an early court date for the hearing.

This however would seem to be a question of waiting months rather than weeks with the slow legal processes.

My lack of progress towards my operation was becoming an acute worry to me, and with my advancing years, I wondered if I was ultimately to be turned away as being too old. To live my life in a half-and-half state seemed more and more a likely scenario and more and more horrendous to contemplate. After all, the main reason for all I had recently undertaken was the question of gender identity and self-identity. How could these be resolved without the ultimate step?

The mood swings occasioned by my hormone treatment were accentuated by my ennui at the impasse with my pension lump sum. Something needed to be done urgently for my own well-being and my state of mind. I therefore, in anticipation of an early settlement on the financial issue, made a further appointment to see Dr Russell Reid at his Earls Court consulting rooms in London for September 1995. This at least made me feel that things were still on the move.

My finances, with only my pension coming in, were proving to be a major worry. I signed on as unemployed but received no benefits or financial help because of my small pension income.

Appropriate new employment was proving impossible to find in these days of high unemployment, and doubly so with my advancing years and half-and-half state. Ideally, I would have liked a part-time job which would have provided me with new interests and covered my shortfall in income.

At least, I was able to concentrate on this autobiography for a while.

Despite my solicitor's optimism that my case was heading towards resolution, it continued to drag on with little sign of completion. I began to worry that my rearranged appointment with Dr Russell Reid may once again need to be postponed. Meetings with my solicitor were regular, and he seemed genuinely concerned at the intransigent attitudes of the other side.

At one particular meeting with my solicitor, he was studying me intently.

'Tell me, Faye, why didn't you do it years ago?' he asked.

I explained the problems and lack of recognition that had existed until recent times and the fact that it was only now that it was recognised as a medical condition.

'Never mind, you got it right in the end,' he replied.

This little gesture of confirmation did wonders for my self-esteem.

I was determined that my London appointment with Dr Reid was not going to be further delayed, and I borrowed the money from a friend to make the journey. I once more prevailed upon Barbara and Harry's hospitality in London and journeyed down there by car the day before my appointment.

As the time for my appointment was in the afternoon, I had to spend a few nervous hours during the morning. I was not sure what Dr Reid's reaction to me was going to be, and I was still haunted by the subjective attitude of the Leeds psychologist. What would I do if Dr Reid shared his opinions?

The day promised, or threatened, to be something of a turning point, depending on what happened at the Earls Court consulting rooms.

I decided to wear my black costume with a plain white cotton blouse for my appointment, feminine but smart and businesslike. My nervousness during that morning's wait obviously showed, and my sister Barbara, bless her heart, asked Harry to take me out for the morning to get my mind off things. So Harry whisked me off to Walthamstow open-air market for an interesting tour of the various stalls. There followed a spell in a local public house, and after a few lager and limes, I was ready to face the music.

I went into Central London by tube and found Dr Reid's consulting rooms close to Earls Court underground station.

He was busy when I arrived, and my appointment was delayed slightly. My early nervousness had by now all but vanished. Faye was back in control, and my mood was one of anticipation.

As Dr Reid bade farewell to his earlier appointment, he turned to me and gave me a big smile.

'I'm so sorry to keep you waiting,' he said. 'Come inside. You look wonderful'.

What a lovely reception, and I entered his consulting room, full of optimism.

After a preliminary chat, he carefully studied my notes, which contained all my case history. After a while he paused.

'I see that you've crossed swords with my colleague at the gender identity clinic in Leeds,' he said. 'How did you find him?'

I felt a wave of anger at his reference to the doctor who had so callously dismissed me for treatment, a man whose stubborn intransigence had even denied me a second opportunity to present my case and whose name when mentioned brought me to the verge of tears of anger.

'Dr Reid,' I replied softly, and with feeling, 'in line with my new status, I have been reasonably successful in eliminating bad language from my vocabulary. Please don't encourage me to restart by asking my opinions in that direction.'

He smiled and said he understood.

He continued to peruse my records and then announced quite unexpectedly, 'You should have had your operation by now.'

I felt the tears starting to well.

'That's why I'm here,' I replied quietly.

'Well, that's easily solved,' he announced. 'I'll refer you direct to Mr Royle at Brighton.'

Mr Royle is one of the country's leading gender reassignment surgeons, with a high reputation for having perfected reassignment surgery.

I felt an overwhelming surge of relief. To be given such an instant seal of approval from such an eminent specialist in the field dispelled a lot of the lingering doubts that earlier experiences had caused.

Dr Reid said that I should wait a couple of weeks for his reference to reach Mr Royle and then contact Mr Royle's secretary to make an appointment.

I left the consulting rooms on Cloud Nine. I was on my way again; my operation, which had seemed so remote, suddenly now seemed so close. Not only that, Dr Reid also confirmed that he would be contacting my GP to reaffirm my necessary hormone dosage, but also I should stop the Provera as this was having an adverse impact on my weight.

The favourable report to my GP meant a lot to me, as I was conscious of some doubt from her as to my treatment since my dismissal by the Leeds psychologist.

My instant feeling of well-being at the course of events was amazing. I felt I could now totally relax and really start to enjoy my female state. I think the change of my outlook must have been noticeable to Barbara and Harry upon my return to Chingford.

My friendship with Jackie, the cabaret singer, was continuing, and I particularly enjoyed the odd invitations to join them at various performances of their act around West Yorkshire. These provided relaxing interludes while I marked time before seeing the surgeon, and Jackie was proving to be a good, understanding friend.

My appointment to see Mr Royle was duly made for October 1995 in his consulting rooms at Hove on the south coast. So it was away yet again to Barbara and Harry's in London for another overnight stay en route to the Sussex coast.

The weather was surprisingly warm and sunny as I left London, and I resolved to have a walk along the seafront when my appointment was concluded.

Mr Royle was prompt and very businesslike. He carried out a physical examination and announced that he was prepared to carry out the operation provided I lost some weight (that old problem again). He went on to say that at my age, he would have preferred to do the simpler cosmetic operation rather than the full reassignment surgery.

I replied that I wanted the full operation, and in answer to his unasked question, I might never use it for a relationship, but the object as far as I was concerned was to be as complete as possible at the end of the day. I had not come so far to be happy with a cosmetic pastiche. So with a little reluctance, he agreed to the full operation.

I was a little set back by his reticence and even more so by his next announcement.

Before he gave his final agreement to carry out the operation, he wanted further confirmation of the condition in my case from Dr Dalrymple, the gender psychologist in Hove. I pointed out that I had already been given the seal of approval by Dr Reid in London and Dr Costanza at Manchester and that even the Leeds psychologist had acknowledged existence of the condition. Nevertheless, he was adamant that I had to undergo the testing procedure yet again.

Upon leaving his room, I had a quick word with his secretary and pointed out that to see Dr Dalrymple would involve yet another 600-mile round trip from Leeds. She said Dr Dalrymple was holding his surgery at that time and if I called at his nearby consulting rooms, he might be able to see me while I was down there.

She also confirmed that Mr Royle had somewhere in the order of a six-month waiting list for the operation.

Dr Dalrymple's surgery was only a short distance away from Mr Royle's, and as the sun was still beaming pleasantly down, I left my car and walked to his surgery.

Dr Dalrymple's secretary said that he had a full appointment list but that in the circumstances, she would check to see if he could fit me in. After a short wait, I was told that if I could wait awhile, he would see me that afternoon.

He eventually came out and invited me inside. His manner was very pleasant, but I was once more subjected to the long series of searching questions similar to those that I had faced elsewhere. Finally, he dropped something of a bombshell.

'What would you say if I told you that I was not prepared to recommend you for the operation?' he announced.

This was too much at this time; things suddenly seemed to be going in quick reverse. The day wasn't going at all as I had expected. Tears were starting to well as I said quietly, 'I can't go back to how I was, and I don't want to live half-and-half.'

'That's all right. I've nothing other than a favourable recommendation in your case.' he said with a smile.

My relief at this time was subdued as I felt somewhat drained of emotion.

'I'm sorry, but that last question caught my Achilles Heel,' I said by way of explanation for my subdued state.

'Yes, that seems to be the usual case,' he replied.

While I felt that I had passed some form of test with the final question, it had caught me unawares, and the effects were proving hard to shake off. I decided to forego my planned walk along the seafront. I just wanted to get back to my sister's place in London. Even this simple drive back to the capital was to prove harrowing.

Travelling northwards along the M23, I somehow missed my turning on to the M25 London Orbital, which would have enabled me to circumnavigate London to get back to Chingford. Instead, I found myself travelling along the A23 towards Croydon. I decided in the circumstances to take the direct route across the centre of the capital.

Big mistake! It was by now the height of the evening rush hour. It took me over two hours of madcap, nose to tail, nerve straining driving, and jousting through Croydon, Lambeth, Southwark, over Tower Bridge, then through Tower Hamlets, Hackney, Leyton, and Walthamstow to

Chingford. I was shattered, both emotionally and physically, when I arrived at my sister's.

To their credit, Barbara and Harry said they had expected me to be a bit emotional on what was after all something of a major day in my life.

After a nice meal and a few gin and tonics, the fact that I had received the ultimate clearance for my operation, which meant so much to me, began to sink in, and I was back to my normal self. What a day though, yet one more giant milestone had passed!

A few short weeks later, I received notification that my operation was scheduled for 2 May 1996 at the Sussex Nuffield Hospital at Woodingdean near Brighton and that I should attend for blood tests two weeks before that date.

I was also told that it was vital that I stop taking my hormone tablets at least eight weeks before the operation date and that my operation would be cancelled if there were signs in my blood test, which showed that I had taken any hormones within the eight-week period.

There were also details of the hospital, which seemed wonderful, and a charming little handbag-size folding location map.

I took the calendar down from the wall of my flat and marked off a day-to-day countdown to the following May. I also counted down to the time in March when I would have to stop the hormone intake.

I decided that it would probably be easier on my system if I gradually started reducing the hormone dosage from three a day to two in January and from two to one in February before the final cessation in March.

All I needed now was to obtain my court settlement to release the funding for the operation, which was now to cost me £7,000, a thousand pounds more than it would have cost me in 1995, another triumph for the procrastinators.

The court hearing was set for 12 December 1995. The end appeared to be in sight.

I attended at court in Leeds to be met by my barrister. After an initial chat, she went off for preliminary discussions with the judge and the opposing barrister. She returned, looking a bit flustered and annoyed.

'With your agreement, I'm asking for an adjournment,' she told me. 'The judge is not satisfied about your need for the operation, and he is not prepared to take the costing for it into account, so I want the opportunity to obtain and submit a report from Dr Russell Reid in support of your need.' I had little alternative other than to agree, and at least, they didn't want me to see yet another psychiatrist!

It then occurred to me that the continuing delay may mean deferring my operation, but my barrister said that she would submit for an early date for the reconvened hearing, probably in January.

Christmas 1995 arrived, and yet another momentous year was over. The year 1996 held the prospect of being even more momentous, although May seemed a long way off, and the court Case seemed unending.

Nothing had been straightforward so far; I had no reason to expect 1996 to be any easier. I had coped so far however, and things had started to move forward towards the end of the year. Would I be facing the next distant New Year of 1997 complete at long last?

The next court date was set for early February, but this was once more to be deferred, as both barristers were involved in lengthy ongoing cases elsewhere. This was not too bad a blow, as Dr Reid's evidence had not arrived in time for the scheduled hearing.

It was still a major worry that I needed a settlement before mid-April when payment for my operation was due. I pointed this out to my solicitor and also stressed that I was already cutting back on my medication in anticipation of meeting the May operation date.

Then quite unexpectedly in mid-February came the wonderful news. Russell Reid's report had been received, and the opposition, after seeing his report, had decided to accept our offer, which had been made several months before, without the need for a further court hearing.

The settlement had to be reported to the court in early March, but at long last, the question of the distribution of the lump sum was finalised.

Subsequent to confirmation by the court, I called at my solicitors to sort out when payment to me could be made. He informed me that full payment could not be made until the question of legal costs had been sorted out. Yet another set back as I had been led to believe that I would not have to pay back my legal aid costs as my settlement was only a fraction of the amount that I had started out with when action had first commenced.

The good news was that £8,500 could be released immediately, which meant that £4,000 was being held back. So at least, I was able to complete the payment for the operation, so in this respect, it was now all systems go. This at least was a big relief. Everything else could be resolved with the fullness of time. From the £12,500 share due to me, almost £4000 went in legal fees, and my operation cost and attendant consultation fees amounted to £8000. This meant from my original retirement sum of £25,000, I finished with just a few hundred pounds.

On 1 March, Jack took me to Liverpool, where I collected my first female passport from the passport office. They would only issue one valid for one year with an assurance that it could be extended to ten years when I produced a letter from Mr Royle confirming that my surgery had taken place. Not that I had any immediate plans to travel abroad, but it was very handy to have for confirmation of identity purposes.

From Liverpool, we travelled on to Colwyn Bay for a lovely weekend in North Wales, just the break I needed at this particular time. At Colwyn, we met up with several of our mutual friends, and on the Saturday afternoon, when shopping in Llandudno was the plan for the afternoon, one of our friends, Rosalind, and I decided to venture up the Great Orme, the massive headland which overlooks the town.

As neither the tram nor the funicular up the incline was working, we decided to walk most of the way up.

This walk was not such a good idea as I was wearing high heels for what had started out as a stroll around the shops. By the time we met up with the others back down in Llandudno, my feet were killing me, and I had trouble walking.

Jack again rose to the occasion when we returned to the hotel. While I was chatting (standing in my stocking feet) to some of our friends downstairs, he ran me a hot bath and made me a welcome cup of tea. He was always able to do just the right thing at the right time. I was warming to him even more. I hadn't thought what my life would be like without his readily available friendly presence. It would not be too long before I was to find out.

On 7 March, I took my last hormone tablet for some time—one more milestone. I had been warned that my physical female development would start to go in reverse for a while when I came off the hormones, but the prospect of this was balanced by the proximity of the operation and the fact that any reversal would be compensated when I returned to the medication.

I was once more bound for London and my sister's on 15 March, prior to visiting Russell Reid on Monday, 18 March. This was for the preoperation interview so that Dr Reid could assess if I was mentally ready for the big step.

In the event, I was so ready that the interview developed into more of an informal chat. Dr Reid confirmed that I had, during my progress, done everything by the book and that I was more than ready for my operation.

I was by now becoming very impatient for my big day in May, and March passed with social visits to a show at the Leeds City Varieties Music Hall and another visit to the Pennington Midland Hotel in Bradford for an Opera Select evening.

As I progressed through April, eagerly counting off the days, the next major event was one more visit down to Brighton for my blood test at the Manor Laboratories in Hove, and to make the final payment for my operation.

While I was down in Sussex, I took the opportunity to call at the Sussex Nuffield Hospital at Woodingdean to see the hospital where the deed would be done. I was made very welcome, and I was given a conducted tour of the hospital. The place was wonderful, very modern and very comfortable. This all added to my impatience and anticipation.

One more social outing, appropriately to see a variety programmes at the Leeds City Varieties which featured Fay Presto, the post-operative transsexual magician. Then the end of April was near; my long wait was almost over.

CHAPTER SIXTEEN

Fulfilment

Far from Yorkshire's Northern Dales
In sunny Sussex's gentle land
A journey ends, complete at last
By pain and care and surgeon's hand

—Faye Helen Wardle

Just where had all the time gone? Here I was on the Tuesday, 13 April 1996, busily gathering together the bits and pieces that I was to take down to Brighton for my operation.

Just as I was about to check off my list to ensure that I had everything I needed, the telephone rang. It was my friend Gina from Wakefield. Radio Leeds was holding a chat show that morning and required a transsexual for an interview, and was I willing to talk to them? The programme was 'The Morning Show' which discussed current affairs.

My heart said yes, but my head said no, as the last thing I wanted on this particular morning was anything that would interfere with my departure schedule to my special journey.

However, I agreed to speak to the Radio Leeds researcher.

It transpired that within the previous hour, the European Court of Justice had ruled in favour of a transsexual who had been dismissed by the education authority in Cornwall purely because she was undergoing gender reassignment. This decision effectively conferred equal employment rights on all British transsexuals.

I agreed to contribute to the programme, and the researcher said she would phone me back as the programme started.

I rapidly retuned my hi-fi to Radio Leeds and inserted a tape to record the programme.

After the initial preamble on the show, my telephone rang, and it was explained that I would be able to follow the interviews conducted by Ian Timms and that I would be called into the conversation.

First of all, Ian interviewed Madeleine Rees, the Press for Change solicitor from Birmingham, who explained at length the implications of the European Court of Justice's decision.

He then turned to Michael Rubenstein, the co-editor of the Equal Opportunities Review, to investigate the wider implications.

After this, it was back to Madeleine Rees for a further round of questions.

While all this was going on, I was getting more and more nervous, awaiting my turn.

At long last, Ian thanked Madeleine and announced, 'I want to bring an individual perspective in here, and I want finally to look at the experience of one transsexual from Leeds. Tomorrow, Faye Wardle will be in the operating theatre for the surgical part of her change to being a woman. Faye is with me this morning. Faye, good morning to you.'

'Good morning.' The nervousness began to fade now that I was in action.

'Thank you for sparing us some time. Do you see this judgement very much as a good omen coming this morning?'

'Yes, I think potentially it's wonderful news, although it is only one aspect of the discrimination that we do have to tolerate.'

'What sort of prejudice have you had to encounter with your sex-change process up to now?'

'Well, I was very fortunate on the employment front in local government. I wasn't dismissed as such, but there's more than pure dismissal. The attitudes of people perhaps weren't all they should have been.'

'Do those attitudes change, particularly amongst one's close colleagues whom you've had a professional relationship with for five or six years beforehand, when you suddenly announce that you're going through the sex-change process and they drop you like a hot brick?'

'Yes, by and large, that's true, although it is a spectrum of attitudes and some of them have been marvellous and very supportive.'

'How long have you been living as a woman, how long have you been coping with these problems, and how long do you get before you reach the stage you are at now?'

'Well, I've been living as a full-time female for two and a half years now.'

'Is that time enough to work through where you stand among this whole plethora of prejudice and people's reactions to you?'

'Yes, they do normally set down a minimum of twelve months. I would say that two years is actually a more realistic target. I think by the end of two years, you're well established in your new identity and tend to know what it's all about.'

'How do you cope with these reactions because mentally you must want to go home some nights and just scream into a pillow?'

'Not only mentally. I do go home some nights and scream into a pillow, erm . . . you learn to cope, you've got to do, you just strengthen yourself and carry on. You face up to it, although it does hurt of course. You're only human at the end of the day.'

'What do you say now when somebody judges you on what you are rather than who you are?'

'Well, I look upon it as though it is them who have the problem, not me. I'm having my problem dealt with, and if people can't cope, then that's their problem, not mine.'

'When the process is complete, when you've undergone surgery this week, and when it's all finished, Faye, what plans do you have to change the rest of your life?'

'Well, I'm unemployed at the moment, but that is of my own choice because I did take early retirement to fund the operation. I'm playing it very much by ear. The main objective at the moment is to get the operation out of the way, and then I'll look at the rest of my life and get on with it.'

'Is tomorrow very much a watershed then?'

'It's tomorrow I go into the hospital. The actual operation will be on Thursday . . . erm . . . well . . . watershed? . . . erm . . . it's a comma rather than a full stop.'

'Is it that big step? Do you go into hospital tomorrow as somebody and come out in a couple of weeks as somebody else in your own mind? Is that mentally the position you're in, or have you been somebody else for a long while?'

'Of course . . . of course, I think the latter is true. I'm not expecting to be someone else. I'm still me at the end of the day, but psychologically, it's bound to have a tremendous difference.'

'Are you expecting it still to be as much of a day-to-day challenge beyond surgery as it has been up to the point of surgery?'

'No . . . erm . . . '

'Is it going to get better, or is it going to stay the same? really is the question I suppose'

'I'm hoping it will get better. I am still going through a learning process and an improvement process, and obviously things do get better with the passage of time, but the fact that Great Britain is one of the last bastions of bigotry in the world and still thinks of people as Adam and Eve and doesn't recognise the vast spectrum in-between doesn't help matters, and the sooner they do fall in line, the better'.

'Faye, best of luck with the surgery this week, and thank you for joining us on the programme this morning. Interesting thought, isn't it? It is now enshrined that people who are transsexuals now have the same employment rights as anybody else. Should that be the case? Should that have been the case a long time ago? If you have views, call on us with your thoughts for Talk Back, and we'll chat after twelve . . . '

At this point, the plug was pulled on my line, and I was free to continue organising my journey. I didn't find out what responses Radio Leeds had to our chat in their later Talk Back Programme.

At least, the radio show had provided an interesting diversion, which sent me off in good spirits.

By now, it was 11 a.m., just time to dash out to Chapel Allerton to pay some last minute bills.

My taxi arrived at noon, and after making my goodbyes to my neighbour, Anne, I was away on the first leg of my journey of fulfilment.

I was eagerly waiting on the platform at Leeds City Station for the 1305 Leeds City to London King's Cross train some forty-five minutes before its departure.

I nervously thumbed through my pile of magazines as the train sped south, but I found concentration difficult.

Nevertheless, the journey seemed to pass remarkably quickly, and the northern suburbs of the capital were soon skimming by, and we were gliding into King's Cross station.

Down through a crowded King's Cross tube station, on to the Victoria Line Underground to Walthamstow Central terminus. I attracted the odd 'Is it or isn't it?' look from some passengers on the tube, but I now felt confident in the fact that I was on my way to answer part of their unspoken questions!

From Walthamstow Central, I got straight on to the bus to Chingford Mount and was greeted by my sister Barbara and brother-in-law Harry at their flat at 4.15 p.m., quite a rapid journey. So far so good.

During a quiet evening at Chingford, my sister prepared an enormous meal for me in the knowledge that it would be my last for almost a week. This meal together with a couple of gin and tonics helped me to get a good night's sleep, going to bed at 10.30 p.m. and awakening at 6 a.m.

It was now Wednesday, 1 May, May Day, or as one of my friends in Leeds had christened it Faye Day, the day when I was to at last enter hospital for the final reassignment surgery!

I had wondered previously if, when I got to this stage, I would be asking myself if I was doing the right thing.

Somehow, this question never entered the equation. I knew it was right. I just wanted to get there and get it over with.

My breakfast that morning at Chingford was a cup of plain boiled water in accordance with my pre-op instructions. Like any doubt, any hunger pangs were now totally immaterial.

At 8.30, Harry drove me back to Walthamstow Central, and I was away again on the tube, this time to Victoria Main Line Station. In addition to my suitcase that I had brought down from Leeds the day before, I now had the luggage that I had taken down to my sisters on my last visit in readiness for this day.

I struggled up from the tube on to the main line station at 9.35 to find that the train to Brighton was 9.35. Cursing inwardly at just missing this link, I struggled along to Platform 15 to find the train had been delayed and was waiting for me, a good omen.

In glorious spring sunshine, and in high spirits, I sat back to enjoy the journey to the south coast. The passing vista was adorned with blossom trees laden with pink and white blooms and the fresh new green colourings of early spring. My mood was further heightened when a kind middle-aged gentleman helped me to get my luggage off the train at Brighton. He seemed pleased by his gallantry, and I was both grateful and flattered. Being female does carry some advantages!

The taxi rank was just next to the platform. I climbed into a cab and asked for the Sussex Nuffield Hospital at Woodingdean.

'Have you been there before?' enquired my driver as we pulled away from the station.

I informed him that I had called there a fortnight earlier.

'It's a great place,' he said, 'just like a plush hotel.'

I confirmed that this had been my own impression on my earlier visit.

He was very friendly, and I enjoyed our chat on the drive to the hospital. It was all going so well on this my very special day, and the sun still beamed down from a clear blue sky.

I arrived at the hospital at 11.40 a.m. Only twenty minutes early from my noon target.

The Sussex Nuffield is an imposing brick-built brand new building having only opened in October 1995. It lies at the southern side of Warren Road at Woodingdean. At the rear, the South Downs fall away to Rottingdean and the sea some two miles away.

It was this particular stretch of the South Downs which inspired Rudyard Kipling's poem 'Sussex', in which he referred to them as 'Our blunt, bow-headed, whale-backed Downs'. Very descriptive of the soft green folds rolling down to the coast, with the silver blue English Channel beyond.

Just to the west of Rottingdean, on the coast, the towers of Roedean, the famous girls' school, were clearly visible. This seemed appropriate to a trainee female who still had a lot to learn!

My room wasn't quite ready for my occupation, so I was taken to the day lounge and provided with a pot of black coffee. Black coffee was to be my only permissible beverage for the next few days.

I didn't have long to wait before I was shown to Room no. 7 and given time to unpack. My room didn't have the gorgeous sea views that the majority of them enjoyed but overlooked the hospital car park and main entrance.

I was later to be pleased at this location as I had a constantly changing outlook when I was confined to bed, with all the comings and goings outside, whereas those at the other side of the building had a changeless view like a seascape mural, relieved only by the occasional far-distant passing ship.

The room was very comfortable, and the combined wardrobe and dressing table unit along the wall at the foot of my bed housed an attractive table lamp and a colour television, which was complete with Sky TV and numerous radio channels. On the wall alongside the unit was a copy of August Macke's 'Jardin du Lac de Thun', which did much to add extra brightness to the room. The floor was carpeted, the furnishings were all in light pine, and the overall impression was indeed more hotel than hospital.

Various administration procedures followed until Mr Royle, my surgeon, arrived to put a giant dent in my state of euphoria. Why was it that every time I was on a high, something, or somebody, would come along to knock me down? Fortunately, the converse is also true: whenever I'm in the depths, there is always something or someone coming along to pick me up.

This particular experience however really knocked me back for a while.

Mr Royle seemed very disappointed that I had not lost more weight, and for some time, I studied whether he was prepared to operate. I was totally deflated and close to tears by his reluctance.

I told him that I was fitter than I looked, but that I was in his hands. After sitting there quiet for a while longer, he announced that there was a high risk that I would prolapse after the operation, but that he was prepared to operate.

His decision to go ahead surprisingly did little to cheer my new mood, which told me that even at this late stage, I could not take anything for granted. Oh dear, surely I couldn't fail at this point.

The nursing staff were wonderful and did their best to make me feel at ease and to resurrect my earlier good humour, but I suddenly began to feel very lonely, very vulnerable, and a long way from home.

Funny how the surgeon's portents of doom and hesitations had completely turned around my mood!

One consolation was that my friend Julia from Huddersfield was in the room opposite having had her own operation a few days earlier. Other cheering aspects were the cards and flowers which had already arrived from my friends and relatives. I even got a pack of Bovril and jelly from Helen in Manchester labelled 'Just in case the hospital runs out!' A reference to my daily food intake for the coming days. I was also cheered considerably by a succession of telephone calls from people who were anxious to show that they were thinking of me at that time, including a long chat with Jack all the way from Harrogate.

Paulette, another transsexual friend, who was then working in Brighton, called around to visit me and brought me a lovely big cuddly owl to keep me company (she was well aware of my affinity to this particular bird and had seen my large owl collection back home).

The world didn't seem quite so lonely as I realised that there were a lot of people out there who were on my side and rooting for me. A lot of the old confidence and determination began to take over. Overweight indeed! I'd show them I could take the operation in my stride.

A bit of good news that evening was that they no longer used suppositories and enemas for cleansing the system. Instead, I was given a couple of lemon-flavoured laxative drinks, which were quite pleasant to take, and it really worked. They were called Picalax, but I insisted on calling them Poleaxe! I won't elaborate why!

My evening meal consisted of what was to become my regular diet for a while, a cup of consomme soup followed by a little bowl of jelly (hence Helen's postal pack!).

I hung up my outdoor clothing for a while and donned my first of a long succession of nighties. After a short viewing of the Sky Movie Channel, I was away to bed at midnight.

Just how would tomorrow go? It held the prospect of being the most momentous day of my life. Hell, what a change that was in prospect!

I must have been very tired, or they had slipped me a sleeping draft, as despite my excitement, I fell straight into a deep sleep.

I awoke suddenly at 2.30 to dash to the loo, where I was suitably 'poleaxed'. Then I got back to sleep until 6.30 a.m.

Upon arising, I had a good shower and then tackled the shaving of the nether regions ready for the operation. Then I had another 'poleaxed' visit to the loo, certainly no problems in this direction.

It was then simply a question of biding time until zero hour at 1.30 p.m.

I had already removed all traces of make-up and nail polish (the last I would see of these luxuries for a few days) as required by my pre-op instructions.

Julia nipped across to chat for a while, and I was glad of her company as the time dragged by on this particular morning.

I began to have some butterflies (of a completely different type to the ones thirty-eight years before when I was due to face my baptism of professional football—these Brighton butterflies were of anticipation rather than apprehension, or Red Admiral rather than Cabbage White!).

The overall feelings however were of excitement and impatience. Why was the time going so slowly? I had waited so long, yet these last few hours seemed like weeks.

I checked that everything that I might need for my several days when I was confined to bed was within arm's reach of my bed. This resulted in my bedside cabinet being piled high with books, magazines, Walkman tape player, boiled sweets (a permissible luxury), small electric fan, tissues, tapes, etc.

The nurse called mid-morning with a surgical gown, a surgical head-cover, and a pair of surgical stockings, all neatly folded.

Around midday, I was told to change into the gown, headwear, and stockings and get into bed. I was a bit nonplussed by the latter instruction but assumed this was to keep me warm and relaxed.

No lunch today, not even my consomme and jelly, but there again strangely, I didn't feel hungry.

The next stage was the pre-med, not injections as I expected, but in tablet form washed down with a sip of water. Once again, all were very civilised.

Sometime shortly after 1 p.m., I found out why I had been asked to get into bed. Two male attendants arrived and wheeled me out bed and all, a short trip along the corridor and into the surgical wing. 'Faye complete' was now 'fait-accompli'.

Inside the surgical wing, the most striking thing was the decor. Everything was pale blue; the walls, floor, ceiling, and fixtures were all the same delicate shade of powder blue. Perhaps the pre-med was taking effect, or was it the lighting casting blue hues? Either way, it all added to a peaceful unreal atmosphere.

The anaesthetist introduced himself, and I mumbled a brief hello. I was conscious of a sharp pain in the back of my left hand as he took it out of my sight, and I was consigned to a state of instant oblivion. There was no gradual slipping away, no counting backwards with a gradual descent into unconsciousness. It was as though a switch had been thrown, which conferred instantaneous sleep . . .

'To sleep, perchance to dream. Ay, there's the rub;
for in that sleep of death what dreams may come'

(*Hamlet*, William Shakespeare)

My memories of regaining consciousness are somewhat vague.

I was aware of one of the nurses smiling down at me and saying, 'It's all over now, Faye.'

I had lost over four hours of my life but had things happen during that time! The four hours were not all that I had lost!

I was aware of the surgeon approaching me and saying somewhat matter-of-factly, 'Well, you've got what you wanted.' I took his hand and said, 'Thank you', and I thought that I detected a smile.

It was some days afterwards that one of the nurses filled in the gaps as to what occurred in my semi-conscious state.

Apparently, I had come around shortly after 5 p.m., and I did have a short conversation with Mr Royle before he departed. What I don't remember are the events of the next two hours.

I was told that I had sat up holding an animated conversation with the nurses saying how exciting it all was and complaining about being tired. Their response to this was to tell me to go with the flow and sleep if I felt like it, advice which, by and large, I apparently chose to ignore.

At 6 p.m., the catering staff, true to the instructions on my door which said, 'Clear Fluids Only', arrived with a cup of consomme and a bowl of jelly. They were informed by the nurses that I had just come out of surgery and would not be eating. I had protested at this, and to the amusement of all concerned, I had sat up and consumed the soup and jelly and then complained again about being tired!

Some things don't change. You can remove anything except my food!

Jack had then phoned the hospital to see if the operation had gone all right and, to his surprise, had been put through to speak to me direct. I don't remember the conversation, but Jack said I sounded tired! I must have only been half-tired as half of me was still asleep!

I recall drifting in and out of consciousness all through the evening and the following night and my back aching considerably as the various tubes attached to me restricted me to immobile sleeping on my back. There was little pain; the sedatives saw to that, just the feeling of general discomfort. My throat however was very sore, where something had been inserted during the operation.

Friday, 3 May, dawned. I was being fed a regular dosage of antibiotics and painkillers, the worst of these being an injection into the flesh of my stomach. June, the nurse who was responsible for me on this day, took off my surgical gown, gave me a welcome bed bath, and helped me into one of my nighties, my first step back to normality. She also changed my dressings.

I had little interest in viewing my new anatomy at this stage, as it was obviously very swollen and discoloured, and it wouldn't have presented a very pretty sight. It was sufficient to know it was all done. Any personal inspections could wait.

I was now fully conscious, and with help, I was able to sit upright in bed, cushioned by a huge mound of pillows. This was a big relief to my aching back. I had little pain, but the biggest problem was wind. I was encouraged to let this go, and I'm afraid that I wasn't a most sociable person in the hospital for a while!

The fact that I was happily consuming copious amounts of water and black coffee meant that the drip that was preventing me from becoming dehydrated could be removed from my hand, one less tube to restrict my movement.

Lot more cards, including a postcard of my beloved Yorkshire Dales, and more telephone calls from Jack and Sadie, a friend of mine from Leeds, kept me in touch with back home and were immeasurably welcome.

The hospital physiotherapist arrived to give me instructions on breathing and leg exercises to do while I was bed-bound.

Did I feel any different now that the operation had been carried out?

To be perfectly honest, I didn't give it too much thought at this stage. I certainly felt very happy at the way things had gone to date, but generally, I was just carried along with events and the need to concentrate on getting better. The mind was definitely taking a back seat to the body at the moment.

That night, with the help of the nurse, I managed to turn on to my side with a little discomfort and difficulty, to give my back a rest.

This was the first conscious feeling of my new anatomy as my thighs fell snugly together with no appendages trapped in between! A warm glow crept across me as I relished this thought. It was done at long last. I slept well that night.

Everything had gone according to the book so far. Saturday was to bring the first setback.

I awoke feeling very damp; my first thought was that my catheter had ruptured, but as I withdrew my hand from under the sheets, it was covered with blood. I had started to haemorrhage. I pressed the bell, and the nurse arrived. After a quick inspection, she dashed off to return with Mr Royle, the surgeon.

He cut off the dressings, flung off his coat, and began shouting instructions at the nurse. He seemed worried. If he was concerned, it was time for me to worry. I immediately thought of his preoperation warnings, but I had been so careful so far. What could have possibly gone amiss?

The fault was apparently a lesion to the side of my new labia. It was not serious, but it was causing quite a mess. He instructed the nurse that it was going to be necessary for her to hold a pressure dressing to the spot for several hours. I enquired if I could carry out this task myself, and he replied that I could if I felt up to it.

The nurse was told to get me some surgical gloves, and I was told exactly what to do. I felt better being involved in what was going on, and it released the nurse for her duties elsewhere.

Some thirty minutes later, Mr Royle returned to check how I was doing.

'Can I change hands?' I asked, as my right hand was going numb.

'Of course,' he said and carefully guided my left hand across to the pressure point.

He returned at twenty-minute intervals until the early afternoon when he announced with a smile that we had solved it, and I could reduce the pressure. He seemed both pleased and relieved. One benefit of his early work that morning was that he had also removed the two drainage tubes, so apart from my catheter, I was now free of extraneous tubing.

The nurse came back to give me a new dressing, and the mini-crisis was over.

I felt physically drained and very tired.

Julia had been discharged from the hospital during the morning's events, but she had briefly called in to say goodbye and to leave me one of her bunches of flowers.

There were more telephone calls from my friends back home, and Paulette once more called to see me.

However, the day's course of events had left me a poor conversationalist. This seemed strange as I so looked forward to calls whether by phone or personal, but it was symptomatic of the morning's happenings.

At 9.30 p.m. my door opened, and Russell Reid, my psychiatrist from London, called to see how I was doing. I must have looked a sight as he almost didn't recognise me. Without make-up and somewhat unkempt after a trying day, I was a far cry from the height of elegance I had tried to convey at my earlier meetings with him in his Earls Court consulting rooms.

When he left, I lay back and listened to excerpts from the opera *Aida* on Classic FM. I had no trouble sleeping that night; there was no

Aida-like invasion to interrupt the darkness of my own incarceration on that particular night!

Sunday was a fairly uneventful, restful day. I put on some make-up for the first time since the previous Wednesday. This was a big psychological boost for me. The sun was again shining brightly outside, and a bit of good news was that I would be able to have a normal meal from the menu on the Monday evening, a sure sign that my progress was on course. The events of the previous day seemed a long way away.

More telephone calls from my friends back north, and Paulette called with a lovely bunch of flowers. My room was beginning to look like an advert for Inter-Flora. It all made the room look very feminine and again was a big boost to my morale. I went to sleep early at 10 p.m.

I awoke early at 4 a.m. and spent the morning continuing to rest up. At lunchtime, I had my last consomme and jelly and gleefully ordered my evening meal from the menu—melon balls (there's an appropriate line here regarding this particular choice at this time, but I'll pass on it for the purpose of this publication!), followed by chicken breast with a little vegetables and fruit salad and cream for dessert.

The prospect of this meal was bliss being my first real meal since I was at my sister's on the previous Tuesday evening.

Paulette again visited, and we had a couple of games of chess, but I found it difficult to concentrate.

When Sarah, my nurse, came on duty, she removed my dressings and said I could now wear a pair of my own panties. Consequently, I was introduced to the use of a sanitary pad, this very feminine of accessories at the ripe old age of fifty-nine! This was much more comfortable after the bulky dressings. The first thing I noticed was that it was far more comfortable in panties without the previous appendage. Yes, now I was starting to feel different and complete. It was all new and rather wonderful.

I watched sci-fi on Sky TV whilst I waited for my first meal. The meal was wonderful, and I was even allowed a glass of milk before I went to sleep. Life was gradually returning to normal.

My whole progress as Faye, over the past thirty-two months, had been a series of two steps forward, one step back. Since my arrival at the hospital, Thursday and Friday had been steps forward, and Saturday, a step back. As Sunday and Monday had been further steps forward, I should have been prepared for Tuesday's traumas.

The day started well as I enjoyed my first breakfast, porridge followed by boiled fish and coffee (I was now allowed white coffee—sheer bliss).

Yet more cards arrived together with a humorous hospital colouring book from Jackie, which raised a laugh or two. Being a pair of Aquarians, Jackie and I share a similar sense of humour.

I was informed that Mr Royle would be arriving early in the afternoon to remove my surgical packing. I had been forewarned that this was the worst part of the whole process.

A trolley of surgical tools and a large cylinder of gas were brought into my room ready for the surgeon's visit. I had heard that you felt very little once you had a good dose of the gas and air mix.

Lunch arrived. For starters, I had two large tomatoes stuffed with tuna fish, then for the main course, I had stuffed plaice with vegetables. All this 'stuffing' was to prove appropriate for what was to follow!

As my dessert arrived, rhubarb and date crumble, Mr Royle also breezed in.

My dessert was whisked away as Mr Royle was anxious to start work. The gas mask to help relieve the pain had just been fitted as Mr Royle withdrew the packing.

The sudden wrenching pain was excruciating and unexpected as I screamed into the mask and grasped the bedhead.

His next act was to insert a dilator, which occasioned the same pain in reverse. I turned to sob into my pillow as the mask was taken away. As I did so, I caught sight of Jo, my nurse, giving the surgeon a look of disapproval and then giving me in turn a look of fellow female compassion.

As Mr Royle hastily departed, I asked Jo if the gas cylinder was empty as it hadn't helped. Jo said I had taken it very well as the gas really hadn't had time to take effect.

In fairness to my surgeon, he probably worked on the principle that the sooner the job was over, the better for all concerned.

The whole process had taken only four minutes, and I was left feeling breathless and sore. My sweet was returned, and although I ate it, my appetite had been definitely blunted. It could have been worse I suppose. I had at least enjoyed the first two courses!

I have heard it said that the removal of the packing is the nearest experience to giving birth. As I said to Jo, if that's the case, I'm surprised that women ever had a second child!

Jo said she should have got me up then to start walking again and to have a bath, but that she would leave me to rest for a while.

Eventually, Jo returned to get me on my feet for the first time in five days. As Jo helped me up, I realised how weak I had become, and my legs had trouble obeying my instructions to move. After a short shuffle around the bed, I was ready to lie down again. I felt that I would have been better with a Zimmer frame!

As my room only had a shower, I was informed that they were moving me to Room No.3, which had a necessary bath. I was moved, lock, stock, and barrel, in my bed just before the evening meal. After the meal, I was helped into the bath, and I enjoyed the luxury of lying in warm, soothing water. The little luxuries in life like good food and a warm bath, which we tend to normally take for granted, take on a new dimension when you've been deprived of them for a while.

After my bath, I was given my first lesson in dilation from June and Sue, another new experience and one which was to become a matter of regular routine. It was not a very pleasant experience at this stage, as not unnaturally, I was still very tender.

Wednesday dawned. What a week! It didn't seem seven days since I had arrived at the hospital.

I had the luxury of being able to get up and wash myself in the bathroom and to have breakfast seated on a chair, albeit packed with a mound of pillows. Yet more welcome telephone calls from back home.

I had more warm baths and two dilation sessions, which I had to do myself supervised by June and Sue in turn. While it was still a painful experience, it wasn't as bad as I had expected. When June first announced that I now had to do it myself, I said I didn't think that I could, as it is one thing someone else inflicting pain on you, and another thing inflicting pain on yourself. June obviously knew how to handle this situation and calmly announced, 'Fine, just leave it and let it heal over.'

This brought home to me just how important the dilation sessions are, and I agreed to 'go for it'.

On Thursday, David, a male nurse, woke me at 6 a.m., gave me my antibiotics and painkillers, and removed the catheter. This was a painful experience but was over quickly, a bit like a sharp electric shock! It was great to be free of this final tubing and its attendant bag. Thursday had started with a little pain and a lot of relief.

Another major step towards normality was that I was allowed to change out of my nightwear into a skirt and blouse now that I was free of all tubing. Added to this, I had booked for a beautician to visit me to trim my eyebrows at 7 p.m.

Despite my two months without the beneficial effects of female hormones, everything now seemed perfectly normal and very feminine.

Yes, I now did feel different. Gone were the feelings of being something of a half-and-half tweenie. No one could now argue.

It suddenly occurred to me that strictly speaking, I was no longer transsexual, which by strict definition means between the sexes. I was now female, albeit still with a lot to learn, but female. Perhaps not biological female, perhaps not legally female as far as the legal dinosaurs of Great Britain are concerned, but now outwardly as well as inwardly, I was now complete. The body in the mirror now looked totally female, well removed from the Frankenstein mixture of spare parts of recent times.

Friday arrived, and I was excited at the prospect of having a succession of visitors. I ordered a bottle of Cordoniu champagne and a bottle of Cave de Masse white wine together with six glasses.

At 11 a.m., my sister Barbara and brother-in-law Harry arrived with, would you believe, a bottle of champagne. I made them a Buck's Fizz, but unfortunately, I wasn't yet allowed an alcoholic drink myself because of possible side effects from my long course of antibiotics. It was lovely to see them, and they stayed chatting until 1.30 p.m.

Their daughter, Kathie, and her husband, Kenny, who were due to call unfortunately, couldn't come.

Christine from Hospital Liaison visited me to sort out my departure details for the following day. She was followed by a visit from Mr Royle at 4.30 p.m. His attitude had mellowed considerably, and I believe that a lot of his early brusqueness stems from a deep concern for his patients. He told me that I had done very well and that there was now no reason why everything shouldn't be all right, providing I took things steady. I thanked him for all he had done, and he asked me to make an appointment to see him in approximately six weeks time for a check-up.

The beautician arrived to finish off my eyebrows by dyeing them and then a further trim.

She solved the problems of dyeing the odd grey hairs among my brown eyebrows by, first of all, treating the whole brow with facial bleach and then dyeing them dark brown. The difference was quite startling.

More very welcome visitors in the form of Jack and Bette arrived. They were to stay overnight locally and take me back to Leeds the following day. More drinks of champagne and a lengthy chat session. It really was good to see someone from back home, especially dear Jack. What a pity that I could never tell him exactly how I felt about him! Something seemed slightly different in Jack's attitude, or was it just a misplaced female intuition?

I had always felt that he was delighted to see me whenever we met, and he had a charming way of making me feel the centre of his attentions, but something had changed.

I had somehow expected him to have been as pleased as I was at my successful operation. He seemed a bit preoccupied and anxious to be on his way. Perhaps he was tired after his long drive?

I'm glad that I didn't know at the time what was on his mind, or my journey home would have been ruined. I think with hindsight, this was the turning point in our relationship, which would regrettably never be the same.

They made their goodbyes and also made the necessary arrangements to collect me the following morning.

So that was it. On Saturday morning, I packed my cases, said my goodbyes, and left with Jack and Bette. Fortunately, Jack had remembered my two large pillows, so I was well cushioned on the long journey home.

We had a welcome first stop at a service centre on the M11 and then a delightful break at Stamford in Lincolnshire for coffee and a cream tea.

It didn't matter one jot to me that I travelled clad in slippers and surgical stockings. It was just something else to be back in the world at large. I had come through it; I was now complete. The rest was now all down to me.

CHAPTER SEVENTEEN

The Deep Pain of Lost Love

So deep the pain of female love
Yet how sweet these feelings seem
The heartache when the love is lost
And shattered lies the dream.

—Faye Helen Wardle

Back at my flat, it was a time of enforced seclusion and recovery. Jack kept in touch and called around occasionally, and Jackie and Tina paid a very welcome visit and stayed for a long chat, but by and large, I had few visitors. All the promises by various acquaintances to call in and give me a helping hand during my convalescence remained largely unimplemented, but I coped.

I took things very steadily, still scared by Mr Royle's early portent of doom with the warning of possible prolapse, and I took the opportunity to continue with the autobiography on my computer's word processor.

Not long after my return from Brighton, I received a telephone call from the West Yorkshire Ambulance Service asking if I was still interested in the vacancies for ambulance saloon car drivers. I had applied for one of these vacancies the previous September.

I reaffirmed my interest and was invited to attend for an interview in June. This was potentially wonderful news.

Prior to my interview, I made my first visit to the Monday night Leeds Beaumont meeting, clutching one of my pillows to ease any seating problems. Apart from my journey home from Brighton, this was my first re-emergence to the wide world in my new form.

The day of my interview arrived, and I donned my black costume and white blouse that I had worn for my first visit to Dr Reid. This outfit made me feel smart and businesslike and had proved something of a good luck omen in the past. I set off in good spirits but a trifle nervous. I had given them a potted history of my 'change' in my application CV. I was still uncertain how I would be received and wondered if my being shortlisted meant fulfilling a curiosity amongst the interviewers. Admittedly, a paranoiac thought, but it does make you wonder.

I arrived at the Ambulance Station in Leeds where the interviews were to be held. Some of my fears were dispelled at the door where the ambulance worker who greeted me announced, within my earshot, to the main interviewer that there was a young lady to see him. I was very grateful for both the 'young' and the 'lady'!

The two male interviewers were very friendly and courteous and put me at my ease immediately. My fears as to why I had been invited were groundless.

The interview seemed to go reasonably well, and I was informed that the duties consisted of collecting people from their own homes and transporting them to various hospitals, etc. as necessary. For this, I would have a brand new Vauxhall Vectra saloon for my sole use, and for which I would only have to pay for my private petrol. Allied to this, the annual salary was £5,000.

The job therefore offered in one fell swoop a solution to my car and financial problems and would get me out and about meeting people.

Additional to this job prospect, there was the chance of the Legal Aid Board acknowledging my just rights to receive the £4,000 still outstanding from my long court case and also the prospect of some success from my claims against the NHS. It finally seemed that fate had decided I was due for a change of fortune.

I left the interview full of optimism, with a promise that they would let me know within a few weeks.

On top of all these prospects of better fortune, Jack had delayed moving down south to be back near to his wife, as she for her part did not seem keen on the idea. I was sorry for him at this turn of events as it was obvious that he missed her very much. I myself however was delighted as it meant I had his company for a bit longer, and who knows, as I develop more as a female, perhaps he might start to look at me differently. In the meantime, I was delighted that I was still to have his company as a friend.

Jack and I had earlier discussed the possibility of a visit to the United States when I sorted out my finances, and I had enjoyed leafing through the brochures with him and dreaming of such a trip. However, I knew this was still dependent on several things being resolved with my financial settlements, etc. So it was something for future reference.

My first main outing after my operation was to a dinner dance at Ashton-under-Lyne, which was organised by the Manchester Northern Concord. My nether regions were still somewhat tender, and as the seat was a trifle hard in the dining room, I asked one of the waitresses if she could find me a small cushion. She returned with an enormous pillow. Fortunately, most of the amused guests were aware as to the necessity of this padding!

Six weeks after my operation date, I had to return to Woodingdean for my post-operative examination. I stayed at my sister's en route once again and arrived at Woodingdean on time. It was something of a sentimental journey returning to the Sussex Nuffield, for despite the odd hiccup during my stay there, it was after all the place where I found fulfilment.

Mr Royle, my surgeon, carried out the examination and seemed surprised at the way my operation had healed, stating that I must be fit, an opinion which contrasted with his fears the night before the operation.

I took the opportunity to see some of the staff who had looked after me during my time at Woodingdean, and they were able to see me at something like my best, rather than in my unkempt immediate post-operative state.

From Brighton, as I had some time to spare, I had a very pleasant drive along the south coast to Hastings and then circled back to Barbara and Harry's at Chingford. I didn't miss the M25 turn-off this time! Next day, it was on the road again. This time across country to spend a restful few days at Eileen's in Wales, before returning to Leeds.

Life was beginning to seem sweet and complete at long last. Fate, however, was yet again building me up only to slap me down by decimating my hopes on all fronts.

The first blow came from my solicitor in Leeds saying that the Legal Aid Board were insisting on my paying my legal costs which currently stood at well over £3,000. This would leave very little out of my outstanding settlement.

As I had been relying on this money to reduce my load of debts, this would obviously cause long-term difficulties. I felt cheated as my offer in the case, which had been ultimately accepted, had been based on my minimum requirements and assurances from my solicitor that I would not have to pay my costs.

This news was closely followed by news from my GP that the NHS had indicated that they were now finally prepared to accept me for gender reassignment treatment as an extra contractual referral.

As I had by now gone private to secure my operation, this news was too late, and the NHS had outmanoeuvred us and rendered my search for a judicial review through the Birmingham solicitor useless. The solicitor in Birmingham confirmed that the case against the NHS was not now worth pursuing.

This wasn't the end of the bad news; a further letter arrived, this time from the West Yorkshire Metropolitan Ambulance Service, informing me that the standard of applicant for the vacant posts had been very high and that in this case, I had been unsuccessful. I had therefore missed out on the job which had held out so much hope.

I went off with Jack on a visit to the Northern Concord in Manchester feeling really down in the dumps, when Jack delivered the final and most devastating blow.

He told me that as there was now little prospect of reconciliation with his wife, he was going to try to make a go of things with Bette, my speech therapist, who had come with him when he collected me from hospital at Brighton.

My heart sank to a new low at this news, and I battled not to let my feelings show.

I really had no complaints; Jack had never wanted anything other than friendship from me, and it was not unreasonable on his part that he should now want a biological female. But he didn't know how I felt. I was battling on an uneven playing field. I had long expected a clean break as he left to go back to his wife. Instead, he was to linger on partnering one of my friends. So I was losing Jack and my speech therapist; there now seemed little else that could go wrong.

It occurred to me that I was the one who had helped to persuade Bette to come down to Brighton with Jack to keep him company on the long journey.

I had no reason to suspect that things would develop between them. It did explain Jack's preoccupation when they came down to pick me up. I had been so blind and so naive. I still had a lot to learn in this direction.

Everything was going wrong at once. I locked myself away in my flat for several days. Crying was frequent at a time when I should have been rejoicing in my new life and form.

Yes, I was finally as I had always wanted to be, but what else did I have? Where had I gone wrong? Life was leaving me nothing to go with my new status.

I still had a mountain of debts with little or no prospects of any income to help reduce them. I had no employment. My financial settlement from my court case in Leeds was way below my minimum needs, and there now seemed no prospects of any recompense from the NHS for my operation.

On top of all these problems, I had lost the one person who meant the world to me in the cruellest possible way. I was once more at rock bottom. Was I never to find my way? What good was it being a female at last when life had left me so few options?

I met Jack again at a Leeds meeting, and he said he was going away with Bette for a holiday in Tenerife for two weeks. If they had got this far, then things seemed fairly final.

The pain of this unrequited lost love went far deeper than anything I had experienced in my male existence. The one consolation was that I finally realised that my sexual orientation was now right. I was now a heterosexual female with all the needs and feelings that went with it.

I could at least be grateful to Jack for awakening these feelings and helping me to find myself. I sincerely hoped that he himself would find happiness as he deserved it.

But what prospect of my enjoying my new status? In a world full of biological females, just who would contemplate taking on board someone who was less than perfect and who carried the welter of financial problems that I was left with? No, I wasn't much of a catch for any self-respecting male.

As I sat alone in my flat contemplating events and my uncertain future, my thoughts once more returned to suicide as a means of escape. Just who would miss me if I went? There seemed very few. I would probably leave behind more feelings of relief than sadness. Who knows, if there is such a thing as reincarnation, maybe dear old Mother Nature will get it right next time around and send me back as either all female or even all male, anything as long as I was complete from the word go.

But no. The conclusion was the same as on that chilly night at Birch Services just over three short years before. I could certainly not go back, and this no longer presented an option anyway. I didn't have the courage to end it there, so it was once again the third option. The drive was still there to go forward. I must battle on.

I sat myself down and asked myself what was the main thing that I had wanted out of life?

The answer was obvious. My desire to be female was paramount. So what was so bad? I had got my main desire. The impossible dream had happened. With this realisation, I was on the way back. In the words of the song, 'Pick yourself up, dust yourself down, start all over again.'

Some time before Jack and Bette had started a relationship, we had arranged that the three of us would attend a concert at Harrogate Conference Centre, where Lesley Garrett, the Yorkshire soprano, was appearing with the Halle Orchestra. In the event, the concert was now to be shortly after their return from Tenerife.

While they were away, my inclination was to find some excuse not to go with them to the concert, but I had never run away from a situation in my life. I had hidden my feelings so far. I would show that I could continue to keep them secret. I would attend.

What I didn't appreciate was that I no longer had the 'meet things head on' male attitudes and outlook. I was now very vulnerable and increasingly very female. I was now capable of being more easily hurt.

The night of the concert arrived, and I had been invited to Jack's for tea prior to the concert. Bette was now staying with him, and it was fairly obvious that they were now very much a couple, and whereas in the past, when the three of us got together, it had been Bette invited to meet Jack and Faye, now it was very much a question of Faye being invited to join Jack and Bette.

I swallowed hard on this shift of emphasis, and despite Jack's efforts to be his usual friendly self, I began to feel something of an intruder. Despite my enjoyment of the content of the concert, I came close to tears several times as I realised what I was losing in dear Jack. It was all a bit too much, and while I braved out the rest of the evening, once I was on my own, I cried bitterly all the way home in the car.

Shortly afterwards, Jack phoned me to ask if I had enjoyed the concert. He told me how well he was now getting along with Bette and how much he had missed the company of a female since he split with his wife.

He obviously wasn't aware of just how this struck home, and I realised just how he saw me.

Despite all his kindness and tenderness towards me, he didn't see me as a female. I was obviously seen as something short of the real thing.

I was learning to cope with the attitudes of a hostile world, but I had always thought that Jack was different.

When it comes down to it, the old deep-rooted fear of the syndrome must run deep somewhere in all of us.

I found it difficult to speak to him as I swallowed on the tears. He asked what was wrong, but I couldn't answer. I think it was possibly at this time that he finally had a glimmering of just how I felt, and the conversation ended inconclusively.

This situation couldn't go on, and I didn't want our special friendship to end in any form of bitterness. I wanted to remember all the good times. I therefore sat down and wrote him a long letter explaining just how I felt and stating that it was no fault of his as he had never led me to believe that we were anything other than friends. I told him that this was by way of goodbye as I had to get away from a situation that I couldn't handle.

It was some days before Jack got the letter as he had taken Bette down south house-hunting as he had resurrected his desire to move closer to his family in the south of England. He phoned me to say he had received my letter and sounded very subdued. He said that he just didn't feel that way about me and he just couldn't put there what wasn't there and he had fallen for Bette. I thought to myself that just as he couldn't put in what wasn't there, it was even more difficult for me to get rid of what was there in me.

He did say that he hoped that we could stay friends and still see each other occasionally. I left this option open and later phoned him back to say that I valued his friendship and hoped we could still see each other.

A question of the heart overruling the head as I just couldn't contemplate not seeing him at all no matter how much it hurt.

Our regular meetings were now at an end however. No more Wednesday lunchtimes at my flat followed by our trip to Manchester and picnics in Wythenshawe Park. No more lovely Sunday evening meals at Jack's followed by a quiet evening in. No more friendly get-togethers at Leeds and Bradford and no more regular concerned phone calls from him. Something very dear and special was departing from my life, and there was nothing I could do to prevent it.

In fact, with him moving down south, the prospects of any continuing friendship now seemed remote, although he did say that they would invite me down to stay with them sometime. I now felt however that my revelations as to my feelings had somehow devalued our friendship in his eyes, but I couldn't have just let him go without him knowing exactly how I felt. I couldn't have lived without knowing how he felt. Now I at least knew that he wasn't interested in me in the same way.

Back on the domestic front, I did receive a couple of interesting invitations.

Firstly Gina, the organiser for the north-east area of the Beaumont Society, had been invited to attend a day-long health education session at Pinderfields Hospital Wakefield in October. This was organised to increase the knowledge of twenty psychology students on the problems associated with gender identity. Gina phoned me to say that she could cover the transvestite side of things and that if I could attend to cover the sessions on transsexuality and gender reassignment.

As this day-long session wasn't until October, I agreed.

Following on from this, I was invited to give a talk to the Samaritans in Leeds on transsexuality. For this, I said I would like to meet them first to ascertain just what they wanted from me, and arrangements were made for me to meet one of their helpers.

I went down to their offices and spent an enjoyable hour chatting to their representative. He had to be reminded by another helper that he was due on telephone duty. In saying goodnight to me, he said that he hadn't known what to expect when I was due to call, but that he found me to be charming and that he was looking forward to my talk to the group. This was also arranged for October.

This meeting was a welcome boost to my ego at a time when I needed a bit of a lift. If I could impress strangers in such a way, perhaps life may hold something after all?

Just when I was adapting to a very quiet life, I was suddenly to be shot to public prominence.

My solicitor in Birmingham, who had been handling my case with the NHS again, wrote saying that although we had abandoned the idea of a judicial review, we could sue the NHS through the county court to regain my expenditure on the operation. I had written back to confirm my agreement to this course of action as it seemed I had little to lose.

BBC Radio Leeds had obviously heard of the pending action and phoned me to ask if I could attend at the BBC Studio for a five-minute news slot early the following morning to briefly discuss the case, and I agreed.

Shortly after this, Radio Leeds phoned back to say they had decided to devote their hour-long News Talk phone-in programme between nine and ten the following morning to problems in the NHS and that if I could stay on at the studio as one of the panellists.

Again, I agreed. They sent one of their researchers around to my flat to tape some preliminary material.

Next day, I arose early as I had to be at the studio before 8 a.m.

After a studio session with a short interview on the news slot, I was taken back outside and given a coffee while I waited for the nine o'clock programme to start.

Just before nine o'clock, I was taken back into the studio and introduced to Terry Foster, who was the spokesperson for Health matters with UNISON, my old Union. Terry was to be with me on the show to answer the phone-in questions.

The show started with a friendly question-and-answer session between the interviewer, Terry, and me, to set the scene for the phone-in.

The calls we subsequently received were quite interesting and covered the full spectrum, ranging from outright opposition to my case to a high degree of support.

We even had a transsexual phoning from Plymouth, who, while they couldn't receive the programme down in the south-west, had been informed by relatives in West Yorkshire about the programme and wanted to phone to emphasise the problems that gender dysphorics faced in the modern world. It was lovely having a kindred spirit bridging the country to support my views.

The hour flew by, punctuated by a News break on the half hour, and the Interviewer thanked us both and said he had really enjoyed the Programme.

It was as I was leaving the studio area that I was given a big surprise. A posse of people were waiting for me, representatives of the press, someone from Radio 5, and two gentlemen from Look North, the BBC Television Evening News Programme.

I wondered if things were beginning to snowball out of control, but at least, I was now only answerable to myself, being single and jobless. I therefore agreed to a succession of interviews.

After an interview with the press, the Look North Television people did a one-to-one interview with me for transmission later that day and then said they would like me to go out with a camera crew into the central Leeds shopping area to shoot some footage of me going about my day-to-day chores by shopping. After about an hour of being filmed looking at clothes, gazing in shop windows, and sitting at a pavement cafe, drinking coffee, it was back to the studio.

Here, Radio 5 were waiting patiently for me. They wanted me to record a three-way discussion with a lady interviewer in another studio and some male in a studio down south, who I think was some form of government health adviser.

I was placed in a small studio with only the Radio 5 representative, who stood just behind me, and I was installed with headphones and a table microphone. The lady interviewer was very good and very fair, but what a bigot the chap on the other end turned out to be!

In one of those pompous Oxford accents, he announced that he didn't see why the NHS should be held to account to treat these people for what was a fanciful figment of their imagination.

I felt my blood starting to boil, especially as he kept referring to me as 'he' and 'him', until the end when he made things even worse by referring to me as 'he stroke she!'

Here was a man supposedly charged with sufficient knowledge to advise others on health matters expounding opinions that would even have been out of place in rugby players' dressing rooms.

'What do you say to that, Faye?' the lady interviewer asked in response to his bigoted tirade.

As I answered, I recalled one of the little things that Dr Joe Borg Costanza had once advised me at the Portland Clinic: 'Remember, Faye, dignity at all times. You are a lady, so act like one.' I had to remember that, although what was left of Roy deep inside said, 'Let me answer him!'

'Well,' I said, trying hard not to let too much emotion show, 'I'm surprised at his opinions, which illustrate the widespread general lack of understanding of the subject, and I only wish he could have been with me on my all-night crying session at Birch Services Car Park three years ago when I was contemplating suicide to be rid of what he calls the figment of my imagination.' (I was tempted to refer to him as she in retaliation for the way he was addressing me!)

Fortunately, the interview didn't go on too long, and the lady interviewer thanked me for my contribution.

As I took off the headphones, I turned to the Radio 5 chap and asked him if I could have a good swear now that we were off the air to release the pent-up hostility. After I had allowed myself off-air to forget that I was now a lady, he smiled at me and said I had done very well to keep my temper on the air. This was also confirmed later when someone who had heard the broadcast said that I had come across as a fair-minded female whereas the chap down south came across as a narrow-minded bigot.

In my mind's eye, I chalked up: 'TSs 1 Bigots 0!'

All in all, I had been occupied for some six hours in and around the BBC studios and wasn't paid a bean. In fact, all I got in that time was two cups of coffee!

Neither was my work for the day finished there. A press photographer came around to my flat that afternoon to take some stills of me in the garden areas outside my flat.

Apparently, my story had featured on the lunchtime Look North News spot on BBC Television, and I tuned in that evening at 6.30 for the regular Look North half hour of local news.

What I hadn't expected was top billing.

As the announcer ran through what was to be featured on the programme that evening, there was a large still portrait of me as a backdrop, and the number one item concerned the Leeds transsexual who was suing the NHS to recover the cost of her operation.

After showing a part of my in-studio interview, they switched to shots of me shopping around central Leeds. They then interviewed the Leeds gender psychiatrist at St James Hospital, who refused to talk about my individual case and was rather non-committal in his reference to general policies.

When asked by the interviewer if he dismissed people on the grounds of age, he even had the gall to say no and that they would first monitor the individual for twelve months before deciding whether to take them further. He never gave me the opportunity of such a monitoring session. I was simply dismissed out of hand.

After further snippets of my interview, they switched to an interview with Christine Burns, a transsexual from the press for change organisation, who was very good and not unnaturally supportive of my case.

All in all, several minutes of prime news time left me thinking that it hadn't done my case any harm at all. The only downside to my television exposure was that I looked distinctly overweight! I vowed to get down to two things: firstly to some serious exercising to lose weight and secondly to get to work on feminising my voice, which, although it had softened somewhat, was still distinctly male in character.

Work on my voice was now totally down to me as Bette, my speech therapist, now had other things to occupy her time!

Next day, it was the turn of the press. It really was amazing how they all gave different slants to the same story.

The Daily Mail published a disgusting bigoted article, which insisted on referring to me as 'Roy', 'he', and 'him'. The only saving grace was that it carried a rather nice colour picture of me from those that had been taken outside my flat.

The Daily Sport, latching on to my earlier footballing experiences, carried the headline 'Soccer Star Loses Tackle'. Far from being annoyed at this article, I got some amusement from it, and at least, they referred to me in the feminine gender.

By far, the best article was the one contained in the Yorkshire Evening Post (surprisingly the same paper that had done the earlier 'Call me Madam' story), which carried a long factual account of events, without any sensationalism, and the same picture as the Daily Mail, only this time in black and white.

I was pleased that the local paper had at least got it right, as that would be the one seen by local people who knew me personally, particularly my family.

As most of the papers had referred to me as 'brunette', I took the opportunity to change my hairstyle and colour and purchased a lovely short strawberry blonde wig. This gave me a boost and yet one more new image.

As for my weight loss programme, the nurse at my local medical practice had concluded that it was a lack of serious exercise that was causing problems rather than my eating habits, and she included me in a weekly all-female aerobics course at the local Scott Hall Sports Centre. I combined this with a follow-up swimming session at the centre's swimming pool.

One enjoyable aspect of this was that I was able to enjoy a shower afterwards with the other girls as of course I was now without the hindrance of unladylike appendages that had worried me at my earlier swimming session at Rotherham, when the changing facilities were communal and I was in a pre-op state!

Besides this exercise programme, I still had regular sessions on my exercise cycle, and I had started going walking again in my beloved Dales with my friend Tina, a pursuit that I thought I had left behind in the 1960s and that would be lost to me in my new form.

Tina also took me along to dance sessions at Pudsey Civic Centre and the Ritz Ballroom at Brighouse, again a pursuit that I thought was abandoned to a previous existence. The main problem on the dance floor was to remember not to try to lead and to adapt to dancing mainly backwards. Another problem was that I towered over most of my partners.

It was something wonderful to be returning to a more active life. It was also encouraging how I was being accepted more readily in the wider world.

The day-long course for the psychologists and nurses at Pinderfields Hospital arrived and proved a very positive and rewarding experience.

I had prepared a paper to accompany the talk that I gave, and my presentation on the subjects of transsexuality and gender reassignment was generally well received. Gina had added one or two others on to our team, and they had also prepared interesting presentations on other aspects of the syndrome and its effects and on transgender matters in general. I'm sure our combined efforts opened a few eyes on the whole spectrum. A particular interesting point was that they had invited a young lady from St James Hospital in Leeds to assist my presentation, no less a person than the assistant to the Leeds psychiatrist at St James Hospital responsible for transgender matters. Yes, the same psychiatrist who had denied me treatment. What an irony that his assistant was now assisting me with my presentation!

As a result of this course, I was invited to give a similar talk to the Wakefield Samaritans at the beginning of December.

Before this, I gave my presentation to the Leeds Samaritans, my first talk all on my own, rather than as one of a team. Again, this seemed to go down very well, although I don't know if there was any significance in the fact that the audience was mostly female. I was rather amused by the attentions of the course organiser. He had asked me before the talk if I needed anything, to which I replied, 'Just keep me supplied with coffee.' He took this literally, and every time I emptied my cup, it was whisked away to be refilled.

I was having problems with my Sierra car. It was now out of MOT and road tax, and it was getting something towards the banger stage. I laid it up and switched to public transport. There was still no sign of my final financial settlement from the court case on my lump sum. My solicitor said the matter was with the Legal Aid Board, who were working out the final sum due to me after the deduction of costs.

I had been led to believe that I would not be facing any costs, but I would have to wait the Legal Aid Board's decision. I was dependent on the final settlement to finance a replacement vehicle.

Financially, life was still a struggle with my pending action against the NHS offering, the only light at the end of the tunnel. How much easier my life would have been if I had been able to keep the few thousand pounds that my operation and the attendant costs had taken away! I valued my operation as priceless, but it hurt that so many of my transsexual acquaintances were being treated on the NHS without any cost to themselves, and I was left with financial hardship.

As for my physical and mental well-being at this stage, I was now conscious of something wonderful developing.

I now more than ever felt totally female. It was almost as though my earlier male existence had never happened. It felt wonderful, and the feeling of appropriate well-being is difficult to describe. With these feelings came extra confidence and increasingly natural feminine behaviour.

More and more, I was just able to be myself, and my acceptability as female was now widespread and mostly without question.

There were still the odd bigots waiting, with limited minds and vision, to snipe at my confidence, but these were now few and far between.

At this stage, did I have any regrets apart from still missing my family? The only regrets centred around the fact that I had not been able to change over earlier in my life, as I was now beginning to realise just what I had missed, all the wasted years when I had tried so hard to be something that just wasn't me. The only positive aspect from those years had been my family, which is something that I would not have wished to change.

Jack and Bette had moved down south to the Channel coast, and he had phoned me to say goodbye. He also said he hoped that I would go down to spend a few days with them as soon as I was able. His call reminded me just how much I was missing him despite my expanding social life, and it was one more excuse for a little cry when his call had finished. I had come to know one of nature's few truly gentle men, and I had to let him just drift away. The only consolation was that I couldn't do anything to prevent it. If there are to be any men in my life, then Jack has set quite a standard for them to live up to.

At least, I still had his friendship and concern, albeit now distant, and I resolved to not let it be too long before I visited them.

How did I feel about my friend Bette? Well, I certainly couldn't hold her success with Jack against her as he had been footloose and fancy-free when she stepped in. However, I envy all natural-born females their biological format, and in Bette's case, I now had additional reason to allow the little green goddess that lies within all females (including myself) to tinge my opinions. If she ever hurt Jack in any way, however, then she would almost certainly see my female fury unleashed!

I had avoided making an appointment to see Dr Russell Reid for my post-operative meeting, in the hope that my settlement would be through to finance my visit. I now felt however that I could delay this visit no longer and made an appointment to see him in London on 29 December. There were only two problems with this arrangement. My sister Barbara could not put me up at this time, and I was still without my own transport.

However, I had imposed on my sister rather a lot in 1996, and it was no great hardship to use the train to travel down there. While at first, I contemplated doing this round trip from Leeds to London and back in a day, it occurred to me that here was an ideal opportunity to journey on to Jack and Bette's and spend a few days with them if they were agreeable. I dropped a line to Jack, and he phoned to say that he would love to have me visit for a few days.

So it was away again on the Leeds-London intercity that I had last used way back in May when I was en route to my operation.

Russell Reid was his usual charming self and seemed genuinely pleased with my progress to date.

He was also pleased to lend his support to my imminent action against the NHS and to support my GP's attempts to get me speech therapy on the NHS. My future visits to him would now only need to be on a once-a-year basis.

This was something of a seal of approval from my psychiatrist, by way of saying that I was ready to go away and just live my new life.

Away from Earls Court, a hectic dash through the rush hour tube traffic to Waterloo, and I was away to the south coast. Jack was waiting to greet me on the station platform.

Nothing had changed for me as far as Jack was concerned. The old feelings were still there, but I was learning to accept the situation, and he obviously did still value my friendship. Bette was with the car in the station car park, and they whisked me off for a delightful meal in a charming local hostelry.

The next five days were idyllic—a visit to a Mozart Concert in Bournemouth, seeing the film *First Wives Club* at a Bournemouth Cinema, visits to the New Forest, and walks along the seafront. All this was interspersed with several lovely meals out. Just the type of mini-holiday I needed, and the weather was so kind.

All too soon, it was time to return home. I thanked Bette for her hospitality, and her extended invitation for me to return seemed genuine enough, even though I think she sensed how I felt about Jack. Jack carried my case down on to the station platform and gave me a quick farewell kiss. I was once more close to tears as I watched him returning over the bridge to his car.

The 'if onlys' returned to haunt me again. Mother Nature's cruel side again got me wondering why it is that the chemistry that makes someone attractive to a person seldom works both ways, one more area where she has been remiss in her designs. Or is it that this is one more test area for us mere mortals?

Boarding the train back to Waterloo, I found a vacant seat next to a charming young Asian lady, and we struck up a conversation.

To my surprise, she announced that she was a gender identity specialist, and she was journeying up to London to attend a gender conference.

My response was to ask if she was sending me up, but she seemed surprised and delighted when I informed her of my own condition, and we enjoyed a lengthy exchange of experiences on our journey. We both agreed that on a train full of people, it was some coincidence that we had been seated together. It's a funny and sometimes small world that we live in.

Yet another Christmas looming. How the years seemed to be flying by! I didn't relish the prospect of spending Christmas on my own, but this was eliminated when I received an invitation to join Jackie and her family for Christmas Day. I gratefully accepted. This was quickly followed by a similar invitation from my friend Tina, which unfortunately I had to decline in view of the earlier invite. It was wonderful to think that I had such friends thinking of me at this family time.

The final balance of my court settlement arrived, but there wasn't much left after the 3,000 pounds plus had been deducted for my costs. If my former wife had faced similar costs, it meant that the results of my former partner's action had swallowed up almost a third of my pension lump sum in legal fees. What a sad loss! There was just enough in my final settlement for me to buy a small second-hand Austin Metro, so at least, I was mobile again.

There now only remained my case with the NHS to resolve and hopefully finding employment.

My aerobic course terminated in December, and I passed the ensuing fitness tests at my GP's with flying colours, although controlling my weight was still proving a problem. I resolved to start the new aerobics course in January and to continue with the swimming and line dancing.

Christmas Day at Jackie's was lovely, and I was made to feel a real part of the family. On New Year's Eve, I went with Jackie and Nick to one of their cabaret appointments in Yeadon to greet the New Year in lively fashion.

So that was it for 1996. What a year! The year when I was at long last fulfilled in my quest for identity. The year 1996 had been a year of resolution; 1997 offered a year of consolidation, and who could say what else?

CHAPTER EIGHTEEN

A Settled Life at Last?

It was the Best of Times
It was the Worst of Times

(*A Tale of Two Cities*, Charles Dickens)

Early in 1997, my finances were helped slightly by my GP placing me on the sick for 'post-operative recovery'. This was by necessity only temporary, but it meant that I was getting a little benefit at last.

In early February, there was a spate of publicity for a doctor and a school teacher who were undergoing male to female gender reassignment. I was once more surprised at the press's insatiable appetite for this type of news articles. As a result of this renewed public interest, I was invited to appear on the 'Time the Place', morning television chat show on ITV.

This involved travelling down to London by train and an overnight stay at the Bloomsbury Crest Hotel, all at the expense of Anglia Television.

During a delightful evening meal at the hotel, I ordered a bottle of wine, and I was informed that as a result of their current promotional offer, I qualified for a free additional bottle of wine. I asked if this could be corked later for me to consume in the hotel's bar. I floated into bed on that particular night!

After an early morning call the next day, I readied myself for my appearance on National Television. After breakfast, a car collected me from the hotel, and I was whisked away to the nearby ITN headquarters.

I was placed strategically at the end of one of the rows of studio seats and was introduced to John Stapleton, who was hosting the show. He was charming and did much to put me at my ease.

During the first half of the programme, John concentrated on the bigots who were sounding off, speaking, with a singular lack of understanding, on their opposition to people seeking treatment for the condition of gender dysphoria. As the programme broke for the period of advertisements at the halfway stage, John turned to our side of the studio, which obviously had a fair sprinkling of transsexuals and announced, 'Right, in this half, it's your turn to have your say, and I'll be starting with Faye.'

I didn't have time to get nervous as John stationed himself by my side ready for the restart. I had no forewarning as to his questions, but there was only one which threw me a bit. This was when I was asked if I had any regrets.

This was a no-win question as to say no would mean I was discounting my family whom I had left behind and to say yes would indicate that I had made some form of mistake in pursuing a resolution of my problem.

I therefore gave 'no' as my initial answer but immediately qualified it with 'That's not strictly true as obviously you have some regrets, but as for having any regrets at the course of action to get where I am today, then I have no regrets.'

I hoped this was non-committal enough to satisfy both sides of the equation.

The half-hour programme flew by, and I was left with the impression that we had given a good account of ourselves and that the exercise had been a positive contribution to understanding of the syndrome.

After the programme, we were invited to the 'green room' for refreshments and a further informal chat with our host John Stapleton, and then I was whisked away to Kings Cross station and was on a rapid journey back to Leeds.

As I queued for a taxi at Leeds City Station, a young lady next to me in the queue said, 'Excuse me, but weren't you on the Time the Place this morning?' I confirmed that I was on my way home from the show, and she added, 'I thought that crowd at the other side of the studio were a right set of bigots!' The lack of understanding certainly isn't universal.

As a pictorial record of my progress to date, I booked a photographic session for a portfolio of photographs. Shortly before this appointment, I was to unwittingly self-inflict a rather painful injury.

Awaking in the middle of one particular night, I felt the need to pay a call, and journeying to the bathroom in the dark in a half-awake state, I caught my foot a glancing blow on the architrave of the bathroom doorway.

It was fairly obvious from the pain, and the odd angle of my little toe, that I had broken this little digit. I strapped the little toe firmly to the next toe. My GP, when I called to see her, confirmed that it appeared broken, but that we couldn't do anymore than I had already done by binding it firmly to its neighbour.

When the photocall came, I was therefore dressed up to the nines in black evening dress and diamante jewellery, but wearing my old moccasin carpet slippers for footwear! This caused much amusement in the studio, and fortunately, there were no full-length shots to advertise the anomaly.

As part of the photo studio session, I had been given a makeover, and I returned home feeling 'all dressed up and nowhere to go'. I phoned around my friends, who all had prior commitments for the evening.

When I phoned Jackie, she said that they were committed to a private 'gig' at Yeadon, which had been booked the previous New Year's Eve when I had been with them and that had it been a public function, then she would have been delighted for me to have gone with them, but she couldn't invite me to a private function.

I sat for a while watching television and resting my damaged foot, when, just as I was about to change out of my finery and remove the make-up, the telephone rang. It was Jackie. Apparently, the first thing that the people who had booked the function had asked them upon their arrival was, 'Where's Faye?' as they had expected me to be with Jackie and Nick.

So without any more ado, I was away to Yeadon for a lovely night out. I even struggled into my high heels as I wouldn't be on my feet too much.

There was one interesting episode during the early part of the evening. While Jackie and Nick were away changing, I was seated on my own at the artistes table, and it was obvious that I was the subject of attention at a nearby table, where two young couples were holding an amused conversation and continually glancing my way.

Oh dear, I hoped they were not going to spoil my evening by their attitudes. Just then, the hosts entered and came straight across to my table saying how lovely it was to see me there and offering to buy me a drink. They were followed by a stream of people who came across to chat and make me feel very welcome.

There was obviously some confusion amongst the nearby foursome at the reception I was being given, and I think there was a glimmer of the fact that they were the odd ones out, not I, a minor victory for tolerance and understanding.

I was continuing to have problems with water retention and swollen ankles as a by-product of my hormone treatment. However, I was beginning to be worried about skin discolouration to my shins and calves. I pointed this out to my GP, and she shared my concern. As a result, she arranged for me to attend the nearby Chapel Allerton Hospital for an exploratory scan.

I had a worrying week waiting for the examination, and in particular, I wondered what would happen if I had to cease the hormones. My GP had already said I should not take any more until the problem was resolved.

I attended the hospital and was subjected to a full-leg scan from the groin to the ankles. Despite the worry, I was grateful for the fact that I was post-operative as explanations may have been necessary as I was stripped down to my knickers!

Finally, the examining doctor announced to my great relief that the scan had shown no abnormalities.

I called at the hospital's cafeteria, and when the young girl on the counter asked what I would like, I replied a double gin and tonic, but that I would settle for a cup of coffee!

Jackie continued to help me widen my circle of female friends and introduced me to Avril, who, like Jackie, is an attractive blonde.

On one evening when Jackie's husband, Nick, was away on business, Jackie, Avril, and I had a lovely evening, chatting and drinking until 5 a.m.! As Jackie's son Philip had some of his friends staying at the house, Jackie, Avril, and I all tumbled into the only remaining bed for what was left of the night.

Next morning, Jackie arose early as she had to be available to answer the phone, and she suggested that Avril and I avail ourselves of the big Jacuzzi next to the bedroom. This we certainly did and enjoyed a pampered morning of relaxed bliss in foaming, bubbly soapy warmth, which Jackie adorned by sending up a large bottle of champagne with dishes of strawberries and cream—what luxury!

Later that day, I was driving Avril home, and we were talking about people's attitudes and levels of acceptance.

'Well, I've accepted you,' Avril announced.

'Good grief, Avril,' I said. 'I've only known you twenty-four hours, and we've slept together and had a bath together. How much acceptance do you think I need?'

We had a good laugh, and we've remained firm friends.

As part of the routine procedures, I was called to take a medical to ascertain my fitness for work as a result of my benefit claims. I had now completely recovered from all after-effects of the operation, and I was informed that as I was now fit for work, I would not receive any further benefits.

The major stumbling block to any progress and indeed to my very existence was still my parlous financial state.

All the old bills and commitments were still there, but now that I was without the benefit of sickness allowance (and I could hardly argue with the fact that I was fit enough for work), I just could not pay everything from my pension. The difficulties of my transitional state were compounded by these money shortages. This had the obvious knock-on effect for my social life, which was becoming non-existent.

My superannuation pension was now my only income, and I just couldn't cope with the outgoings exceeding the income. Life was one long series of robbing Peter to pay Paul, and my outstanding debts, far from decreasing, were increasing.

I was desperate for additional income, and it suddenly occurred to me that I could now understand why some females, and even some post-operative transsexuals, turned to prostitution in their desperation. Who knows, had I been younger and more attractive, even this would have seemed a tempting proposition. Yes, I was becoming that desperate. With such desperation comes a lack of self-esteem and self-respect.

Surely, there must be some employment for me. I still had much to offer on the job front.

Scanning the papers for job adverts became a daily routine. Given that I was unlikely to find an employer willing to take a chance with a gender-reassigned female fast approaching retirement age, I began to search for some type of work where I could possibly work from home on a self-employed basis.

Even this was easier said than done, but one particular advert caught my eye.

The Yorkshire Evening Post newspaper (ironically again the one that had done that 'Call me Madam' article on me when I worked with the council) were looking for direct delivery agents to organise delivery of their newspapers from their own homes, with commission based on the number of copies distributed.

It was in effect self-employment as the paper charged a reduced bulk rate, and it was up to you to get the papers out and collect the cash. This offered prospect of a weekly profit of £87 for every hundred papers delivered over the six nights.

If I could deliver around 120, this should just about bring in the extra £100 per week that would make all the difference.

I put in an application and was awarded a round on the nearby infamous Scott Hall Council estate. Not ideal, but very handy.

I had decided to deliver the papers myself to maximise any profits, but getting the money in was very difficult. In the first week, I was thirty pounds down. This turned out to be the usual shortfall, and the monies owing to me rapidly exceeded over 200 pounds after several weeks. It was fairly obvious that the majority of the debtors had no intention of paying for their papers.

I was even cheated out of twenty pounds at one house. I called to collect their outstanding payments, which amounted to six pounds sixty pence. I was invited inside by the male occupant, and I began to feel uneasy as I saw he had another seedy-looking male companion with him inside. A twenty pound note was placed on the table, and I counted out thirteen pounds forty in change which the first male pocketed. When I reached for the twenty pound note, it had gone, obviously surreptitiously removed by the second man.

They both insisted that I had taken the £20 note, and as the situation was beginning to turn ugly, I left, not only without their payment, but with them still having the change I had given them. I reported the incident to the police, but at the end of the day, it was my word against theirs.

Allied to the problems of getting the money in, I was subject to verbal abuse and stone throwing from the local youths while I was doing my rounds. I could but wonder just what discipline, if any, some of these yobos were taught, as often their parents were standing by and watching. I had no doubt that I was meeting first hand some of the no-hope criminal classes of tomorrow. My experiences on the Scott Hall Estate did much to reduce my sympathies for the underprivileged social classes, although I would not wish to generalise as there were odd gems amongst the darkness, people who deserved better but were trapped amongst the no-hopers.

My confidence and spirits were yet again at record lows. I still had not found a solution to my financial woes, and I once more felt very much alone and vulnerable. Thoughts of suicide returned yet again. After all, what was left for me to live for? Despite now having the physical format that I had always desired, life was still offering me nothing to go with it except an ever-increasing load of debts.

There seemed no avenues of escape from an impossible situation, which if left unchecked could only worsen. Despite all my efforts, I was caught on what appeared to be a downward spiral.

Arriving home one Saturday evening in June, wet, tired, and hungry after a particularly harrowing delivery round in the rain, and after mainly futile attempts to get some money in, I placed a piece of pork under the grill of my electric cooker and went into the lounge to sit down for a few minutes. The inevitable happened: I dozed off to suddenly awake to smoke filtering across the lounge. As happens when suddenly awakened from a deep sleep, I was at first momentarily bemused by this fact and then shot to my feet as I remembered the pork that I had left cooking.

I flung open the kitchen door to be engulfed in thick black swirling acrid smoke. Choking, I rushed away to the bathroom, soaked a bath towel in water, and placed it over my head as I entered the kitchen. The cooker was a ball of smoke and flames. I flung off the electric switch and dashed for the safety of the hallway and a few lungful of fresh air before re-entering the kitchen to fling the wet towel over the cooker.

This did little to stop the blaze, so after again leaving the kitchen to draw breath, I flung several bowls of water from the kitchen sink over the cooker which finally quelled the flames.

I staggered out of the flat on to the communal landing, gasping for air. My neighbour Anne came out to see what the fuss was about, took me inside her flat, and made me a welcome cup of tea.

'Have you seen your arm?' she asked.

It was only then that I noticed a large burn down the inside of my left arm. Anne carefully helped me dress it, but the burn mark was still clearly visible some months later.

I returned to my flat to open the windows to clear the air, to be confronted by a new further problem.

In my haste, I had left the kitchen tap running full belt, and the plug was in the sink. The overflow couldn't cope, and the kitchen floor was awash, and the water had run through to my hallway. All this, whilst obviously down to me, was the last straw.

Even then, I still managed to laugh as Anne withdrew a blackened grill pan from the wreckage of my cooker, and as she surveyed the black cinder in the centre of the grill, she pronounced, 'I think your pork is a bit overdone!'

There was an obvious irony in my current status by the fact that after all my life's experiences, all my studies, hard work, and a long list of qualifications, I was ending up delivering newspapers, in one of the city's worst areas, a job usually undertaken by schoolchildren to do for pocket money when they completed their school day. Could I sink any lower?

I was tired, weary of battling against societal attitudes and the welter of problems. My resilience and fortitude had gone; I had had enough. I could not even produce the floods of tears, which had usually preceded a return of my determination to succeed. I had even lost interest in continuing my work on this account of events, which usually offered a diversion, and work on the autobiography ground to a halt.

I lost the ability to sleep, and the inadequacy of the three or four fitful hours that I was getting was beginning to reflect on my general appearance and energy levels.

On top of all this, my solicitor in Birmingham reported that there was no progress on my court case as she was awaiting events elsewhere on similar cases before progressing mine.

I was beginning to despair at my chances of success in this direction as I felt some of the initial impetus had been lost. Events were to prove this foreboding correct.

At least having control of newspapers meant I was able to keep up with local news and job opportunities, and if there was to ever be any form of resolution to my problems, I must continue to seek work somewhere to replace the newspaper job. There was still the faint glimmer of hope that at the times when I was down that was the time when events usually took a turn to pick me up, and I must still try to give the Fates some help. The little demons that waited to knock me down when I was on top also made sure that when I was at rock bottom, there would be a leg-up in some shape or form.

After all, hadn't my life been one long roller-coaster ride of ups and downs? Perhaps yet again, there was to be a rise in fortune although I just couldn't see from which direction.

A possible job front seemed to be to consider seeking employment with the city council again. Perhaps not back in the Planning Department, but something more in keeping with my current status? After all, I had the advantage of having worked with the council for twenty-seven years. I was therefore very much the 'devil they knew'.

I carefully studied, without too much hope, a long list of council vacancies in the Evening Post and dismissed one after another, when I came across the Social Services section in which were five advertisements for vacancies as sheltered housing wardens to various council properties. A job I could cope with, so I phoned for the forms and applied for all of the five warden posts at different locations around the city.

I didn't hear anything by way of a reply, which didn't really surprise me. It seems I was the devil they didn't want to know!

A regular break to my day-to-day worries came when I was able to attend the aerobics and swimming classes at nearby Scott Hall Sports Hall, and I particularly enjoyed the conversations with the ladies in the classes who had befriended me.

I had mentioned my applications for the warden posts in our conversations, and one of them produced an advert for a scheme supervisor at a sheltered housing complex with Yorkshire Metropolitan Housing Association at one of their complexes at Morley in South Leeds.

My friend Jackie had already phoned me to let me know about this job advert, but I had decided that if I couldn't raise interest from the council, I was unlikely to stand any chance with a housing association. However, given that it had again been drawn to my attention, I decided to apply. Perhaps the fact that it had twice been drawn to my attention was an omen.

Some little time later, I was both delighted and surprised to receive a response inviting me for an interview and asking if I would first of all meet their Mr Les McCall at the complex to view the rent-free accommodation that went with the job.

I had a reasonable knowledge of Morley town from my time in the South Leeds Development Control team during my time with the council, and I attended the site meeting on a lovely summer afternoon in early July.

Both the complex and the flat were lovely, and the location and surrounding area were far removed from the dubious environs close to my own flat at Potternewton.

I also got along fine with Les McCall, who was very friendly and put me at my ease. It was all so ideal. I would receive the flat rent-free and a gross salary of approx £400 a month. I would also have a worthwhile interesting job based at my own flat, a solution to all my problems in one fell swoop.

My feelings as the time for the interview approached were mixed. I had a feeling that I was once more having a carrot dangled in front of me to be ultimately cruelly snatched away. I thought back to the time in North Cornwall and my more recent experience with the West Yorkshire Metropolitan Ambulance Service. At least this time, I was ready for the anticipated forthcoming disappointment of denial. Experience was making an incurable pessimist of me.

The interview lasted a full hour, and I pulled no punches. I hid none of my past and pointed out that what the job needed was someone with the capabilities and upbringing of a male combined with the caring and responsible instincts of a female and that they wouldn't find many with all these attributes. Les McCall was one of the interviewers, and they were very fair and respectful in their conducting of the interview.

After my previous interview techniques of 'I can do this job, so please give it to me', this time, it was a slightly different approach more in the order of 'I'm not going to get the job, so this is what you're missing.'

They were very non-committal at the conclusion and said they had others to see and they would let me know the outcome the following day.

As I left the office, there was a charming young lady waiting her turn for interview, and it occurred to me that I was in competition with several biological females who were all probably younger than I.

I left with a feeling of doom. The job was so ideal, and yet how could I possibly be expected to get it?

I went around to Jackie's that evening and told her that I was dreading the phone call the following day as I couldn't take the anticipated disappointment. I said that if I didn't get this job, I was going to stop trying.

Jackie, as she had done so many times tried her best to cheer me up, but I was building myself up for one more knock-down.

When the phone rang the next morning, my heart fell to my shoes when it was Les McCall on the line, and I began to shake fearing the worst.

I was almost ready to join in the anticipated format of 'Well, you did very well, but the standard of applicants was very high, and unfortunately in this instance, you have been unsuccessful, but please don't let this put you off applying for any future vacancies we may have'—the standard gentle let-down.

'I'm pleased I've caught you,' he said, 'as we would like to offer you the job.'

My heart took a giant leap, and the feeling of elation was enormous.

'Just a minute,' I thought. 'This isn't in the script, has he phoned the right person?'

'Oh . . . Oh, that's wonderful' was my immediate and inadequate response.

'I read that paper of yours,' he went on, 'and I found it very interesting and informative.' I had left a copy of the transcript for one of my talks on transsexuality with him.

'Well, you should find my book interesting then,' I replied.

'You're doing a book?'

'Yes, an autobiography. It's been waiting for a happy ending, and you may have just provided it.'

'I'm very pleased,' he said. 'We will be in touch to confirm your appointment.'

This really did seem too good to be true. It was almost as if the Fates were saying, 'Now, can you see what we were saving you for?'

My feeling of well-being was instant. I was on cloud nine, and it brought it fully home just how much being jobless and the subsequent financial problems had adversely affected me and my moods. Now, see me go!****

I was straight on the phone to Barbara and Harry in London, Eileen in Wales, and Jackie with the news, and they all shared my pleasure.

I did my paper round that afternoon with a distinct spring in my step. It wasn't too bad doing it now I knew that it was only temporary, and I resisted the temptation to put two large fingers on the front of my car! When I returned to my flat, tired but happy, there was an enormous bunch of flowers waiting on the doorstep. The note read as follows:

'It couldn't happen to a lovelier person, from Guess Who'

I phoned Jackie, as I knew it was just the kind of thing she would do.

'Could I speak to Guess Who please?' I asked as she answered the phone, and we shared a good laugh.

What a good friend Jackie is! I think she was as pleased as me with the new job. It nicely rounded off a major day in my life and heralded yet one more new direction for my life. I had a feeling that a giant corner had been turned.

The next couple of weeks, before starting my new job, were spent decorating the new flat and gradually moving my furniture and effects across Leeds to Morley, halcyon days of hope for the future, which only a short time before had seemed so bleak.

Eileen, the outgoing warden at the complex made me very welcome, and I was pleased that she was to stay in the flat next to mine. Only reaching the compulsory retiring age of sixty-five had necessitated her ceasing work. Eileen said she was ever so pleased that it was I who had got the job as she hadn't liked what she saw of some of the other applicants. A nice compliment, even if a little backhanded.

My star was really on the rise, and the residents of the complex accepted me from the outset. I even got one or two nice compliments from the male residents.

Immediately before my transference to Morley, I received a letter from Social Services of Leeds City Council asking me to attend for an interview for one of the jobs I had applied for some weeks before.

I had to decline on the basis that I had already secured employment, and it occurred to me that jobs are a bit like buses: you wait ages for one, then two come at once!

Shortly after my move to Morley, I was yet again contacted by Radio Leeds to join in a three-way discussion on a transsexual news item.

I was rapidly becoming their local regular consultant on the subject.

After a month in my new post, the on-off holiday that Jackie and I had recently contemplated came about, and the two of us went off to Ibiza for a week. It was my first real holiday for some years and my first abroad as Faye. I was able to use my new passport at last.

I had some reservations about Ibiza as our choice of destination as it would inevitably evoke some bittersweet memories of my earlier family visits.

However, it reaffirmed my love for this particular Island, even though it was now swamped by the ubiquitous over-commercialised tourist trade and was far removed from the unspoiled paradise that it presented way back at the time of my first visit in 1971.

1971! Where had the time gone? Was it really twenty-six years ago?

We managed to book into a lovely hotel on the south side of San Antonio Bay. I got a certain amount of mischievous amusement from the fact that one or two hotel guests obviously had their doubts about the towering burly blonde. I added to their confusion when I donned my swimming costume (I could almost hear the 'where has he put it?' from the doubters!), and I added to their confusion by sunbathing topless by the swimming pool, and proudly airing my firm 44C boobs in public for the first time.

Jackie was amused by the pleasure I got from their confusion. I could now enjoy displaying my female attributes at last!

I really enjoyed showing Jackie around the island, and she shared the eerie fascination that I had with Es Vedra, the giant rocky island which rises sheer from the blue Mediterranean waters just off the western coast of the main island. At the time of our visit, there was a sepulchral stillness in the atmosphere, and the rock was in silhouette against the evening sun.

Local legend decrees that this particular outcrop was used as Bali Hai in the film *South Pacific*. Certainly, there is a cathedral-like splendour to its vast aloof mystical form, and anyone who believes in Ley lines or earth forces must see this rock as a centre of mystical energy, akin to Stonehenge in Wiltshire, Ayres Rock in Australia, or Mont St Michel in France.

I took the opportunity to have a sentimental journey one afternoon and went off on my own in our hire car to Playa den Bossa, where I had spent so many happy times with my former wife and family. It was a ghost that I had to try to bury. You cannot run away from your past life, and there were aspects of it that I still missed so much. It's a great pity that there could not have been some way that my old life could have accommodated the new happier me. However, it had all passed, and after a few minutes of quiet reflection and a couple of quiet tears on our old beach, I was up and away back to my new life again. Life is for living, and I still had a lot of living to do!

Resident on Ibiza was Trish, yet one more friend of Jackie's.

Happy-go-lucky Trish with her natural flair for comedy, and a delicious sense of humour, is a former Ice skating star, and we hit it off from the outset.

We met a few other expatriates on the Island, who all made me feel so welcome, and I contemplated that had I not received my lovely new job, the prospect of staying on the Island would have probably proved irresistible (a definite touch of the Shirley Valentines).

I gave a silent vow to return at the earliest opportunity to this welcoming island, where I had always felt so much at home, and indeed effervescent Trish extended an invite for me to revisit any time.

Shortly after my return from Ibiza, I was to receive some very bad news from the solicitor in Birmingham. A letter arrived to say that she did not feel she could obtain renewed legal aid on my case, and with the timescale since the NHS decision, she felt my chances of success on my case were small enough to not justify legal aid.

Given the length of time it had taken for her to come to these conclusions and the recent restrictions on legal aid, I felt I had once again been a victim of our iniquitous legal system, irrespective of the merits and justice of my case. The whole of my reassignment process had been one long series of bad timings or being in the wrong place at the right time or the right place at the wrong time!

I was understandably very disappointed as I had become so convinced about the merits of my case, that I considered a favourable outcome was just a question of time. My biggest disappointment however, which overrode the financial loss, was the fact that the Leeds psychiatrist was getting off the hook. I wanted so badly to get him into court, to get him to try to explain his subjective dismissal of me for NHS treatment.

On the financial side, I consoled myself that the £7,000 plus that having to go private had cost me was small price for the result of the finished product and the contentment it had given me. Going private had also at least provided me with the finest treatment and top surgeon.

Another bit of news which put everything into perspective was that my dear friend and former work colleague with the Planning Department, Malcolm, wrote to say he had terminal cancer of the pancreas and could I pay them another visit at Stratford-on-Avon as soon as possible. It was with a somewhat heavy heart that I travelled down there at the end of October 1997 to spend the weekend with him and his wife, Sheila.

As it turned out, I was extremely cheered by his fortitude and attitude, and we had a charming weekend visiting Shakespeare's birthplace and the villages of Upper and Lower Slaughter in the Cotswolds. My beloved Dales are far from being the only touch of heaven in this underrated country.

Seeing Malcolm's fortitude and his efforts to put his work in order while he could, I was once more reminded of one of the old sayings: 'I used to complain because I had no shoes and then I met a man who had no feet.' To put it another way, no matter how bad things may sometimes seem, we should all count our blessings. I learned much about strength and fortitude from Malcolm and his wife, Sheila, on this visit.

My dear friend lovely Jackie and her family finally secured the move of abode that they had been seeking from their lovely house at Horsforth in Leeds to Doncaster, where her husband could be near his new place of work. This wasn't quite as convenient for me to visit, but it wasn't too far for me to travel down the M62 and A1.

I took a day off work and helped them move, and I was given the pleasant task of driving their lovely big Jaguar car down to South Yorkshire. My worries that my best friend might gradually be growing away from me was allayed to a large degree by her invitation for me to join them on Christmas Day again. I gladly accepted as I didn't relish spending Christmas Day 1997 on my own.

After a hectic day of furniture moving, her husband, Nick, took all of us out for a delightful and welcome Indian meal at a gem of an Indian restaurant he had found near their new home.

It was only a few weeks before that Jackie and I had been bewailing our respective problems of unemployment on my part and lack of progress on their move to Doncaster on Jackie's part. In just a few short weeks, we had both found solutions to these problems—further evidence that you can never be sure what lies just around the corner.

Dear Jack visited me for a short stay at the end of November after he had been visiting his father in Harrogate.

It was lovely to see him again and stirred the old feelings I had for him yet again. While out of sight is certainly not out of mind; being within sight can however be more painful.

Bette phoned while he was with me and told me that she hoped I was looking after her man. I didn't need this reminder of just where he belonged, but it warmed me a little that she saw it as necessary to remind me!

He brought a video and photo album with him of the month-long holiday which they had taken earlier in the year in the United States. It was the holiday that he and I had talked about going on someday before he went off with Bette, so it was a bit of a bittersweet viewing. I was surprised by his comment when we were looking at the photos when he said quite wistfully, 'We almost got there, didn't we?' I was tempted to respond, 'Well, it was no fault of mine that we didn't!' but I could never get cross with him.

There are times with Jack when I think that had I been a complete biological female, then I might have fitted the bill for him. But who knows. Still it is always lovely to see him even if only for a short time. He was with me for only twenty-four hours, then Bette got 'her man' back.

There was more good news for me at the beginning of December, which helped to compensate in a small way for the demise of my court case. I received confirmation from the local health authority that they had amended their protocols, which had dictated that only patients accepted by the Leeds gender psychologist could receive any gender-related treatment such as speech therapy, so I would be able to have this therapy on the NHS in Leeds.

I felt that I had broken the god-like restrictions imposed in Leeds by the gender psychiatrist who had come close to ruining my life and who I had learned had imposed similar subjective judgements on other individuals.

I don't think it was coincidence that from cases he had recently accepted, it was apparent that his hitherto restrictive subjective assessments had relaxed. I like to think that all the noises a certain Leeds transsexual had made about his judgements had brought about a more liberal approach to acceptance. If so, a lot of my troubles had been well worthwhile, even if it was a bit late to help me personally.

I met one of the transsexuals whom he had recently accepted for treatment, and I was informed that the Leeds psychiatrist was coming up to retirement within the next few weeks and that his successor who seemed more tolerant and enlightened was wanting to review the cases who had been rejected by his predecessor.

There is the prospect therefore that although acceptance of my case would come too late to be of much practical use now, it would nevertheless remove the stigma of having been unacceptable originally to my native authority, a little bit like being pardoned after serving a long jail sentence for a crime you didn't commit!

I also heard that the retiring psychiatrist was allegedly suffering from cancer of the prostate. Given the way he had adversely affected so many aspects of my life, any sympathies on my part would be hypocritical. Suffice to say I would not even wish this particular ailment on the worst of my enemies, and given that he has during his duties at least helped some gender dysphorics to find resolution, then I hope he recovers to enjoy his retirement.

However, these sentiments are not intended to forgive him for his professional shortcomings with my case. I cannot envisage anything which could redeem him in my eyes for those.

The only stipulation by the local health authority at this stage was that my referral for speech therapy must have the support of my new GP at Morley. My new GP was delighted to proffer such evidence, and she penned an appropriate letter of support to the authority. I had indeed been fortunate to find such a pleasant and supportive GP so close to my new home.

Early December occasioned a visit from my line manager, Les McCall, to tell me that my probationary period in my new job was over and I would henceforth be on the permanent staff, another small step on my settling into my new life. He asked me if I was still interested in football, given that he comes from a footballing family, and I produced a list of forecasts I had prepared for the 1998 World Cup Finals in France to confirm my interest.

He was a bit perturbed, given his Scottish background, to see that I had forecast an early exit for Scotland. A few days later, I received a letter from him at the Leeds Office confirming the end of my probationary period. The final paragraph made me smile however. It read as follows:

' . . . However, your appointment as football pundit is to be placed in abeyance until June 1998. Time will tell.'

This friendly informality, even on such a letter, was a real breath of fresh air to someone used to the starchy formality of local government. This organisation was one after my own heart, and I was becoming increasingly at home with them. After all, was it not my own philosophy to take work with a smile and to build up a friendly team spirit? I was now with an association which put these principles into practice.

I gave two more lectures on the subject of transsexuality at Bradford University and Wakefield. These, together with my spots on Radio Leeds, were becoming regular enjoyable interludes and were helpful to spread understanding of the syndrome.

Christmas 1997 loomed large (is it my imagination or do the celebrations start earlier and earlier as the years pass?) and was preceded by a long telephone chat with Trish in Ibiza. I felt quite envious of the warm weather which she told me they were having on the island (she had found it necessary to wear a sweatshirt poor thing!).

Yet one more invitation to visit the island was extended to me, and I promised to try to make it in early 1998. It was lovely that my range of new friendships now extended internationally.

I had one more small task to complete before Christmas. As I wanted to give my three children some money with their Christmas cards, I decided to deliver them to my old house direct rather than risk them in the post. I therefore waited until late one Monday evening when I would be unlikely to bump into any of the family.

It was the first time I had been back to the old Homestead for over four years, and it felt strange driving down the little muddy private road that I had taken many hundreds of times before. Never before though had I had to make the journey surreptitiously.

I was very pleased that little seemed to have changed. I parked a little way from the house, walked up to the back door, and quietly slipped the three envelopes through the letter box. I could see my former wife through the window sitting inside the house, and she looked well.

There was a pile of compost bags in the rear garden area, which suggested she was still looking after the gardens, and a new burglar alarm with a small light had been installed high on the wall.

The little Fiat Uno was still parked outside the garage where it had always stood.

As I turned away, I was suddenly bathed in bright light from an automatic wall light, but this did not provoke any interest from within. I was able to quietly slip away with a mixture of sadness at the aspects of my past life that I had lost and still missed and pleasure that everything still seemed normal and shipshape back in the old homestead. One small point of difference that I noticed was that the muddy back lane was much more difficult to negotiate in high heels than it ever was in male footwear!

The week before Christmas saw my first office party with my new employers. As there were large numbers of the staff that I had not met, I was invited to go straight down to the office for 11.30 a.m. and go on to the venue with the Leeds office staff for the meal which was due to start at 12.30.

Setting off in my finery, a black trouser suit in this case, at 11 a.m. for the fifteen-minute journey into the centre of Leeds, I was appalled to see that traffic at the end of my street was at a standstill. Apparently, some unfortunate person had fallen off a bridge on to the Inner Ring Road in central Leeds, and as the police had cordoned off this section, traffic across all south Leeds was backed up for some five miles. The queue at the end of my street was therefore extending all the way from the centre of the city.

I was sat on the bus for eighty-five minutes, and upon arriving in the City Centre, I dashed straight round to our luncheon venue.

Despite this breathless and hectic start, I was made very welcome at the function, and I was made to realise just what a lovely crowd I was now working with.

There was a friendly camaraderie of a type that I had only experienced twice before, first time being amongst the small crowd at our remote RAF unit on the Baltic and second time during my time with the members of the Masonic Order.

After the Christmas meal and festivities, I was invited to join some of them for a drink at the nearby Viaduct Public House. Inside the hostelry were large groups of young men who had obviously had more than their fill of the brewers products and were in very high spirits. As I was enjoying my drink, one of the directors from my new firm came over to me and asked if I was all right, obviously conscious of the number of nearby 'rowdies'.

I replied that I was all right, and he added that they all felt very protective towards me at Yorkshire Met, a nice thought that I appreciated, and which I like to think was aimed as much at my femininity as at my transsexuality.

Off to Jackie's for Christmas Day, a lovely lunch, and a dip in their lovely new indoor heated swimming pool, luxury indeed and a real Christmas novelty.

As on the previous Christmas at Jackie's, overindulgence was the order of the day, and my diet went to pot temporarily.

For the first time ever, I spent New Year's Eve on my own. A quiet evening was interrupted by a telephone call, which took the edge off the year end. It was my friend Malcolm's brother phoning from Stratford-on-Avon. He told me that Malcolm had passed away that morning, and he wanted me to know the funeral arrangements.

I was naturally very saddened by the loss of someone who had somewhat unexpectedly turned out to be a true friend. I would like to think that he has now got the place he deserves in the next world that he fervently believed in and that he now has the time and wherewithal to complete all the little things that he had wanted to do during his retirement, and which by and large he had been now cruelly denied in this life. Now finally detached from the mortal body that had restricted his activities towards the end of his days here, I'm sure there will be a place where he can now find his own fulfilment.

One of my first appointments in 1998 was therefore to be attendance at his funeral service on Tuesday, 6 January, at the United Reform Church in Stratford-upon-Avon. I was both moved and struck by the service. In particular, during the address, an account was given of Malcolm's early life difficulties. I felt very humbled at having known someone who had turned problems into triumph in the way he had.

He had earlier, in Leeds, said of my condition that it must have taken a lot of courage for me to live as I was previously. This acclaim now takes on more meaning having come from someone who during his life had reinvented the word and meaning of courage. Like so many others who knew him, my life is less richer without his understanding and worldly wise presence.

In mid-January, I had occasion to visit my GP to collect my hormone prescription, and she informed me that she had received a letter from the authority about my speech therapy. It transpired that they were asking for psychiatric and social work assessments prior to my being included for speech therapy! Far from being justifiably upset by these requests, I was highly amused.

I had been on hormone tablets for almost five years and had lived as a full-time female for four and a half years. I had passed through four of the country's foremost gender psychiatrists and had full gender reassignment surgery by arguably the top surgeon in this field. I had run the full gamut of what society could throw at me and come up smiling. I had been in love as a female. I was accepted by hospitals, universities, and Samaritan groups to give lectures on the subject of transsexuality and my experiences. I had appeared on television shows and many times on Radio Leeds, who now treated me as regular consultant on such affairs. I had secured employment as a female in competition with biological females. I was accepted as a female by my residents at work, by my employers, and by my numerous new friends. I had been to numerous functions and dances as a female. I had attended all-female aerobic and swimming classes and been fully accepted. Yet the authority wanted proof that I was serious about being female and the need for speech therapy!

I had not stood on my head on top of the Eiffel Tower as a female nor swum the English Channel as a female. Perhaps this was where I had been remiss! Anyway, their request had given me the best chuckle I have had for some time.

My GP shared my amused astonishment at their requests and felt sure that the evidence on my medical file should meet their needs without my having to undertake further assessments. Unfortunately, my medical file had not yet arrived at my new GP's.

She summed the situation up when she said that after all, I was only looking for some fine-tuning, as she thought I had done so well so far. Maybe if the authority continued their procrastination, then eventually they would have a justifiable case for not treating me on the grounds of senility!

It certainly seemed as though something, or somebody, resented the effort I was making to break into the NHS system in Leeds.

The need for help with my speech was brought home yet again the very same evening.

I could not get my car to start in the local Kwik Save car park after I had been shopping at the supermarket. The nearest public phone was several hundred yards away. I phoned the AA Breakdown Service and spoke to a pleasant young man.

'Whereabouts is your car, sir?' he asked.

'It's miss actually, and it's in the Kwik Save Car Park in the centre of Morley,' I replied.

'We don't have that on our lists. Can you give me a street name?'

'Sorry, I don't know this area very well.'

'Can you find the name of the street and phone me back please, and I'll get someone to you straightaway.'

So off I toddled all the way back to the car to find the street name.

I returned to the phone box to be answered this time by a female voice, who wanted all the particulars over again. After I gave her my membership number, she asked, 'Are you on your own, sir?'

I was growing weary of being called sir. 'Yes,' I replied.

'Then we can't attend to you, sir, as this is a single membership in the name of Miss Faye Wardle.'

I sighed and entered into the routine explanation of gender reassignment and everything changing except the voice. She was most apologetic and asked, 'And where is your car now, Miss Wardle?'

'In the Hope Street Car Park,' I replied, satisfied that I at least now knew the name of the street.

'Oh, is that the Kwik Save Car Park?' she asked.

'I think I've just come full circle,' I replied as I explained my earlier conversation with her colleague. She seemed amused and promised there would be someone there in approx thirty-five minutes.

Sure enough the mechanic arrived and soon had me mobile once more. It had been a funny sort of a day!

The end of January brought another invitation to give a talk at Bradford University for 25 February.

The year 1998 was safely underway. The last few years had been times of transformation, fulfilment, and consolidation. Now, this year offered promise of a more normal, steady life. I felt as though I had emerged from a long dark challenging tunnel into the sunlight. Life is good and is for living. As I looked back at some of the traumas of recent times, they all seemed a necessary part of the learning curve to the course I had taken. Now, I could at last look to the future.

CHAPTER NINETEEN

Whither Now the Butterfly?

So whither now the butterfly
Newly emerged to the morning air
Its zig-zag course no clue shall give
To come to light we know not where

—Faye Helen Wardle

As I conclude this narrative of my life's journey to date, I am sitting in my new flat at Morley with the prospect of finally a settled and contented, if potentially lonely, future.

I can but still wonder if my life has any new twists and turns.

I am blessed with good friends and neighbours and the understanding and support of some of my relatives, my new employers, and my GP. Yet I am haunted by the continuing absence of my children. It is now almost five years since they last had any contact with me.

Just how are they developing?

Just what do they think of their old dad?

I am now finally more than content with my new life and form, but I am deeply saddened by the price. By the pain it was necessary to inflict on others. Was it really so wrong for me to want to find out how my life should have been even at this late stage? Had I not made a valiant attempt at living the vast part of my life in the wrong gender? Why then should I be so condemned for seeking a little personal fulfilment and happiness, to belatedly sample how my life should have been?

If my course of action is seen as selfish by some, then so be it. What I have done has not been easy and was not undertaken lightly. Only I can know the pain of the costs.

It was not as some have accused 'a flight of fantasy', but a successful attempt to bring some ease to a lifetime's torment.

In this context, I have one small message for the brother and sister who have condemned me and want nothing to do with me now. It says in the Bible, 'Let he who is without sin cast the first stone.' They each have their own skeletons-in-the-cupboard from their past lives and yet seek to condemn me for seeking belated resolution to a medical condition that has haunted me for a lifetime. My conscience is clear. I hope they feel they can say the same.

As I have heard it said, this life is not a rehearsal, and we only get one chance. We have each therefore to find our own way in this mixed-up mortal coil.

I am however also deeply angry.

Angry with nature for not getting it right first time. If she is indeed a female and a mother to boot, then she is deeply remiss in some of her maternal design duties. Why, oh why, couldn't she have given me a mind to fit the body or a body to fit the mind from the outset? Either way, I would have not had to endure a lifetime of confused torment and have had to inflict the pain of loss on my dear family.

I could have been happy as a male if only nature could have blessed me with a male mind to go with the male body, and I could certainly have been happy if nature had given me a female body to go with the female mind from the outset. Unfortunately, the best she could do was a hybrid of the two—a confused mishmash of something beyond the comprehension of myself, society, and the medical profession.

I am angry when I think of the years that I have been deprived of. Of my missing girlhood, love, and the many female experiences and womanhood that should have been. What a sad, sad loss! Yes, I feel deeply, deeply cheated.

This anger is only heightened by the feelings that my new form and life is right. This is how it should have been. But it is all so late. My new experiences have only reinforced my feelings, not now of what might have been, but of what should have been.

The anger I feel however is not paramount, but it nags repeatedly at the back of my mind, that part of my mind where there's now a little empty prison where I used to hide and condemn my female self. This prison is not now completely empty for there exists the many echoes of my past.

No one, with the possible exception of another transsexual, can understand the feelings of having been cheated by life. Yet it is something wonderful to have finally found myself. This is me; I have nothing to prove to anyone. I do not have to work hard at being someone who doesn't feel to be me. How wonderful it would have been to have always felt this way!

While there have been times in the past when I felt like two people in one body (from confusion, not schizophrenia), I am content that my whole being is now female, both inwardly and outwardly.

What leads me to these feelings? Quite simply whilst as a male, I was continually haunted by the need to be female, as a female, I have neither desire nor inclination to return to male. My mind and body are now congruent and at ease.

With these feelings of appropriateness comes a happiness which transcends all pain, all regrets, all anger, and some of the sadness.

What could eliminate the last elements of sadness?

The obvious possibility that my children may come to understand, may wonder how their old dad is making out in his new format, and may contact me and establish ongoing contact. I realise this is asking a lot, and their absence from my life may be a continuing price for me to pay. If this is so, then again so be it. Others may condemn, but only I can know the necessity of the course I have taken and the personal contentment I have gained.

If my children are wondering why I have made no attempt to see them, I do not see it as appropriate that I should add to any of their sense of loss by imposing on their lives uninvited. They know I am always there if needed.

My deep regrets at my lost girlhood and womanhood are greatly tempered by the many and varied experiences during my time as a male.

I have nothing to be ashamed of in my male existence, far from it. Just how many females have the advantage of having spent time on the 'other side'? Could they enjoy the experience of soccer trials with a top professional football club? Could they experience the excitement of serving in RAF Electronics Intelligence on the former Iron Curtain? Could they experience the special masculine camaraderie of Masonic life?

Could they enjoy the undeniable privileges and freedoms that society conveys on the male of our species? Or even more overridingly important, enjoy the many delights of fatherhood (second only to motherhood) with three delightful children?

What of my married life?

I do have very much to be grateful for, almost a quarter of a century of largely happy times. It was not without its problems, but what marriage is?

It was only this nagging inappropriateness within me which brought about the unavoidable sad demise of our marriage. To have attempted to continue would not have been fair to my lovely wife and family, nor indeed to myself.

I do not like to dwell too long on which way I would have gone if I hadn't finally faced myself and the truth. I couldn't have gone on as I was. They must surely have sensed my increasing unhappiness which had nothing whatsoever to do with any of my family, but was entirely down to me.

Perhaps if my former wife and my children find time and inclination to read this account of events, there may be a glimmer of understanding, of compassion, and perhaps an easing of the pain I have obviously caused.

I have done as much as I possibly could for my former family, would that I could have done more.

So whither now for Faye, now that the butterfly has emerged from its cocoon?

I have no grand expectations. I would dearly love, even at this late stage of my life, to experience the love and affection (emotions which are every female's birthright) of a partner who would be prepared to accept and treat me as the female I am. Perhaps out there is one such hero, but I have no grand illusions, being well used to life's disappointments and societal attitudes. I am after all 'the unknown', someone who is different from the norm and therefore someone that society prefers by and large to ignore.

My experiences have shown that I can love as a female and that such love is very deep, very profound, and of a type unknown to the mere males. It is a love based not on the male's primary driving instinct, the need for sexual fulfilment, but on a female's deep empathy with a fellow human being of the opposite gender and the female need for tender loving care. I have not completely lost hope of rekindling these feelings somewhere along the remainder of my journey, but I am also prepared for the more likely scenario of a life on my own.

The new employment has given me some purpose in life and has considerably eased my financial problems. I am aware how fortunate I have been in this respect given the current dearth of job opportunities, my advancing years, and the prejudices and misunderstandings which pervade society. I am deeply indebted to the company for having had the heart and vision to give me a chance. I intend to repay their trust during what remains of my working life and hope my work will enable me in turn to return to sheltered accommodation as I myself later enter into old age.

So, with the mixed blessing of hindsight, has it all been worthwhile? I think the answer to that question lies in that state of deep inner contentment, which now pervades my whole being. It's been a long and difficult journey. It hasn't all been Chanel and Roses, but I made it.

I have bridged the huge chasm between the sexes. I have experienced life on both sides of the great divide and feel so much the wiser. What a far better place this world would be if everyone were endowed with a glimpse into the other gender. A little understanding is what we all lack.

It is not an easy world for both males and females. Both have their problems and difficulties. Both are so different, not only physically but also in so many other respects. Small wonder that there is so much intersex conflict and misunderstandings.

A recent television programme, and successful book, was intriguingly entitled *Women Are from Venus and Men Are from Mars*, and it dealt with differences between the sexes in a light-hearted way. There are times though when the sexes do seem to be worlds apart.

The analogy is even more appropriate to the attitudes of the two sexes when you consider that Venus is the Goddess of Love and Mars the God of War. Need I say more?

These differences make the whole search for sexual equality a nonsense. Each sex has its own attributes and abilities. We should all be delighting in and utilising these basic differences. Sorry, girls, but there are many areas where the boys are superior, but the male ego must also appreciate that there are also many areas where the girls leave the boys well behind. Equality? Who needs it—VIVA LA DIFFERENCE! (anyway, girls, my mischievous side tells me that for us equality with the inferior male would be by and large a backward step!).

I did also hear that little girls grow up, but being a little boy is a job for life! I would not wish however to be flippant about the question of equality of opportunity, which is a separate and ongoing issue.

As I have attempted to punctuate this account of my life to date with little snippets of poetry, I believe the following anonymous poem, which originated from a transgendered person on the computer internet and which was recently brought to my attention, perhaps sums up succinctly my current feelings in relation to my new form:

I think I'm finally starting now to like myself at last
It wasn't always so you know I lived a confused past
But now my femininity is evident you see
I like the way I look and feel I like the real me
I like the softer texture of my epidermis shell
The glow that it now radiates just suits me very well
The growth of fleece and mane that once proliferated so is
diminished to a soft fine fuzz and mostly does not show
I sport a rounder fuller look in legs and hips and thighs
and somehow round about the face there's a sparkle in my eyes
My chest has now expanded a soft mound of bosom shows
The changes are quite evident from head to polished toes

My journey is not over and the changes are not fast
But I think I'm finally starting now to like myself at last

(Anon)

I think this poem says it all, and I am indebted to its unknown author. I can now start to like myself at last, both in mind and in body. The reflection I see in the mirror is female, I can identify with it, and it is me. The changes are wonderful and very fulfilling.

How do I now see myself?

Self analysis is always difficult. As poet Robbie Burns said, 'Would that we could see ourselves as others see us.'

I used to like to think of myself as something of an iron fist in a velvet glove, outwardly soft but inwardly hard. Well, having had the opportunity to sample life's slings and arrows to the full, I now think I'm more of a sponge fist in a velvet glove, outwardly soft and inwardly soft but capable of a lot of absorption.

I can look back with sadness and some regrets, but with a lot of pride. If my experiences do anything at all to help understanding of the syndrome of gender dysphoria or help others experience the condition, then so much the better, and that alone makes this exercise more than worthwhile.

I have tried to show the ups and downs of an involved existence, both the joys and the sadness, the achievements and the failures, the laughs and the tears. It is not intended to be a tale of self-pity, rather a tale of triumph against the odds, an account of success but at great cost. A story of a long, long journey littered with obstacles.

And what did I find at the end of the road? Myself.

The self I had sought all my life with at times little prospect of finding. Yet there it was so near and yet, for most of my life, so distant.

We do live, as the twenty-first century gets underway, in more enlightened times where society is gradually learning to accept the multitude of differences within the spectrum of humanity.

My heart goes out to those kindred spirits who in the past were not blessed with the opportunities which I have, albeit belatedly, received, and who were condemned to a full lifetime of unresolved confusion without ever experiencing just how their lives should have been.

My heart similarly rejoices, with a mixture of a little envy, at the opportunities which are unfolding for currently young and future kindred spirits. May they all find rapid resolution to their needs.

I shall continue helping the fight for equal civil rights for transsexuals, until such time as the narrow-minded legal dinosaurs and politicians of Great Britain drag this wonderful country of ours out of the nineteenth century and into the twenty-first century. Too many of our legislative ideas and principles are bogged down behind outdated Victorian principles and bigoted ideals.

Other countries unfettered by the dogma of the ages have no difficulty at all in conveying civil rights to transsexuals in their new gender, whilst our own government blunders on like some small-brained dinosaur. Fortunately, we all know what happened to the dinosaurs: they became extinct because they were unable to adapt to changing times.

I certainly do not intend to climb back into my cocoon now that my transition is nearing completion, and I will continue with others to pursue our just rights.

I remain deeply disappointed and frustrated at the ultimate climb down and the sheer discriminatory injustice on my battle with the National Health Service for the funding for my operation, even if it was only to prove that the Leeds psychiatrist was wrong in his uncaring dismissal of my case. How I would have liked to get this self-appointed god into court for his comeuppance, not only for my own satisfaction, but also for the many others that he had submitted to his unfair, restrictive, subjective judgements.

To my mind, the situation is simple. In cases of gender dysphoria, you either have the condition or you don't. If the case is proven, then you are worthy and deserving of treatment. It is a proven *medical* condition and therefore as deserving of treatment as any other medical condition.

To deny a true gender dysphoric appropriate treatment and consideration is a cruelty of the deepest magnitude and runs a very high risk of driving the unfortunate individual to the only remaining course, that of suicide.

Statistics do not unfortunately show how many people have solved their problems of gender identity by taking their own lives. If they did, the medical profession and society at large might wake up to the seriousness of the whole business. Many decisions on suicides are given as 'suicide while the balance of the mind was disturbed'. I wonder in how many cases, it was the balance of their whole body that was disturbed, and not their minds? I can't believe that society just doesn't care.

However, I am equally convinced that the Leeds judgement on me was based on financial considerations at the time of my consultation. Given restrictions, the psychiatrist must of necessity be choosy, and I know for a fact that he later accepted people for treatment who were not within the parameters that he applied to me back in 1993.

I like to think that the waves that a certain Leeds transsexual was making had led to a more accepting attitude at the Leeds Clinic. If this is so, then not all the noises I have made were wasted.

I know of no other branch of medical science where age and physical appearance are factors determining suitability for treatment. Inclusion of these factors as determinants is discrimination of the worst kind and deserves the utmost condemnation. These factors when applied to gender dysphorics only reinforce, and pander to, the male attitude of just how a female should look in their eyes.

Success as a male-to-female transsexual does not depend on whether you look like a beauty queen at the end of the day, but on how you can survive as an individual in your new format. I hope I myself by my efforts have proven this particular fact. Females do come in all shapes and sizes, and femininity owes more to behaviour than appearance.

Neither is it sufficient to dismiss an individual from treatment on the basis that 'you have managed all right in your biological sex so far, so there is no reason why you shouldn't continue in it'. This is akin to telling a shell-shocked soldier that because he has always acquitted himself well in the face of enemy fire, then there is no reason why he cannot go back into the firing line! He, of course, is no longer capable, and a caring society would acknowledge that he has done his best, afford our soldier all necessary treatment, and send him home where he belongs.

So it is with our transsexuals. Is it really asking too much that when an individual can no longer bear the dysphoria that has haunted him (or her) all their life, the society should say you have done your best, and it is time for you to go where you belong?

The Leeds psychiatrist *was* wrong in his refusal to treat my proven case, and all the people who were expecting me to fall flat on my face during the conversion process were wrong. I can stand tall and thumb my nose at all of them (in a ladylike way of course!).

I am female, and I have always been female, it's just taken me a little time and effort to prove it!

Yes, you should have seen the caterpillar, but I can assure you it intends to continue to develop into one hell of a butterfly!

> All my life I have been searching
> Now that I am a woman it is all clear
>
> (Princess Amalfi, *The Last Unicorn*)

Postscript (Written June 2005)

Well, it has just arrived from the government-appointed Gender Recognition Panel—my gender recognition certificate, dated 22 June 2005, stating quite simply that legally I am now recognised as a female and entitled to all the same benefits and freedoms of any other female. My new birth certificate will now follow. Thus has been removed the final obstacle in my search for my true gender. This certificate is number 000526, so I am one of the first to be so recognised. At sixty-eight years of age, it has arrived rather late to be of much practical use to me personally, but it pleases me to think that I have helped pioneer an easier course for future gender dysphorics. It is a condemnation on this and earlier governments that it took many years of pressure from individuals and the European Parliament in particular to bring about the necessary legislation for gender recognition. In this connection, I have only one thing to say to the successive governments responsible for the delays. Welcome to the twenty-first century!

CHAPTER TWENTY

Epilogue

It is now June 2007, some fourteen years since I started on the long journey of conversion and some nine years since completion of my foregoing life story. I have now moved into my seventies.

I have retired (2002) from my work with The Yorkshire Metropolitan Housing Association, and I now live in a lovely rented bungalow in the beautiful village of St Neot in Cornwall, which in 2004 was voted 'Village of the Year for England and Wales' and only last year was voted as National village of the Decade. When I retired, I had been based in one of the Yorkshire Metropolitan complexes in Huddersfield, some sixteen miles south-west of my home town of Leeds. The need for this transfer from Morley, in August 1999, was once again a victory for the mindless vandals who pervade modern society.

In November 1998, I had occasion to stand up to a crowd of young yobos who were running rampage through my complex at Morley. My reward for this was that they came back later and vandalised my car (deja vu from my experiences at Potternewton Heights). This continued to be the order of things for the next few months, so I took the opportunity to transfer when it was on offer. When I look around at the onset of a lawless society, I can but fear for the future of our once proud safe country. I am now however settled into my lovely new bungalow in an area of the nation as yet still unaffected by the lawless masses.

My life has now settled into a steady pattern. The village where I now live is delightful, and the villagers are very friendly. I join in many activities around the village, including the annual pantomime, the

Christmas concert, the local art class, and the local church choir. I also help to organise the Local Produce Market and have also only this month been elected to the Parish Council. Yes, I have finally 'arrived'.

The government after dragging their feet in considering the question of civil rights for transsexuals, considered a recent White Paper on the subject, and this resulted in a draft bill 'The Gender Recognition Bill'. The House of Lords has approved the new legislation to grant us full civil rights, and the bill went forward for the Royal Assent. Formal legislation was finally approved, and I will now have full gender recognition and a new birth certificate. I am finally legally female.

My development in the female state continues, and I am still battling against the two main obstacles—my tendency to put on weight and my voice. The speech therapist has done much to help inflection, intonation, and resonance, but raising the pitch of my voice has proved far from easy. I have even tried singing lessons in an attempt to raise the bass baritone nearer to the contralto levels. These lessons helped my singing voice considerably but unfortunately had little impact on my day-to-day voice pattern.

My speech therapist therefore arranged (via my GP) for me to have surgery to alter my vocal chords and raise the pitch. I saw the surgeon, and it was undertaken recently at Leeds General Infirmary. The operation was a bit horrendous as it was carried out only under a local anaesthetic and took the best part of two hours. The big consolation is that early indications are that it has been a success, and I have lost a lot of the lower register to my voice. The softer, higher voice is very encouraging and far more feminine than my previous voice.

The operation was done on the National Health under the recommendation of my GP and the Leeds Gender Identity Clinic (yes, the same clinic which denied me my earlier treatment).

Whilst I was recovering in the hospital, one of the nurses asked, 'Is that it all finished now, Faye?', and I replied that it should be the last piece in a very big jigsaw.

I still have not managed to attract a steady boyfriend, and indeed at my advanced age and with my history, I think I can dispense with any hopes in this direction.

I do however now have a very dear male friend who has accompanied me on many outings and holidays over the last nine years. He does not see our relationship other than as close friends, and I respect this situation as I value his companionship and the respect he has for me. I would not wish to do anything which would mar the special relationship which we have enjoyed. Perhaps if I had been a biological female, I may have been better able to fill the void in his life that the death of his wife, whom he obviously loved dearly, has left.

He recently retired and moved down to Cornwall. He shares my love for this particular county, and I missed him very much when he moved. However, now that I myself have moved down to the south-west, we continue to enjoy each other's company from time to time. I consider myself fortunate in that having enjoyed Jack's company for several years, I did not think I could find a friend who could match or surpass dear gentle Jack. I am pleased to say that I have been proven wrong. If, however, my latest companion, like Jack, finds himself a permanent biological female or tires of my friendship, then I am now a realist. I will at least be ready for this eventuality and will know when it is time for me to move on.

After retirement, I did for a while try a partnership in a local dress agency in Yorkshire, but this didn't work out and only added to my debts.

One major surprise just before retirement was when I had a visit from my friend Chris Eagle. He had with him a very tall, well-built young man. When Chris asked me if I knew who it was, I replied that I had no idea. Chris announced it was my eldest son.

I had not seen him for over eight years, and he has grown into a fine young man. He had called to ask me to sign a form on behalf of his mum. He was quite amiable and spent a good hour chatting. I ascertained that my second son was pursuing a career in computing and my daughter was seeking a career in the fashion industry. He himself had obtained a B.Sc. degree and was currently job hunting.

This reassuring news from my family came at a time when I was a little bit down in the dumps having not heard from my dear friend in Cornwall for several weeks. While I have no reason to believe that my son's visit was nothing more than a 'one-off', I was very relieved to be given the impression that I had not been totally discarded by my children.

I recently had some very good and some very sad news. The sad news was that my dear brother Bernard passed away after a short illness. I was not able to attend the funeral, but my former partner and eldest son attended. The wonderful news was that my second son who was living with a very nice girl had had a son, my first grandchild. My thoughts are with both my brother's family and my son's new family. More recent news informs me that my son's partner is expecting a second child.

My daughter is living in London and has developed into a lovely successful girl. All this news of my family comes from my sister Barbara as I still have had no contact from my children.

During the last twelve months, both my eldest sister and brother have passed away, leaving only three from the original seven children.

I have managed to make a molehill out of the mountain of debts that I have borne since the events of the 1980s, but finances are still very tight. I still do the odd singing gig (an activity I have not covered in the foregoing and which merits a separate chapter!). For transportation, I was in 2000 lucky enough to obtain a lovely Audi saloon at a bargain price, which I have recently replaced with a newer similar model. I can now travel in a comfortable and reliable vehicle.

I can look forward to the rest of my retirement with confidence, and I have various plans for things to keep me occupied here in this lovely part of the world. The biggest possible obstacle is loneliness, but who knows what the future holds?

I think it is appropriate to leave the final word, and a final poetic contribution, to a fellow Yorkshire lady of previous times:

Riches I hold in light esteem,
And Love I laugh to scorn;
And lust of fame was but a dream,
that vanished with the morn:
And if I pray, the only prayer
That moves my lips for me
Is, 'Leave the heart that now I bear,
And give me liberty!'
Yes, as my swift days near their goal,
'Tis all that I implore;
In life and death a chainless soul,
with courage to endure.

Emily Jane Bronte, 1818-1848

Yes, life is good and is for living, and I go forward to a new future full of optimism. Many aspects of the troubles that I have encountered along the way now seem like a distant bad dream. I can look back at it all, with a lot of pride and some regrets. But the conclusion must be that it was all so worthwhile. The ends did, for myself, justify the means.

God bless my family, my friends both old and new, and all those who have helped me along my journey.

Lightning Source UK Ltd.
Milton Keynes UK
UKOW040614100413

208974UK00002B/83/P